CONQUERING UNEMPLOYMENT: THE CASE FOR ECONOMIC GROWTH

Also edited by Jon Shields and published by Macmillan for the Employment Institute

MAKING THE ECONOMY WORK

Conquering Unemployment: The Case for Economic Growth

Edited by
Jon Shields

M
MACMILLAN in association with the EMPLOYMENT INSTITUTE

First published in book form in 1989

Published by
THE MACMILLAN PRESS LTD
Houndmills, Basingstoke, Hampshire RG21 2XS
and London
Companies and representatives
throughout the world

Printed in Hong Kong

British Library Cataloguing in Publication Data
Conquering unemployment: the case for economic growth
1. Great Britain. Unemployment. Implications
of theories of economics
I. Shields, Jon II. Employment Institute
331.13′7941
ISBN 0–333–47134–2 (hardcover)
ISBN 0–333–47135–0 (paperback)

COUNCIL OF THE EMPLOYMENT INSTITUTE

(as at 1 June 1988)

cont. overleaf

The Employment Institute is a research organisation promoting study and debate about the best methods of reducing unemployment without setting in motion an inflationary upsurge. Its staff conduct in-house research on barriers to employment growth and arrange for the publication and discussion of pamphlets by distinguished outside contributors.

The Trustees and advisory Council of the Employment Institute are listed on the previous page.

The Employment Institute's series of pamphlets and other publications are available to the public on payment of a yearly subscription. Requests for further information about the Institute should be addressed to:

Employment Institute
Southbank House
Black Prince Rd
London SE1 7SJ
Tel. 01–735–0777

Contents

List of Tables

List of Figures

Preface

This book and its companion volume *Making the Economy Work* portray major aspects of the Employment Institute's published output in its first three years. The books draw on the series of policy pamphlets produced by the Institute to explain why alternative prescriptions to 'monetarism' could have avoided the massive rise in unemployment in the early 1980s.

The policies recommended cover both 'macroeconomic' and 'microeconomic' solutions. Broadly speaking, the contributions in this book look at the macroeconomic side, whilst those in *Making the Economy Work* concentrate on microeconomic or structural issues such as policies towards the regions, the influence of the trade unions on wages, profit-sharing between workers and owners and special programmes for the long-term unemployed.

This book considers whether the government should increase its own expenditure levels or reduce tax rates in order to stimulate economic activity. Authoritative authors discuss how the government should set interest rates and what its attitude should be to the level of the exchange rate. Answers are given to criticisms that unemployment could not be reduced by active government policy without reigniting inflation. It is shown just what went wrong with the 'good housekeeping' and 'tight money' approaches of the first Thatcher administration.

The aim throughout has been to tackle complex economic issues in as readable and non-technical a manner as possible. This does not mean that jargon has been wantonly jettisoned where it actually helps the reader, nor that arguments are only superficially displayed. The contributions are intended to be meaty, but not tough.

Many people have had a hand in the production of these readings. The authors toiled willingly but without financial reward and often under uncomfortable pressure from myself, Richard Layard and other trustees. Brenda Haddou, Sandra Cox, Michelle Bailleux and Harbans Chana processed various of the manuscripts with remarkable patience. Mark Cornelius provided invaluable support and advice.

The views expressed remain the responsibilities of the authors themselves; the errors either theirs or mine.

May 1988 JON SHIELDS

Notes on the Contributors

Charles Bean is Reader in Economics at the London School of Economics. He is a Council Member of the Employment Institute.

Willem Buiter is Professor of Economics at the University of Yale and also a Council Member of the Employment Institute.

Andrew Britton is Director of the National Institute of Economic and Social Research and was a Trustee of the Employment Institute from 1985 to 1987.

Gavyn Davies is Chief UK Economist at Goldman Sachs and a Trustee of the Employment Institute.

Rudiger Dornbusch is Ford International Professor of Economics at Massachusetts Institute of Technology.

Rt Hon. Edward Heath, MP, a patron of the Employment Institute, is the Conservative Member of Parliament for Old Bexley and Sidcup. He was Leader of the Conservative Party from 1965 to 1975 and Prime Minister of the United Kingdom from June 1970 to February 1974.

1 Introduction

Jon Shields[1]

In the winter of 1971–2, the level of unemployment in the United Kingdom broke through one million. Newspaper headlines shrieked disbelief and horror. The budget of March 1972 saw the government apply its third dose of 'reflation' inside a year. Unemployment began to fall.

In the winter of 1981–2 the level of unemployment reached three million. Newspapers reacted with little more than resigned acceptance. The government declared its determination not to deviate from its existing policy of 'disinflation'. Unemployment continued on an upwards course for a further four years.

Within a single decade, the public seemed to have undergone a total reappraisal of its attitude towards the concept and desirability of 'full employment'. Soon talk that unemployment levels of three million or worse might be around 'for ever' could be guaranteed to attract support in pub, common room and debating chamber.

The contributors to this book do not, and never did take such views seriously. Nor did a great majority of the economics profession. By coming up with the most radical notions and making most of the noise, fatalists adhering to old-fashioned 'monetarism' or the developing 'new classical' school may have appeared to make most of the running amongst economists in the debate about the potential effectiveness of economic policy. But the vast majority of experts continued to believe that governments could influence the level of unemployment – for good or for evil. To them, 'full employment' was still an attainable and legitimate goal.

The response of these 'mainstream economists' to the policy failures of the previous decade was neither to throw up their hands in despair nor to rip up the whole edifice of their previous beliefs. Instead, they sought to identify with care what specific features of economic behaviour had led to the breakdown of previously successful remedies. They worked to refine their models of the economy to take into account in a more effective way certain key elements, such as the way in which expectations about inflation and policy were now being formed, and the growing importance of financial markets and mechanisms.

The refinements made to their models did not cause them to lose faith in the basic lessons learnt and, where necessary, put into practice by governments since the depression of the 1930s. The models continued to show that the level of output produced by the economy and the employment levels sustained are substantially affected by the amount of money being spent in the economy. This in turn can be heavily influenced by the spending and taxation decisions of the government. It was the Thatcher administrations' decisions to ignore these lessons that had in part been responsible for the substantial rise in unemployment in the early 1980s. End these policies and unemployment could be made to fall again.

Not that many 'mainstream' economists in the mid-1980s thought that the road back to full employment and low inflation would be a quick or easy one. The tendency of the economy to erupt into bouts of inflation demanded new remedies. Controls over wage or price increases might have to be extended rather than rolled back. Any stimulus to the economy would have to be directed specifically towards or 'targeted' at those areas where there was surplus capacity, so as not to create new inflationary pressures. The impact of policy changes on expectations and international confidence had to be faced squarely.

These policy prescriptions took into account the new synthesis that was emerging at a theoretical level. Whilst mainstream economists still rejected the notion that there was a simple, causal link between the growth of the money stock and the rate of inflation, many now accepted that money *did* matter. The rapid accumulation of sterling assets could spill over into spending and prices. Furthermore expectations could be generated in a variety of ways. The mechanisms involved could not always be boiled down to a simple set of rules, particularly if these implied perpetual myopia. Instead expectations could well be formed in very sophisticated ways. In some circumstances, this might amount to true 'rationality'. If economic agents made mistakes, they could learn from them, and this would include any misreading of the intentions or commitments of government.

When it came to the determination of prices, however, the teachings of 'Keynesian' economists since the war still seemed to be relevant. Prices, and particularly the price of labour (wage rates) did not always move quickly enough to allow markets to 'clear'. Often it was the quantities traded (or the levels of employment and unemployment) that took the strain. New advances helped to explain in theory why this universally-observed phenomenon occurred in practice. Imperfect markets sometimes played a role, also revealing why the economy did not always tend to the equilibrium position implied by models assuming universal perfect competition.

These features of modern economies meant that the tools of postwar macroeconomic policy still had their uses. By adjusting levels of government expenditure and taxation and by operating in domestic or external financial markets governments could, at least in the short term, manipulate output as well as prices. If markets were shocked out of equilibrium by external forces, governments could take it upon themselves to shock them back in again. Sometimes a government's freedom of action would be limited by the markets' ability to 'see through it' and fear of incipient inflation, but policy activism could still play an effective role.

This synthesis at both theoretical and practical levels may have been favoured by the economics profession. It did not, however, receive any acknowledgement of support from the Treasury or 10 Downing Street. Their public doctrine in the early 1980s continued to be that of 'TINA' – 'there is no alternative' to maintaining tight 'housekeeping' limits on spending and borrowing and enforcing strict guide lines on monetary growth.

In these circumstances it was hardly surprising that there was considerable frustration within the economics profession, rising in some cases to desperation. Unemployment continued to rise and the costs of policy failure escalated. The message was simply not getting across to policy makers. Any criticism by the profession was subjected to immediate denunciation as symptomatic of political subjectivity or Keynesian revisionism.

If the profession was failing to make its mark on policy, so were adherents of similar views in Parliament, industry and the country at large. Divisions amongst the parliamentary opposition, amplified by the vulnerability of the 'wet' wing of the Conservative party, meant that any alternatives advanced to the government's 'monetarist' policies could easily be attacked as incoherent and inconsistent. Similarly, although both the trade union movement and large numbers of employers were highly critical of the effects of economic policy on public procurement, interest rates and the exchange rate – and hence on unemployment – they failed to demonstrate their unity of argument and purpose.

This highlighted the need for new vehicles to identify and channel the common elements in these alternative proposals and to articulate their strengths. If the majority of respected economists could be shown to support an alternative set of policies which were recognisably the same as those being advocated by a majority of Westminster politicians, both sides of industry and other influential groupings, perhaps the pressures on the government to change the course of economic policy would achieve a new coherence. The potential benefits were enormous. With unemployment at over three million rather than at the level of one and one-quarter million it had been in 1979 – and even neglecting all the personal, social and output costs of unemployment – the Exchequer was wasting expenditure at the level of the annual education budget each year, just keeping people idle.

The Employment Institute set out to assist this process of explanation and co-ordination. In a series of articles and statements, some published by its sister organisation Charter for Jobs, contributors from across the political and industrial spectrum as well as professional economists set out the economic facts behind the rise in unemployment and confirmed their common belief in alternative policies.

The readings in this book and its companion volume *Making the Economy Work* represent one part of that process. Most were originally published in the Employment Institute's pamphlet series. They include contributions from one of the leading political figures of the last two decades and from a major figure in the trade union movement, as well as eminent economists. The strength and diversity of support attained by the Employment Institute are also evident from the membership of its Council (see in the prelims).

THE PROBLEM

Before considering the proposals emanating from the Employment Institute in greater detail it is helpful to home in on a few statistics. Unemployment levels are not measured with great precision or consistency in the United Kingdom. The monthly count of unemployed benefit claimants has been subject to some twenty changes in coverage over the last six years because of revisions to administrative procedures or definition.[2] Many categories of involuntarily unemployed people have always been left outside it. A more comprehensive count may well have reached a peak of over four million in the mid-1980s rather than the official peak in unemployment of about three-and-a-quarter million.

In addressing the arguments of those who claimed that 'nothing could be done' to combat this unemployment, the following main points have always tended to emerge:

1. Not four years before the three million figure was published unemployment levels, on similar methods of counting, had been in the region of one and one-quarter million. Even at that level, there were few signs of 'overemployment' with fewer reported labour shortages, lower levels of capacity utilisation and stronger balance of payments than in the previous 'economic peak' of 1973.
2. No other country experienced as quick or savage a deterioration in unemployment as the United Kingdom in the world recession of the early 1980s.
3. Almost all the net job losses in the United Kingdom – numbering over two million – were in manufacturing, which suffered disproportionate and probably temporary damage as a result of the substantial rise in the real exchange rate, itself strongly influenced by government policy.
4. Similar fatalism had been expressed during the last bout of mass unemployment in the United Kingdom in the 1930s. Yet unemployment had then stopped rising after four years and a rapid decline had set in. This was well before rearmament and war had effectively eradicated unemployment completely.
5. Inflationary pressures had been substantially reduced by the early 1980s, the country's net foreign assets were rising and public expenditure was actually falling as a proportion of national income.

Plant was lying idle, queues for the few job vacancies were enormous and the infrastructure and public sector were crumbling. So why not use the government's spending powers to put people to work and hence generate additional demand to get industry moving again as well? This is the central issue addressed by this volume.

SOUND CURRENCY AND FULL EMPLOYMENT

Rudiger Dornbusch is best known amongst economists for his contributions to economic theory. His predictions and explanations of the temporary rise in the value of a country's currency that would follow from the use of monetary instruments to tighten economic policy became universally recognised in the early 1980s as 'Dornbusch overshooting'. But his interest and understanding of the course of economic policy and developments in Europe is also substantial, exemplified by his involvement in the expert group writing for the Centre for European Policy Studies in Louvain which has produced a stream of positive policy prescriptions for the countries of the European Community in recent years.

Few could therefore have been better placed than Dornbusch to highlight the problems faced by the UK economy under the 'monetarist' regime of the Thatcher administrations. Although he is an advocate of a 'tight money' approach, Dornbusch, in his contribution to this volume (Chapter 2), knocks on the head the notion that there was no connection between inadequate demand in the United Kingdom in the early 1980s (itself reflecting in part the stance of government policy) and high unemployment. He shows that the urgent need during this period was in fact to *increase* expenditure levels and so raise output. The chapter ridicules those who considered growth rates of 2½ per annum to be adequate for the economy – a judgement shown in recent times to have been more than justified by the performance of the economy in 1987 when a 4½ per cent growth rate was achieved without noticeable strains on the economy and to the predicted accompaniment of falling unemployment.

Dornbusch points out glaring inconsistencies in the attitudes of government ministers towards the case for growth. They can be totally dismissive of the advantages of higher growth if this is achieved through policy intervention, while being uncritically accepting of growth achieved through higher exports – even though the inflationary consequences of each are likely to be identical.

Dornbusch powerfully dismisses the use of high unemployment as an instrument in bringing down inflation once the threat of hyperinflation has been tamed. But if unemployment is either an ineffective or immoral weapon for the government to use in trying to achieve a stable price level, what might be used instead? Dornbusch sticks by the merits of tight controls on monetary growth, albeit with sufficient flexibility to absorb economic shocks. This would permit advantage to be taken of favourable opportunities on the price level (perhaps falling oil prices or a rising exchange rate) to achieve periods of relatively costless disinflation. The intention would be to bring about step reductions in the rate at which earnings were rising during these periods. Incomes policies might also have a role to play.

The key to policy would be the use of monetary instruments to prevent a collapse in the exchange rate alongside expansionary fiscal measures to raise output. The choice of which fiscal measures to use would depend on their effectiveness in increasing employment, their net exchequer cost and the ease with which their effect on the public sector deficit could be unwound.

This concept of 'targeting' the choice of fiscal measures in ways which would maximise employment for minimum cost recurs throughout this volume. It is further elaborated in *Making the Economy Work*.[3] As Dornbusch points out, the 'economic' output of traditional employment programmes – in terms of their measured contribution to Gross Domestic Product – might be small, but employment programmes could put hundreds of thousands of people back to work without increasing the public sector deficit by much more than the additional 3 per cent of GDP which Dornbusch recommends in his two-year programme of fiscal expansion.

Of course, massive expansion of such programmes to the point at which the *guarantee*[4] of a place could be given to the long-term unemployed might raise questions about permanence and about compulsion (the threat that benefit would be withdrawn if an offer were refused). It would be better, however, to square up to such issues, rather than simply to allow a further twist to be added to a benefit culture of automatic entitlement to benefits which could be likened to mass *un*employment programmes.

GOVERNMENTS CAN AFFECT EMPLOYMENT

Central to Dornbusch's arguments is the certainty that government decisions on tax, public expenditure, the budget deficit and monetary growth *do* affect both the inflation rate and the level and composition of activity in the economy. The notion that monetary and fiscal policy are useless because they will not affect the decisions that private sector agents make is dismissed as the artefact of highly stylised models and of only limited relevance to the real world of poor information, uncompetitive markets and sticky prices.

Gavyn Davies develops this theoretical theme in Chapter 3. With care and clarity, he reduces the arguments advanced by the 'new classical' or 'new monetarist' economists on whom the Thatcher governments have drawn to a set of testable claims and falsifiable assumptions. The tests are failed; the assumptions are rejected. 'Keynesian' remedies can still work after all. With a few lessons learnt on the way, governments still do have the power and ability to influence if not fully to manage the economy.

Davies first addresses the captivating notion, recorded by David Ricardo in the nineteenth century and now embraced by some followers of the 'new classical' school, that changes in government borrowing can have no effect on the economy because ultimately all borrowing will have to be paid back. Since everyone knows that it is taxpayers who will ultimately have to pay, they will fully and immediately react to any increases in government borrowing by increasing their own savings. A decision to increase public spending will therefore be offset automatically by private saving and there will be no effect on overall demand or output in the economy. The problems with this appealingly simple idea are that it requires not only incredibly far-sighted taxpayers to make it work but also ones who either live as long as Methuselah or are perfectly altruistic in their attitude to the need of their taxpaying descendants. They also of course need to be able to adjust their spending and saving decisions at the drop of the Chancellor's briefcase.

Not surprisingly, Davies gives the whole idea little credence. This sort of 'fiscal crowding out' is a nonsense. He goes on also to dismiss the more sophisticated notion that *financial* crowding out will automatically render fiscal policy ineffective through its impact on interest rates and the exchange rate. In general, he concludes that it will not; and particularly not if the appropriate choice of monetary policy is made.

More importantly, however, Davies proceeds to investigate whether, given that fiscal policy *can* influence demand, it can be operated in such a way that real output and employment will be affected rather than the price level and inflation. In classical monetary theory, it cannot. Perfect knowledge and perfect certainty mean that only real variables determine real output and the money supply (or growth) determines prices (or the rate of inflation). But new classical economics is not that simplistic. Perfect knowledge is understood to be an impossibility. Into its place steps 'rational expectations' as the mechanism through which information about the rest of the economy and its future course is transmitted to the individual or economic agent.

Under 'rational expectations', any view about the future which affects current economic decisions will not be formed in an *ad hoc* way, but using the best predictive tools currently in existence and bringing to bear all the affordable information currently available.

Economic agents (such as you and I) do not make systematic errors in such predictions because we learn by experience to revise our models and forecasts. Davies carefully draws out both the plausibility of these mechanisms and their implications. He finds that on both theoretical and empirical grounds it is unlikely that economic agents can or do form their expectations 'rationally'. It is therefore irrelevant that one ultimate implication of rational expectations might be to render ineffective any attempt by the government to manage the economy against the predictions of economic models.

This is a crucial conclusion. Much of the invective heaped by the new classical economists on policy makers has rested on the notion that they are misleading themselves in believing that they can 'fool' economic agents and markets. But markets (and policy makers) do not always get things as right as they could. They may indeed sometimes be systematically wrong.

The message that Davies picks up from the rational expectations 'revolution' is not that agents will *always* be as sensible or 'rational' as they might, but that they *may* be sometimes. This means that it is dangerous for policy makers to assume that others will *always* make predictable mistakes. It also means that an assumption that agents will continue to form their expectations in a 'non-rational' way should not be allowed to permeate the construction of models of economic behaviour. Thus the theory of rational expectations turns out to provide some important messages for economic policy determination, but not to provide the strong pillar of the new classical case that its supporters would have us believe.

What of the other pillar of the new classical school: the assumption that the economy operates (or ought to operate) according to models of perfect competition with perfectly flexible prices? This receives much shorter shrift from Davies. The assumptions are exposed as little more than mathematically convenient artefacts. Davies shows that many prices, and particularly the price of labour (the wage rate) do not in fact adjust quickly to ensure that a balance is always achieved between supply and demand. If, for instance, a large shock is experienced on the demand side of a market, large imbalances can exist for a long time. This means that when some, perhaps largely external, event influences the labour market, involuntary unemployment can and does frequently occur. It may be that market forces would ultimately bring about a full adjustment, but the time taken for the adjustment process to work might be extremely long.

It is this long and costly delay which provides the most persuasive reason for government intervention. Governments can sometimes offset the effects of sticky prices on the output of the economy by stimulating aggregate demand. This might slow down further some of the price adjustment that would otherwise have taken place, but by raising productivity levels it can even render some of that adjustment unnecessary by validating higher costs and real wages. Government action can also ameliorate the impact of the adjustment process by, for instance, providing employment programmes for the unemployed which do not impinge on other parts of the labour market.

The structure and operation of product and labour markets fail to support other preconditions of perfect competition. The economy is not made up just of small, atomistic agents. Markets tend to be dominated by a few fairly large producers or unions. Imperfect competition and, particularly, oligopoly is the rule. In these circumstances, not only is it easy to observe real-world examples of price stickiness, but also to construct convincing models of why it should happen. Davies shows how involuntary unemployment can thus easily become entrenched. It falls to government to dislodge it.

With the 'new classical' case for the ineffectiveness of policy in the short run so comprehensively debunked on theoretical and practical levels, it remains only for Davies to survey the empirical evidence. Although in the end he does not find existing tests to offer conclusive proof either way it is noticeable that, as the econometric tests have become more sophisticated, so each new piece of evidence has been more damning to the 'new classical' case.

What about the long run? Can governments interfere with the long-run trade-off between unemployment and stable inflation, so that unemployment can be permanently reduced without sending the inflation rate into an upwards spiral? The main task must be to try and reconcile the normally inconsistent demands of employees and producers over the appropriate level of the real wage: preventing the leapfrogging of wages and prices. Incomes policies can play a role, as can the closing of the gap between each party's aspirations by reducing unit costs to the employer (lower labour taxes, improvements in the skill levels of the available workforce) or the demands of potential employees (increasing their readiness to work at proffered wage levels). There is much scope here for government action.

The central role of the Davies text is to re-establish the case for policy activism rather than to indulge in specific prescriptions or suggest a new framework for decision taking. Those tasks, as they relate to macroeconomic remedies, fall instead to the next three chapters in this volume.

MEDIUM-TERM EMPLOYMENT STRATEGIES

Chapter 4 considers whether there is a case for reforming rather than abandoning the government's Medium-Term Financial Strategy (MTFS). It identifies what positive and productive elements might be rescued from a structure that seemed to promise a great deal in the struggle to rid British economic policy making of its volatility, however damaging its final impact may have been. Could the failures of the MTFS be ascribed simply to the wrong choices of objectives and instruments? After all, the frequent haphazard reversals in direction characterised by a succession of 'mini-budgets' and crisis-induced gyrations in monetary policy in the 1960s and 1970s certainly called for some new structure to be devised.

The first issue is to establish what the purpose of a 'framework' or a 'strategy' for policy might legitimately be. The identification of specific and feasible objectives seems to provide a sensible starting-point. But the MTFS specifically ruled out as unrealistic the setting of goals for what most would see as the primary (if not the sole) aim of economic policy: the achievement of low unemployment and high output.

The assumption that underpinned the MTFS was that macroeconomic policy was powerless in these areas. Davies has shown how ill-founded this assumption was, a point easily confirmed by reference to a host of historical and international parallels. But the architects of the MTFS were adamant that only the control of inflation was a worthy and attainable objective. Even that should not be specified as a quantifiable target, but only be seen as an ultimate aim which would be achieved by adherence to a sequence of specific targets for 'intermediate' variables, notably the rate of monetary growth.

With such restrictive and arms-length objectives, it was hardly surprising that the MTFS should produce such poor outcomes for output and unemployment. That has not inhibited its supporters from pointing out its relative success in other fields: there is now a much greater confidence within financial markets that the government will stick to its guns; oscillations in economic policy have become much less frequent; predictability within both fiscal and financial policy has increased; and there is a greater likelihood that the two will be used in supportive rather than opposing modes.

At the same time, ironically, much of the Chancellor's freedom of action has in fact been preserved. Nigel Lawson has never felt constrained to frame his budget in such a way that the precise fiscal targets set out the previous year will be met. He has exceeded by substantial amounts the targets he has set for the money stock, sometimes reducing interest rates while the degree of monetary overshooting is increasing. He has even felt free to 'move the goal-posts' of policy by selling off public sector assets or redefining money. In many ways, the policy decisions of 1983–8 seem more akin to old-fashioned fine tuning of the economy to balance out inflation and growth than adherence to fixed financial targets.

If these are successes what special ingredients have made them possible? Two vital elements of the framework which have fostered confidence but permitted flexibility are identified as: a time-scale which is long enough to help economic agents plan beyond the current year (even if not in complete certainty); and a commitment by the government about the direction in which levers of economic policy would be moved if the outcome differed from expectations.

If the Medium-Term *Financial* Strategy were therefore to be replaced by a Medium-Term *Employment* Strategy it might usefully take such criteria as its starting-points. Such a strategy would give guidance about the government's expectations for the major components of the economic outlook over, say, a five-year period. Inflation, output, employment and unemployment would all be covered. But the outcomes would clearly be dependent on, amongst other things, the operation of economic policy itself. This would bring the government into the business of clearly stating its own objectives and the means it would be using to bring them about. It would have to provide some form of 'feedback rules', stating how it would react to deviations from its expectations, including the way its priorities might change if it became clear that its objectives were inconsistent or simply unobtainable.

Turning the behavioural assumptions of the MTFS on their heads, it is suggested that the most appropriate single *objective* for a Medium-Term Employment Strategy should simply be the level of unemployment. Other objectives, such as a desirable level of inflation or a sustainable balance of payments position, would be better handled not as targets in their own right but as constraints. If these seemed likely to be breached, this would limit the speed at which the central objective could be reached. Furthermore, and again learning from the lessons of the MTFS, unique targets would not be appropriate: better to specify ranges within which outcomes would be acceptable. Discretion within these ranges could safely be left to the government of the time without inciting the distrust of the markets.

Having set up a framework for a Medium-Term Employment Strategy, the chapter proceeds to show how it might work in practice. Precise objectives are specified for unemployment, ranging from an 'ambitious' five-year schedule (equivalent to the best of past achievements) to a cautious figure almost certain not to provoke strains elsewhere in the economy. Limits on acceptable out-turns for inflation and the balance of payments are carefully determined.

Last, but by no means least, a set of policies for bringing about the unemployment reduction are explored. These involve not only the stimulation of aggregate demand by increases in targeted public expenditure and reductions in taxes on employment, but also a raft of 'supply side' measures to prop up the workings of the domestic economy and prevent the constraints from biting.

We have now moved a long way from the notion that the government can do nothing to improve the economy but 'stand clear', to one where it is back as an active economic agent, albeit one concerned as much with the importance of others knowing what it intends and is doing as with the operation of policy itself. Its responsibilities stretch into all areas, with no ideological inhibitions about staying clear of the arena within which industrial and wage decisions are made.

THE STATE OF BRITAIN TO COME

This wider, more optimistic role for government policy is explored further in Edward Heath's contribution to the current volume. As the first postwar Prime Minister in the United Kingdom to experience the trauma of an unemployment level of over one million, he is only too aware of the misery and waste that such unemployment can bring and of the breadth of policy action that is needed to counter it. His approach is uniquely compassionate and comprehensive.

At the heart of Heath's prescriptions lies the need for a return to a forward-looking and energetic industrial policy. He emphasises the need to help large, as well as small companies to prosper and to work with the grain of industrial innovation and development as pioneered by the approach of the Scottish Development Agency. His vision embraces the fostering of European-wide industrial units to take advantage of an emerging 'home' market of 320 million people rather than the passive acceptance of aggressive take-overs by overseas interests. Industrial policy cannot be framed in isolation from developments in other, 'competitor' countries. However much the government may believe in 'playing by the rules' of non-intervention, it cannot force those rules on others. The result is that, too often, British companies have found themselves unable to compete on level terms precisely because of the lack in the United Kingdom of the government support that is taken for granted elsewhere.

Conflicting interests may set governments on collision courses in industrial policy. When it comes to macroeconomic policy, however, Heath sees a clear role for co-operation between governments. High unemployment is not a problem in Britain alone. Nearly all major countries would gain from higher rates of activity in the world economy (not least the United States, whose domestic priority should be the curtailment of their own public sector deficit). A co-ordinated reflation in industrial countries other than the United States would be the answer.

What would be the United Kingdom's contribution to this? As a patron of the Employment Institute and the associated Charter for Jobs campaign, Heath endorses their calls for a removal of the financial straitjacket on government borrowing. One major result of this would be that a programme could be undertaken which would guarantee the offer of a temporary job or place on a training scheme to all long-term unemployed people. This would place investment in people alongside investment in physical capital as one of the prime aims of policy. The development of a National Training System would cement the case for the raising of our educational standards to the level of 'best practice' in France, Germany, Switzerland, Japan and the United States.

Heath's call is for a general return to policies of national consent. Only in this way can those who feel outcast and neglected be brought back into the fold.

FULL EMPLOYMENT AND THE BALANCE OF PAYMENTS

Andrew Britton's concern (Chapter 6) is with a more specific impediment to maintaining a high rate of growth and restoring the economy to full employment. It is one that plagued the British economy throughout the 1950s and 1960s, but which some hoped the move to floating exchange rates in the early 1970s would banish for ever from the nightmares of policy makers: the current account of the balance of payments.

Experience has now shown that substantial balance of payments deficits and surpluses can persist for a number of years (there is, besides, no reason why a zero balance should be 'correct'). Far from triggering the sort of adjustment in exchange rates that would ultimately lead to the resolution of balance of payments problems, the policy origins of payments imbalances have sometimes led to perverse movements in exchange rates. More to the immediate concern of UK policy makers, adjustments can simply be delayed. When they do come, movements in the exchange rate can be sharp enough to cause considerable disturbance to the domestic price level and rate of inflation.

The UK current account of the balance of payments has recently been marching ever more swiftly into the red. Andrew Britton's problem is not so much how to deal with this on its own (which he ascribes to the legacy of the high exchange rates and low level of demand of the early 1980s) but how to counteract the far more severe pressures that are likely to accompany any change of policy which would be directed towards achieving still higher rates of economic growth. As he points out, the non-economist might be forgiven for thinking that the obvious way of reconciling high unemployment and potential difficulties with the balance of payments might be just to put the unemployed to work making goods for export. If only one could do this and not have to worry about the responses of the market and the appetite of the newly-employed for imports!

Britton is in no doubt that a fall in the real exchange rate (the nominal exchange rate corrected for changes in relative price levels) is a necessary condition if the United Kingdom is to return to full employment. How can this be achieved without provoking an inflationary spiral? Wage cuts (or a slower rate of wage inflation than obtains overseas) could in theory produce the required effect without any change being necessary in the nominal exchange rate. But, in practice, they could cause tremendous disruption and take years to effect – and there would still be the problem for policy of maintaining an appropriate level for the exchange rate against possible upward pressure. In fact the whole question of actually being able to secure a given rate of exchange is an extremely open one. Co-operation with the IMF or the authorities of the European Monetary System (the EMS) might provide possible mechanisms for engineering an appropriate fall in the nominal rate if that is the chosen course. Either approach would secure Britton's approval. But neither these nor the achievement of lower rates of growth of wages should be seen as policies in their own right, able to deliver the required levels of output and employment.

Instead, a mix of policies is required. There must be some measure of fiscal expansion involving lower taxes or higher public expenditure. The elements of this should, however, be chosen not only with an eye to their power to generate employment (the 'targeting' approach outlined above) but also to the way they could help prevent an inflationary spiral being set up by a fall in the nominal exchange rate. Indirect taxes might be cut, for instance, or subsidies implemented on consumers' expenditure. Cuts in employers' contributions to national insurance would score highly on all counts.

Other policies supporting the overall employment-creation strategy might involve enhancement of industrial training to attack the problem of skilled labour shortage or the encouragement of capital inflow to raise managerial standards. But the needs of the balance of payments itself may benefit from being faced directly. If we are going to gain effectively from an improvement in industry's overall competitive position, brought about by a reduction in the real exchange rate, industry may need help to put in place the necessary changes in a speedy fashion. Government would be trying not to interfere with industry's long-run decisions about products, pricing or investment, but it could offer adjustment assistance. It could also encourage import-substitution through an improvement in the information supplied about British suppliers.

What emerges are the basic elements of a comprehensive strategy for attaining the twin aims of full employment and balance of payments equilibrium.

THE PLAIN MAN'S GUIDE TO FISCAL AND FINANCIAL POLICY

Expansion of the economy through the easing of fiscal policy (higher government expenditure or lower taxation) has been a common theme of all the contributions so far. The task of Charlie Bean and Willem Buiter (Chapter 7) is to formalise what rules might sensibly guide the size of response necessary while preserving fiscal and financial responsibility.

Their first step is to take us back to basics. What do we mean by the public sector, by expenditure, revenue and deficits? Do different items of expenditure and revenue have different effects on the economy, depriving summary measures of the fiscal balance of any ability to assess in a unique sense the effect of a fiscal package on the economy?

By explaining the operation of the 'balanced budget multiplier' and the varied effects that increased public sector provision can have on private sector expenditure decisions, they demonstrate just how complex the process can be. But it is not just the expenditure and revenue decisions themselves that can affect the outcome. The theoretical mechanisms that might cause monetary effects to overturn entirely the impact of fiscal changes are examined. It is revealed that this itself is a matter of policy choice. The arguments advanced by Davies (Chapter 3) are endorsed: it is perfectly possible to let monetary policy 'accommodate' economic changes brought about by fiscal policy rather than suppress them. Similarly, the much-heralded but little-analysed effects of public expenditure or taxation on *supply*, through the incentives they provide for different types of economic behaviour, can in theory substantially alter the eventual outcome of budgetary changes.

Having shown that the 'mix' of policy does matter, Bean and Buiter extend the Davies arguments to provide quantitative estimates of the impact of different methods of financing and of different monetary regimes. Using a structural model of the economy, they show that a permanent rise in the level of exhaustive government expenditure at less-than-full employment can shift employment levels higher, but the extent and permanence of this (and the effect on inflation) are considerably affected by the choice between tax and debt financing and the targets being used for monetary policy.

So life is complicated. Does that mean that there are no simple universal rules governing fiscal policy that would be better obeyed than avoided? At the least, perhaps the authors could offer a few generalities about the public sector deficit (however defined) that could help a responsible Chancellor restrain the enthusiasms of his high-spending colleagues? Not, it turns out, as far as the day-to-day operation of budgetary decisions is concerned. Clearly, aggregate demand should not be stimulated by expansionary fiscal policy when the economy is at or approaching full employment. But it is only the threat that a spiralling debt burden could ultimately induce the government to undertake inflationary monetary policies (monetising too much of the debt) that provides a long-term limit to the size of fiscal deficits that can be sustained (assuming that default is not an option). The authors show that, to be consistent with a given, low rate of inflation, the required average size of the *primary* deficit or surplus (excluding interest payments) will depend on the level of real interest rates, the potential growth rate of the economy and the velocity of circulation of money. At current debt-income ratios and primary surpluses it turns out to be *deflation* rather than *inflation* which is the risk. Moreover looking at measures of the 'permanent' rather than conventional public sector financial deficit indicates that for much of the 1970s and early 1980s the public sector's overall financial status was improving, with its net worth probably growing.

The message is therefore supportive of the qualitative line developed by all the previous authors. Whilst it may sometimes be right for the government to keep its budget in surplus to prevent increases in the long-run debt ratios that threaten excessive monetisation, fiscal prudence is not a sufficient criterion for successful economic management. Surplus capacity in the economy, including involuntary unemployment, should be brought back into play by selective fiscal measures.

THE FUTURE

Looking back at the three years since the Employment Institute's birth in April 1985 it is possible to gain a certain amount of satisfaction from the changes that have come about in the way that the government has implemented economic policy. The inflexible adherence to inappropriate targets ridiculed by Rudi Dornbusch has completely disappeared. The judicious use of asset sales to disguise rises in the public sector deficit and expansion of special programmes for the long-term unemployed has shown not only that the government accepts Gavyn Davies's contention that it *can* affect unemployment but that it is prepared to use the fiscal instruments he advocates to do so. All the discussion surrounding the 1988 budget suggests that 'demand management' has returned to centre stage with worries about the balance of payments and inflation being allowed to influence but not override the objective of maintaining economic growth.

Certainly the fiscal position has been more restrictive than this volume advocates – and the government's rhetoric has not changed – but each budget has seen a willingness merely to preserve the gains brought about by the previous year's economic growth rather than to improve the public sector's balance sheet even further for its own sake.

At the same time, economic growth has been maintained and employment levels (though mainly in part-time jobs) have been steadily rising. Since late 1986, the government's monthly count of unemployed benefit claimants has been showing substantial falls. These falls have not all been good news: many of the people removed from the count are no less unemployed now than they were while in the count. Only their entitlement to unemployment benefit or their willingness to claim it has changed. However, the very fast growth rate (probably 4½ to 5 per cent per annum) achieved in the latter part of this period has almost certainly brought with it some genuine reductions in unemployment – exactly as predicted and advocated in 'Medium-Term Employment Strategies'.

Will this improved performance be maintained? The recovery currently is under threat from imbalances caused by too heavy a reliance on the unfettered expansion of personal sector credit. The deficit on the current account of the balance of payments is rising rapidly. It is difficult to be sanguine as to how long the financial markets will accept both this and signs of rising inflation without adverse reactions. The exchange rate in the spring of 1988 looks vulnerably high. The recipes offered by Andrew Britton for dealing simultaneously with unemployment and current account problems may soon need to be brought into play. More fundamentally, however, the concerns voiced by Edward Heath about the longer-term health of British industry and the desperate need to raise the quality and quantity of training provision will resound again and again until a genuine change of policies is undertaken.

As the unemployment count descends through the 2½ million mark, the doom-laden prophecies of those who feared it had nowhere to go but up from three million plus are exposed as nonsense. The task now is to send genuine unemployment back down at least to the levels of the 1970s. This book, and the accompanying volume, *Making the Economy Work*, offer the means of achieving it.

Notes

1. Jon Shields, first Director of the Employment Institute, was formally a Senior Economic Adviser in HM Treasury.
2. See Charter for Jobs Economic Report vol. 2, no. 7.
3. See for example Jackman, R. *et al*. (1989) *Making the Economy Work* (London: Macmillan) ch. 9.
4. Op. cit.

2 Sound Currency *and* Full Employment[1]

Rudiger Dornbusch

THE BRITISH EXPERIMENT

The British Experiment is the unfortunate title the Chancellor of the Exchequer, Mr. Lawson chose for his Mais Lecture in June 1984. The title reflects the detachment with which policy makers in Great Britain have fought to transform British society and to stop inflation. There is no question that the Thatcher government has changed the country. The most striking achievements are the reduction of inflation to surprisingly low levels (by the standards of the 1970s) and, to a lesser extent, the consolidation of public finance. These two strategic victories return the country to the position of the early 1970s, undoing the extreme instability of the past decade. But they have not been achieved without costs: unemployment conditions today, in 1985, resemble those of the 1930s. Unemployment, far from being transitory, is becoming a way of life for an increasing number of people.

The increase in unemployment, and the absence of any policy commitment or conception to cope with the problem, must leave any observer in awe. What is there to assure society that the 'experiment' will be called off in time if it becomes evident that the present course cannot achieve a reintegration of the unemployed into normal social conditions? The rules of the experiment, for maximum success, call for stone-walling the very idea of concession. But the policy stance of non-negotiability, of course, also means that failure can be total. Gains, rather than being locked in by a judicious and timely shift in policy, may be sacrificed in an ideological quest for total victory. To convey a sense of the problem, here is an excerpt from Mr. Lawson's above cited speech:

> Stable prices are a blessed condition, but one that we in this country have not experienced other than very fleetingly for 50 years. To achieve stable prices thus implies fighting and changing

the culture and the psychology of two generations. That cannot be achieved overnight. But let there be no doubt that is our goal.

One cannot but note the difference between the approach pursued in the United States and conditions in Britain. I am not only thinking of Paul Volcker, the Chairman of the US Federal Reserve who combines a pragmatic policy approach with a basically uncompromising commitment to disinflation. In the White House too, where the free market philosophy runs at least as high as it does with policy makers in Great Britain, amid union-busting and deregulation there is a keen appreciation of the merits of prosperity. And, for the time being, prosperity is on the move.

The single most important question for Great Britain today is whether an argument can be made for a prosperity policy to build employment opportunities, without threatening the double achievement of disinflation and consolidation of public finance. If so, is this the time to move, or are there further important gains to be reaped from the current course of action?

I do not believe that many thoughtful observers would opt for expansion at any price. That philosophy is bankrupt today, whatever its merit and appeal may have been on past occasions. Today the public would want assurance that a shift in policy is in fact sustainable and does not involve throwing away the gains of the past few years. At the same time it must be clear that the deterioration in economic performance, as evidenced by high and rising unemployment, cannot go unchallenged. Of course, it might be argued that it would be a big mistake to deviate from the set course of policy just as the rewards for steadfastness are about to be reaped. But credibility cuts two ways: the assertion that steadiness of policy will reap rewards in terms of falling unemployment and rising prosperity is still just an assertion. There is little favourable evidence of success so far. On the contrary, it looks as if Mrs Thatcher's Financial Squeeze (MTFS for short) might turn out to be the big blunder of the 1980s, on a par with the mistakes of over-optimistic Keynesian policy makers in earlier episodes. Indeed, unless there is a really big surprise around the corner, that must be the verdict.

Much the same problem, though on a more moderate scale, is faced in all of Europe, but few countries have achieved the consolidation the United Kingdom can point to. The closest comparison is Germany where fiscal stabilisation and the fight against inflation has been pursued with less rhetoric but with as fierce a commitment and determination. Significantly, in Germany there is now much public support for a programme of fiscal expansion to promote more rapid recovery.

In the light of the obstinacy of British policy makers in the face of a dramatic unemployment problem, it is worth remembering some comments of John Maynard Keynes under very similar conditions in 1929.[2]

> Except for a brief recovery period in 1924 before the return to the gold standard, one-tenth or more of the working population of this country have been unemployed for eight years – a fact unprecedented in our history . . .
>
> Was there ever a stronger case for a little boldness, for taking a risk if there be one? It may seem very wise to sit back and wag the head. But while we wait, the unused labour of the workless is not piling to our credit in a bank, ready to be used at some later date. It is running irrevocably to waste; it is irretrievably lost. Every puff of Mr. Baldwin's pipe costs us thousands of pounds . . .
>
> It is not an accident that the Conservative Government have landed us in the mess where we find ourselves. It is the natural outcome of their philosophy:
>
> 'You must not press on with telephones or electricity, because it will raise the rate of interest.'
>
> 'You must not hasten with roads or housing, because this will use up opportunities for employment which we may need in later years.'
>
> 'You must not try to employ everyone, because this will cause inflation.'
>
> 'You must not do anything, because this will only mean that you can't do something else.'
>
> 'Safety first! The policy of maintaining a million unemployed has now been pursued for eight years without disaster. Why risk a change?'

Table 2.1 offers a perspective on key economic indicators in the past fifteen years. The striking success at disinflation is quite obvious, as is the reduction in the budget deficit. The counterpart is the huge increase in unemployment. Figure 2.1 shows inflation and unemployment to document the pattern since 1970. The figure reminds us that twice in the past decade the inflation rate was at or above 20 per cent. The return to such instability is an important objection to any

Table 2.1 Main economic indicators

	1971–80	*1980–4*	*1985 (forecast)*
Unemployment rate (%)	4.1	9.8	13.0
Inflation rate (RPI, %)	13.3	9.2	5.2
Budget deficit (% of GDP)	3.3	3.7	2.6
Public debt (% of GDP)	57.4	48.6	NA

Source: European Community, *European Economy*, November 1984 and OECD, *Main Economic Indicators.*

***Figure* 2.1 Inflation and unemployment**

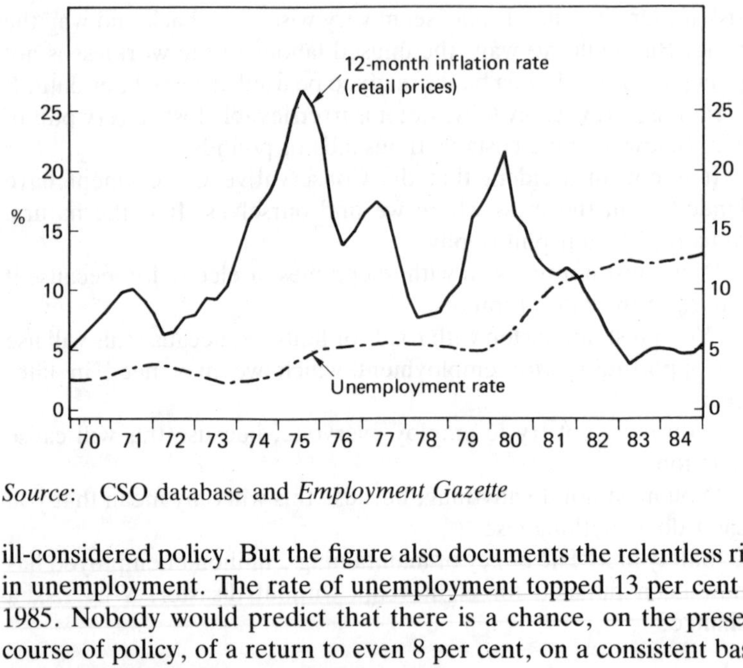

Source: CSO database and *Employment Gazette*

ill-considered policy. But the figure also documents the relentless rise in unemployment. The rate of unemployment topped 13 per cent in 1985. Nobody would predict that there is a chance, on the present course of policy, of a return to even 8 per cent, on a consistent basis of measurement, in the foreseeable future.

The budget and public debt figures in Table 2.1 deserve special attention. In 1970 the public debt amounted to nearly 75 per cent of GDP whereas now it is around 50 per cent and will decline on present policies. The budget deficit has been cut since 1979/80. That reduction, while aided by North Sea oil revenues, is striking, since it occurred in the face of a poor macroeconomic performance which meant a reduction in the effective tax base. Furthermore the sharp cut in inflation did not help cure debt problems because it stopped the inflationary erosion of debt burdens. If adjustments are made for the effect of inflation on debt service and for the effect of economic slack on revenues and unemployment benefits, the budget figures on an adjusted basis now show a surplus. If the economy were using all available resources at reasonable capacity levels, the impact on budget revenues would be more than sufficient to balance the budget.

The impressive results in the area of fiscal consolidation are offset by extraordinarily poor performance in other areas. The youth unemployment rate in 1985 is over 25 per cent. The extremity of the unemployment problem shows up similarly in statistics on the fraction of the unemployed who have been out of work for more than six months or even a year. Already in 1983 more than half of the unemployed had been out of work for more than six months, and more than a third for as much as a year or more. Since then the position has, of course, deteriorated further.

WHERE DOES THE UNEMPLOYMENT COME FROM?

Between 1979 and 1985 unemployment rose by nearly eight percentage points, from just above 5 per cent to over 13 per cent. It is certainly important to know why unemployment in the late 1970s was nearly double the level of the early part of the decade, but that is not the immediate concern of current policy options. There is wide consensus that supply-side factors account for a significant part of that increase. In the period to 1980 increased real labour costs because of labour taxes and unwarranted real wage increases reduced employment. Increases in structural rigidities and regional problems aggravated the reduction in labour demand. The existence of an improved level of unemployment benefits and perhaps the fostering of an 'unemployment culture' may have worked to raise the fraction of the labour force that 'chose' to be unemployed. These microeconomic factors are important, but they share the characteristic that they accumulate over time, sometimes even in an offsetting manner, so that their net impact over a short interval is in fact difficult to document.

Careful studies of unemployment since the 1950s have singled out and documented the role of microeconomic factors. I would not challenge the common belief that microeconomic factors account for a good part of increased unemployment. But the interesting finding is that, whereas demand factors explained less than one-third of the change in unemployment in the period 1956–79, in the period between 1979 and 1985 they account for 70 per cent.[3] In the last six years, macroeconomic factors have simply swamped all the microeconomic determinants of unemployment. Our focus here is primarily on the dramatic rise in unemployment in the 1980s which occurred simultaneously in the United Kingdom and all over Europe. The important issue is to understand the massive rise in the past six years where (counting discouraged workers) perhaps as many as fifteen out of every 100 people cannot get jobs. Here macroeconomic developments are the explanation.

The rise in unemployment in the United Kingdom over the past six years can readily be explained by the decline in employment, which in turn can be traced to the combination of slow growth in real demand for goods and services and growth in productivity. Spending growth has been slow because monetary and fiscal policy, the exchange rate and growth abroad combined into an unfavourable setting for spending on British goods. The growth in productivity, with both labour-shedding and genuine improvements in production, reinforced the impact of slow demand growth by making it possible to produce the same amount of output with less labour.

Econometric evidence leaves little question about the influence of four key factors on changes in the unemployment rate:

1. Real appreciation of the exchange rate, or a loss of external competitiveness, shifts demand from UK goods to those produced abroad. Hence real appreciation leads to a rise in unemployment.
2. Fiscal policy has an important effect on real demand, employment and hence unemployment. Specifically, an increase in the cyclically adjusted budget surplus via increased tax rates or cuts in public spending will raise unemployment.
3. Growth of the world economy is also a significant, though quantitatively small, influence in determining employment. Stronger growth of the world economy expands foreign demand for UK goods and thus helps create employment.
4. Monetary policy is one more critical determinant of employment and hence unemployment. It is difficult to assess the various channels through which monetary policy works. But there is little disagreement that tight money would find its expression in increased real interest rates and reduced real credit availability.

Through both channels there would be a reduction in spending by households and firms and hence reduced production and employment.

THE ROLE OF OUTPUT

There are two strong facts that emerge from a study of unemployment behaviour. First, growth of real spending and income must be sufficiently high for unemployment not to increase. Growth of productivity, among other factors, reduces labour demand over time at each level of production and hence raises unemployment. To overcome this adverse trend, output growth must be sufficiently strong to create a demand for labour that matches the growing labour supply. If growth falls below this threshold level, unemployment will be rising because the growth of labour demand is simply not sufficiently high.

The second fact is that, following a shock, unemployment does not tend to return automatically or spontaneously to a normal level, whatever that level might be. Following an increase in unemployment due to some disturbance, only growth above trend can bring down the unemployment rate; it will not decline spontaneously, at least not over a span of a few years.

These two facts have important implications for unemployment policy and in other countries are well appreciated as constituting lesson number one of the political or election business cycle. The lesson is this: to reverse the impact of a recession that has raised the unemployment rate above its normal level, growth must *exceed trend* for some time. The extra growth is required to drain the unemployment pool by an extra dose of labour demand. Failure to have growth above trend simply means that the unemployment rate will stay higher permanently or at least for quite a few years. The reason is, in simple terms, that the market for labour is very different from the market for fresh fish. In the fish market price adjusts so that all fish finds its way into the frying pan. Not so in the labour market. Workers need not take any pay cut just to remain employed: the social arrangements today provide for unemployment relief that has as a cost reduced the flexibility of real wages and thus increased the risk of unemployment. Collective bargaining adds a distinction between those who have jobs and therefore have an interest in protecting their standards of living, and those who are unemployed and hence do not sit at the bargaining table.

Figure **2.2 Actual and trend real GDP**

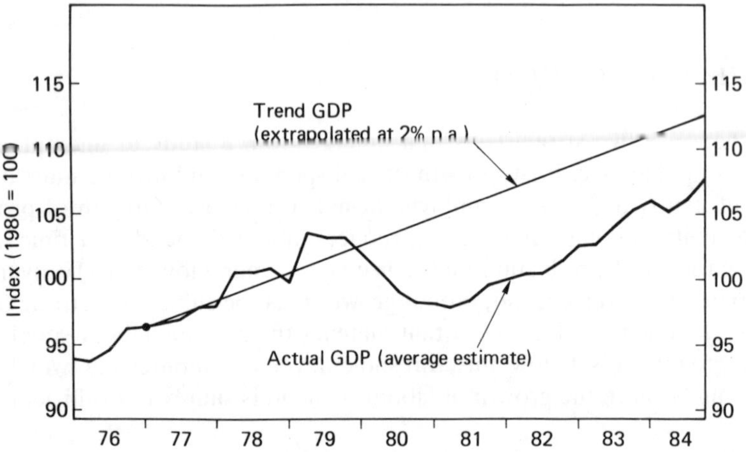

Source: CSO database and *Economic Trends*.

If the trend growth of output were 2 per cent per year and for some years the economy fell below that growth trend because of a recession, then it would never return to trend output unless there were a few years of *catching up*. Failing the extra growth, the economy would simply be growing at the trend rate, but at a lower output level than potential. The difference between potential output or trend output and actual output reflects unemployment and the unused capacity that has not been wiped out. Everything else aside it is obvious that such a policy amounts to wasting scarce resources.

The point can be best appreciated in terms of Figure 2.2. Here we show the level of actual real GDP (*including* oil) and the level of trend output or potential output. To calculate trend output it is assumed that the first quarter of 1977 reflects a normal level of employment and output and that the trend growth rate is a modest 2 per cent per year. The discrepancy between trend output and actual output is the GDP gap – the loss of output due to macroeconomic policy. Corresponding to the output gap there is a gap for employment. If, in 1985, output were at the trend level, capacity utilisation and profitability would be higher, employment higher and unemployment lower. In fact in 1984 the output gap was 6 per cent even on the very modest 2 per cent trend growth assumption. If trend growth were reckoned at the more realistic rate, given the expansion of

North Sea oil production, of 2.25 per cent per year the gap would be 8 per cent.

Figure 2.2 shows at once the problem of never making up for the 1979–81 decline in output. The British economy since mid-1981 has grown at about 2.4 per cent per year (including the effects of North Sea oil), slightly above the trend, but the loss in output accumulated before is still around today and, indeed, unemployment is even higher because the growth of 2.4 per cent has not been enough even to keep unemployment constant at the high level to which it had been driven.

Explaining the decline in real activity in 1979–81 is easy: there was a massive correction in the cyclically-adjusted budget in the direction of restraint, the real interest rate was pushed up strongly, external competitiveness deteriorated, and world growth slowed down sharply.[4] The combination caused a recession. Subsequent easing of monetary and fiscal policy in 1982–4 and the real depreciation of the currency restored growth, but not sufficiently to wipe out the accumulated unemployment. Growth since 1982 has not been much above the trend rate, leaving the gap unfilled. Hence the problem that we can look backward and say: yes, there has been reasonable growth, and yet we know that something is wrong because unemployment remains at record levels.

The basic point that the recession of 1980–1 was never made up by extra growth is so obvious that one would expect even people unacquainted with macroeconomics to have seized on that point. Yet Professor Sir Alan Walters, in his assessment of the British economy, paints an altogether different picture:[5]

> . . . Britain's monetarist policies have been associated with increasing GDP since the second quarter of 1981 at an average rate of about 2.5 % a year. As a 'small' locomotive, Britain led Europe and most of the OECD countries out of the severe recession of 1980–82 . . . Since early 1983, employment has increased by 613 000 jobs. It is difficult to see how 'inadequate aggregate demand' could be responsible for the continuing high level of unemployment.

Perhaps it helps to think of the question in terms of the Great Depression in the United States. From the trough of the depression in 1933 real output grew at the average rate of 10 per cent per year over the next four years. Even so the unemployment rate was still

Figure **2.3 The employed labour force**

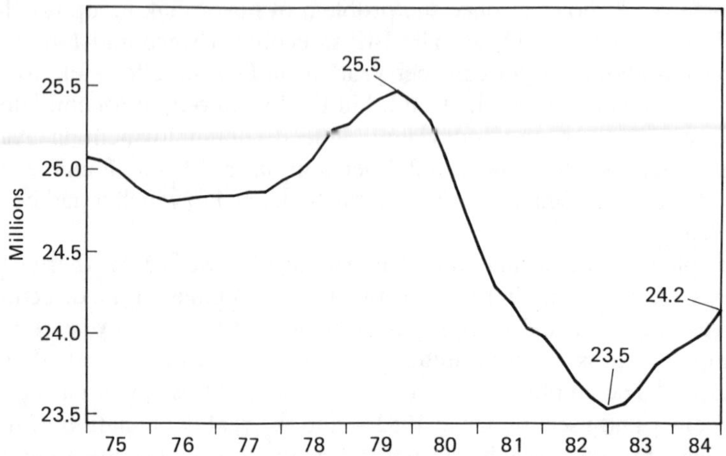

Source: CSO database and *Employment Gazette*.

14.3 per cent by 1937, down from 25 per cent. Does anyone doubt that unemployment remaining as high as 14 per cent reflected the fact that demand had still not recovered sufficiently from the depression level of 1933? In the same way, of course, Britain's employment today – Professor Sir Alan Walters's boom notwithstanding – is lower than it was 10 years ago. Figure 2.3, showing British employment, makes that point obvious.

AN EXPANSIONARY POLICY

The question today is whether policy can and should be used to bring about a spurt in growth that restores the economy to potential output and wipes out some of the record unemployment. The first issue is whether policy can do anything at all to reduce unemployment. The proposition that policy is basically ineffective is attracting a growing number of adherents, more because it is dramatic and conservative than because of significant evidence in its support. The second issue, assuming policy can be effective, is whether a growth spurt would risk sacrificing the success achieved in disinflation, in reduced inflationary expectations, and in fiscal consolidation. If there was a serious chance or even certainty of increased inflation, then there would be a trade-off in choosing between more growth and more inflation, at best an uneasy choice. But in fact the available evidence offers some confidence – not certainty, by any means – that more rapid growth for a while, and of the right kind, need not put at risk the improved inflation performance. The third question is whether a policy-induced extra growth would threaten other important features of the stabilisation effort, especially in regard to fiscal policy. We now review the case against policy action.

THE CASE FOR DOING NOTHING

The case against an expansionary policy has at least six prongs:

1. Increased monetary expansion, while perhaps effective in raising demand in the short run, will inevitably spill over into increased inflation, thus compromising the commitment to disinflation.
2. Fiscal expansion is undesirable because it leads *either* to crowding out via increased interest rates or real appreciation, thus worsening the medium-term natural balance of the economy, *or* else to monetisation, which implies inflation.
3. Fiscal expansion is also undesirable because it undermines financial stability via excessive public sector indebtedness, which is unjustified in view of the fact that easy fiscal policy means, more often than not, wasteful public sector activities.
4. Any Keynesian-style stimulus to aggregate demand would be unlikely to succeed, since firms are employing all the labour they are willing to hire at the going real wage. Unemployment is caused by excessive labour costs, not by a lack of demand. Premature expansion would forestall the necessary cuts in real wages which high unemployment will bring about.
5. The unemployment problem is simply misrepresented. Most of the unemployed are 'professionally unemployed' in the sense that they are workshy. An increase in aggregate demand would therefore encounter supply limitations and hence be primarily inflationary.
6. Policy activism is both ineffective and undesirable because it destabilises the private sector's decision making and interferes with optimal resource allocation and the microeconomic quest for increased flexibility and adaptability.

Each of these points contains at least a germ of truth and it is important to know just how substantive the interlinking objections to expansionary policy in fact are.

Inflation

Consider first the money–inflation issue. The argument that increased money growth finds its way, always, anywhere and independently of the state of economic activity into inflation is an extreme version of the basic monetarist tenet. It would be supported by evidence such as Figure 2.4 (suggested in Professor Sir Alan Walters's article referred to above) where current inflation seems in part to be explained by past growth in money. We show the rate of inflation of the retail prices index and the growth rate of one definition of the money supply M1 (lagged two years). The linkages between current inflation and previous M1 growth are far from tight. In some inflation episodes, for example 1979–82, the picture looks just right to confirm the tight monetarist link. By contrast, in 1983–4 or in 1973–5 the linkage is simply not there.

It would certainly be a mistake to reject a money–inflation linkage altogether. If money growth were permanently reduced and stubbornly kept low forever, inflation would ultimately abate; *ultimately* the oxygen would run out and inflation must come down. Little is known, however, about the speed with which this consolidation would occur and the price to be paid in the transition. The UK experiment (and that in Chile) give, however, some indication. But it is completely clear from all the evidence of industrialised countries that there is no simple, immediate link between monetary policy, expectations and actual inflation. To understand the medium-term behaviour of inflation it is important to flesh out the money–inflation relationship and determine the role of commodity price disturbances (the oil shocks of 1973–4 and 1978–9), taxes, money demand disturbances, aggregate demand, unemployment and the exchange rate in this context.

The fact that inflation is determined not only by money growth but also by other factors makes the case for expansionary demand policy more difficult. If inflation were uniquely determined by money growth, we could simply freeze it and that would look after the objective of price stability. With full success on that front assured, we could use all other weapons to promote growth, profitability and employment. Unfortunately aggregate demand, unemployment and the exchange rate do play a role in the inflation process, and very

Figure **2.4 Money growth and inflation**

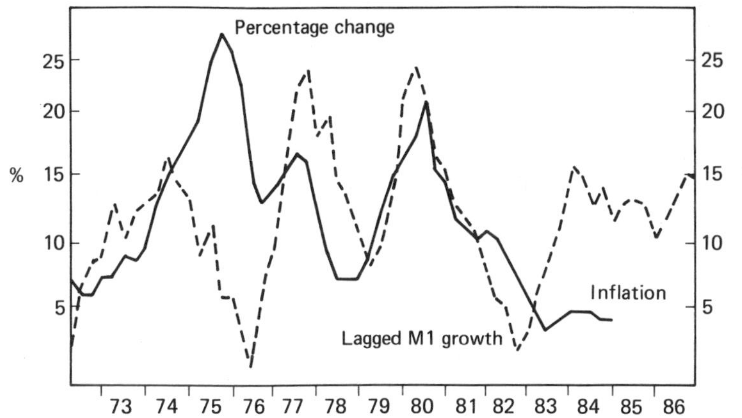

Source: Data Resources International (DRI database).

much complicate the policy problem. The complication comes in two ways: steady, low money growth is no longer sufficient to bring rapid disinflation and the effect of such money growth may, for a while at least, be primarily felt in reduced activity rather than slower inflation. At the same time, more rapid expansion in demand or a higher level of demand (relative to potential output), even with a given money growth, may lead to an upsurge in inflation.

The link between inflation and activity is often presented in terms of a threshold unemployment rate at which inflation remains stable; lower rates of unemployment lead to increasing inflation, and higher unemployment to reduced inflation. Econometric studies suggest that there is, indeed, an unemployment rate consistent with non-accelerating inflation (NAIRU). Estimates suggest that the level may currently be as high as 10 per cent in the United Kingdom (and rising with the actual rate of unemployment). At the present level of unemployment there should, accordingly, be at work a dampening influence on wage settlements and price inflation. In the past two years not much of such a deceleration has been felt, despite high and rising unemployment. One reason has certainly been the continuing real depreciation of sterling over the last few years.

There is another way of thinking about the inflation–unemployment trade-off. Would those who argue against expansionary policies on the ground of inflation anxieties recommend that the government stand in the way of a boom that springs from a dramatic rise in exports or investment? One is hard-pressed to imagine that the Thatcher government would not stand by cheerfully to harvest all the credit for such 'true' growth, and not even think about the inflation issue until such time as it might actually emerge. There would surely be no effort to forestall a rise in growth by an immediate tightening of monetary and fiscal policy, lest rapid demand growth reignite inflation. The issue then is a prejudice about the kind of demand growth, spontaneous versus policy-induced. There is no evidence that fiscally-induced growth (other things equal) is more inflationary than the growth deriving from an autonomous export boom.

If one kind of demand is accepted and another rejected, then the reason is unlikely to be the inflationary impact of strong demand, but must be simply a bias against policy-induced expansion. We return to that question below. But there is a quite different line of argument against expansion, namely that a high level of unemployment, rather than being an unfortunate fact, is in fact a policy instrument deliberately sought and maintained to improve inflation performance. The unemployed are serving in the war on inflation and they will serve for years to come until the disinflationary stance of financial policy permeates the economy sufficiently to allow lower rates of unemployment, consistent with zero inflation. Moreover yet higher unemployment is needed to drive down inflation to zero and to maintain it there. This line of thinking brings up very forcefully the issue of trade-offs.

Whatever significance one attaches to the inflation target, there surely must be some level and persistence of unemployment at which unemployment becomes the priority, even if reduction means no further cuts or an actual increase, in inflation. The question of trade-offs might be avoided by suggesting that in fact there is no trade-off: only a transition to a non-inflationary environment allows a resumption in growth because the very fact of inflation is inimical to enterprise, innovation, progress, prosperity, investment, financial stability and employment. While that idea is, no doubt, in some people's heads, it is of course sheer nonsense at a rate of inflation of 5 or 6 per cent. One would have to believe that any expansion takes the economy straight to double-digit inflation to take this view at all seriously. Yet another way of trying to avoid the dilemma is to believe that, indeed, there are trade-offs, but that the investment in disinflation would be entirely lost and would have to start all over again, unless the course were seen through all the way to zero inflation. But clearly at zero inflation exactly the same arguments would be brought: expansion threatens the great sacrifices made in securing price stability. For some people any year is simply the wrong time to think about unemployment.

Mainstream macroeconomists no longer believe that there are simple, sure ways of controlling inflation, other than to sacrifice all other objectives and single-mindedly use all instruments to counter shocks and disturbances to the inflation rate. The need for attention to monetary growth is widely accepted, though mainly in the way practised by the Federal Reserve in the United States, with substantial discretion and occasional 'money blips'. Beyond that it is, of course, accepted that unemployment and the exchange rate are particularly important influences on inflation. A steep collapse of the exchange rate would unavoidably increase inflation. In the same way a reduction of unemployment would reduce the disinflationary pressure in the economy and, if carried too far, would certainly be inflationary.

The inflation problem, in this perspective, is best dealt with in a twofold way: on one hand, we should avoid overheating; on the other hand, we should use favourable opportunities (oil price declines, appreciation) to achieve some disinflation and hence reduced rates of wage inflation. But within these broad parameters there is a basic acceptance of the idea of trade-offs and the potential for policy to expand demand, in the face of very high unemployment, without the risk of a sharp escalation of inflation. One would certainly add that the policy mix employed to bring about expansion can be designed to minimise the inflation risk. The issue then is the right monetary–fiscal mix, and the right kind of fiscal incentives which in conjunction with incomes policy promote growth. Of course, incomes policy has a bad reputation, but it is perhaps not quite as bad as that of monetarism.

Difficulties with Fiscal Expansion

Basic objections to deficit finance as a stimulus to aggregate demand centre, rightly, on the potentially hazardous effects of deficits. These side-effects arise either because deficit finance may carry the seeds of financial instability because of excessive debt accumulation, or because of the fact that debt finance distorts the allocation of resources between the present and the future, the government and the private sector. These issues have attracted a great deal of attention in all industrialised countries and are now at the centre of discussion in the

United States, where it is strongly felt that the deficit finance strategy, while immensely successful in terms of growth, must be used with care.

The financial instability problem arises in the following manner. The accumulation of debt brings with it the prospect of increased future taxation to service what appears to be an ever-growing debt. As more and more debt accumulates, the high debt service requires levels of taxation that ultimately become intolerable because they affect the efficiency of the economy and private sector enterprise. This burden of taxation cannot be thrown off, assuming no growth miracle or the discovery of natural resources yet untapped, except by repudiation of the debt. As the discussion of the 1920s in Great Britain makes quite clear, repudiation or use of once-for-all 'capital levies' on wealth do not command great popularity, mostly because they might become a habit.

One way out in some countries has been to have bursts of inflation. The process starts with an accommodating monetary policy which pushes down nominal interest rates in the face of inflation. With negative real interest rates the debt falls in real terms even in the face of a continuing deficit. Inflation turns out to be a way of servicing debt, but the economy adjusts. Bond holders realise their fate and debt turns to shorter maturities so that market rates can more readily adapt to the inflation risk. As financial markets adapt to the deficit strategy, more extreme bursts of inflation are required to wipe out public debt, and the very expectation of these policies causes capital markets to turn their attention away from the financing of productive capital to the far more important issue of predicting the course of deficits and inflation. Foreign exchange crises ensue and real interest rates soar and collapse alternately; resources are devastatingly misallocated as the capital market becomes the Casino Royale where the Chancellor of the Exchequer is the croupier. In the end it is clear that avoiding the destructive taxation required to service the debt, by recourse to a strategy of inflationary debt liquidation, carries with it even more staggering costs. Fiscal consolidation, even taking into account the painful costs, becomes a more credible and, in the long run, more profitable strategy.

All this is a fair description of Argentina, but it has very little to do with public finance in Great Britain *today*. This is the case because, in good part, high inflation in the 1970s has already reduced the debt to GDP ratio by quite a margin. Today, the debt ratio is low by comparison with earlier years and the real cyclically-adjusted budget is in surplus. Despite a decade of normal budget deficits the debt to GDP ratio today is nearly a third lower than it was in 1970.

While the fiscal picture does not justify any great concerns of financial instability, there is a quite different aspect that does need mentioning. Mr J. de Larosière, at the time managing director of the IMF, made himself a forceful spokesman for the position that a penchant for deficit finance ultimately distorts the economic landscape, and that a return to fiscal orthodoxy is required on efficiency grounds. Here is what he had to say:[6]

> For a variety of reasons the traditional stigma attached to fiscal deficits and growing public debt gave way to a certain nonchalance on the part of policy makers. Fiscal deficits no longer required justification, and they did not seem to have undesirable political repercussions, even when they occurred during non-recessionary periods . . . Traditional principles that had held that no deficit was justified if associated with unproductive investment, current expenditure or revenue, were insidiously abandoned in favour of fiscal activism that made full employment and the expansion of welfare programs predominant objectives of economic policy.

An active expression of these concerns is, in the UK case, the build-up of government outlays. Whereas in 1960 they were a bare 32.4 per cent of GDP, by 1984 they had risen to nearly 45 per cent. The counterpart of this level of spending is taxation, present or future, and these high levels of taxation in turn affect economic efficiency. Supply-side economics represents a revolt against this unstable trend of growing government and deteriorating economic performance.

Much of this concern is perfectly valid; the problem is what to do about it. The correct view is to consolidate the public sector over time, weeding out inefficient programmes and using every opportunity that presents itself to retire debt. But such a course of consolidation cannot be pursued blindly, seeking budget improvement irrespective of the state of the economy. Such blindness might well worsen the fiscal picture even further as deteriorating economic performance, stagnation, lack of investment and lack of jobs erode the revenue base and sharply increase the need for public programmes. Even on a course of fiscal consolidation there must be room for deficits, even large deficits, required to keep the economy on a course of prosperity. As Professor Giersch, the leading German supply-sider has argued, *increased* cyclical deficits today (of the right kind) are investments in prosperity fully in line with a conservative fiscal policy.[7]

If neither financial instability nor the objectives of fiscal consolidation stand in the way of a cyclically-motivated expansion, what other objections might there be? The chief remaining concern is *crowding out*. Here the concern is that public sector deficits require financing. They absorb scarce resources and lead to competition in capital markets where government debt diverts saving from capital formation or net foreign lending. To the extent that deficits are not matched by increased domestic saving, they imply that investment or net exports must be crowded out. The crowding out emerges from competition for scarce saving, which drives up interest rates and draws in foreign capital, thereby appreciating the real exchange rate. A reduction in investment is, of course, highly undesirable, since it reduces growth of activity and jobs. To the extent that net exports are reduced, this implies an immediate fall in activity for at least part of manufacturing.

Whatever the cyclical merits of increased deficits, the crowding out issue is a serious one to contend with. One answer to the crowding out problem is to recognise that with the expansion of output and employment there is a rise in incomes and hence a rise in both tax collection and in saving. These will not increase sufficiently to close fully the budget and saving gap, but they will go some way. Furthermore the rise in interest rates induced by fiscal expansion does depend on monetary policy. In the extreme (an unwise choice) the impact on interest rates could be entirely neutralised by accommodating monetary policy. At the other end strict adherence to monetary targets would mean higher interest rates and exchange rate appreciation. There is room between these extremes to look for a policy mix that strikes a balance between the interests of efficiency and price stability. The example of the United States documents in a particularly forceful way that one can have an investment boom in the middle of an extreme fiscal expansion. One reason for this is that the very fact of a sustained expansion is a forceful incentive for investment that may well outweigh some increase in the cost of capital. Another is that, in the United States, investment incentives have helped to offset increased capital costs. The crowding out argument, on the investment side, therefore is primarily an argument for the right kind of mix. Of course, the US example also shows that fiscal expansion draws in foreign saving as the current account deteriorates.

Policy Effectiveness

Whereas the previous objections to policy action focussed on negative side-effects, perhaps the most basic challenge comes from an entirely different perspective: monetary and fiscal policy, it is argued, are useless because they will not affect the decisions that private agents make. Either these policies have no effect at all or they are ineffective because the inefficiency they involve makes everybody worse off; they cannot do anything for the better and therefore the economy should, for best results, be left to look after itself.

There can be no question that this kind of thinking has significant intellectual support and cannot be dismissed as a crackpot idea. But the appeal to 'rational expectations' must also not overshadow the fact that this kind of thinking is quite extreme. It is entirely correct when executed in the framework of highly stylised models, where economic agents are optimally informed and can without constraints of decentralised decision making, information costs or lack of access to capital markets, pursue their optimal decisions. But none of these ineffectiveness results have been demonstrated for anything more closely resembling the world we live in. It may be a puzzle why the unemployed do not succeed, via aggressive wage cuts, in placing themselves in jobs, but it is a fact. Once we accept the fact of wage-price stickiness, the edifice of rational expectations/market equilibrium collapses and the case for policy activism maintains most of its Keynesian vigour. It would be a silly mistake to believe that modern macroeconomics has learned nothing from the rational expectations/market equilibrium school. But it would be equally wrong to suppose that developments of the past ten years have vindicated the main tenets of this movement. If anything the past ten years in the United States confirm, in the most striking way, mainstream macroeconomics.

The main argument of the rational expectations/market equlibrium school of thought is that private agents set wages and prices optimally so as to achieve, at each point in time, the profit- and utility-maximising levels of output, employment, consumption and investment. Their information is as good as that of the government, and hence no role is left for the government except to distort the privately optimal choices by fiscal moves or monetary surprises. On the fiscal side, the predominant idea is that fiscal policy does not have any effect because the public that receives tax relief recognises that they themselves (or their heirs) will have to pay for the present relief via increased future taxes. Hence they will not respond to reduced taxation by increased spending, but rather will increase saving to set aside resources to pay the future taxes. Similarly, increased government spending cannot be expansionary because the implied future taxes tend to reduce private spending. If anything this effect is compounded since government provision of goods and services, in many cases, merely displaces the private provision, though perhaps not with equal efficiency. In this setting the government is viewed with hostility since anything government can do, the private sector can do better. The extremity of the argument reminds one of the great rift at an early postwar meeting of the libertarian Mont Pelerin Society: at issue was whether the British navy should rent or own the battleships.

The impartial observer must feel that all this cannot be very serious and certainly not the best that economics can offer as policy guidance. The sad fact is that it remains the height of academic fashion, even if the lack of empirical support, after fifteen years of assertive research and advocacy, has begun to create a problem of credibility. It is worth noting, though, that Professor Thomas Sargent, one of the leaders of the rational expectations/market equilibrium school expressed an early scepticism as to the applicability of these ideas to the case of Great Britain.[8]

> . . . it is difficult to interpret Thatcher's policy action in terms of the kind of once-and-for-all, widely believed, uncontroversial, and irreversible regime change that rational expectations equilibrium theories assert can cure inflation at little or no cost. This is not to render a negative judgement on Thatcher's goal or her methods, but only to indicate that the preconditions for the applicability of rational expectations 'neutrality' or 'policy irrelevance' theorems don't seem to exist in Margaret Thatcher's England. Where these conditions are not met, rational expectations equilibrium models imply that contractionary monetary and fiscal policy actions are likely to be costly in terms of real output and unemployment.

The foregoing discussion has offered some perspective on the difficulties surrounding an expansionary policy stance. Some of these are purely imaginary, others reflect a well-founded concern for inflation risks and the need to watch closely long-term fiscal balance and efficient resource allocation. With these concerns in mind we now turn to the discussion of a reasonable programme for prosperity.

WHAT KIND OF EXPANSION?

Once it is accepted that policy can and should do something about the unemployment problem, matters stop being easy. The choice of policy mix is a political decision involving trade-offs between efficiency and equity. But it also involves an economic problem of determining the relative impacts of the mix upon inflation, short-run employment, and medium-term growth effects. We will deal here primarily with these latter issues. The choice of policy mix involves decisions on the following points:

1. What is the right mix between monetary and fiscal policy? Should money be tight and fiscal policy expansionary, the reverse, or, implausibly, both easy money and an enlarged deficit?
2. Should the programme focus on stimulating aggregate demand or should it centre on expanding jobs from the supply side?
3. If there is policy action on the demand side, should the objective be to maximise the employment impact of a given increase in the budget deficit, or are other criteria (including consumer/taxpayer sovereignty) at least on a par?
4. If policies are undertaken on the supply side is the emphasis on inflation, on employment, or on capital formation?

Inflation and the Mix

The key feature of an expansionary policy mix must be to rule out a collapse of the exchange rate. It is well established, in every banana republic but now also in industrialised countries, that sharp exchange rate depreciation immediately and sizeably adds to the inflation rate. A major depreciation of the exchange rate raises the cost of living because of increased prices of goods that enter foreign trade and because of increased prices of industrial materials that are traded internationally. These price increases directly represent a rise in the inflation rate. But they also spread wider in the economy as they find their way into wage settlements and into the prices of competing products. The exact timing and magnitude of the impact of exchange rate depreciation on inflation may be open to discussion; the fact itself is quite definitely not.[9] The British reduction in inflation owes much to the real appreciation in 1979–81, and the disinflation in the United States, similarly, would not have been as successful without the strong dollar.

What kind of policy can avoid an exchange rate collapse in the course of expansion? The answer is quite unambiguously a policy of relatively tight money and of sufficiently easy fiscal policy. *Monetary policy should be exchange rate oriented*, assuring levels of interest rates sufficiently high to attract the capital flows required to finance the inevitable deterioration in the current account. It would definitely be a mistake to use monetary policy to the extent of seeking real appreciation (as the US policies have turned out to do) since the real wage, if anything, is already too high. The inflation rate is comfortably low so that the emphasis should simply be shifted from inflation to employment, having taken precaution to avoid the most likely risk of exchange rate depreciation.

Of course an easy fiscal policy/tight money mix involves difficulties in the policy framework of monetary targeting. If the fiscal expansion is successful, growth in output and hence money demand may mean increasing the money supply even if the interest rate is allowed to rise to counter exchange market problems. The other difficulty, and this is a more real one, is that increased interest rates would potentially worsen the expenditure mix away from investment towards consumption and government outlays. The details of fiscal policy have to take this risk into account by making provision for compensating investment incentives. Once again, the United States is a case in point: tight money and easy fiscal policy have not stood in the way of an investment boom precisely because the fiscal expansion involved a sizeable incentive for investment. This is in sharp contrast to current British policy.

Much less critical to the inflation issue, though perhaps not negligible, is the possibility of using on the supply side fiscal measures chosen because of their favourable inflation effect. Investment incentives might work to expand capacity and thus avoid bottlenecks. A reduction in excise taxes would directly dampen inflation. A reduction in social security taxes on additions to employment would reduce marginal labour costs and hence might also dampen inflation. It must be clear, though, that here fiscal policy cannot do much, or at least not short of vast revenue losses. The inflation impact would therefore not be the primary criteria of choice among different forms of fiscal stimulus.

Employment Priority?

The big question is whether scarce fiscal revenues should be used with the primary objective of creating employment. The question is important because particular fiscal programmes, specifically special employment programmes, have a much larger employment effect, for a given increase in the deficit, than say personal income tax cuts, investment subsidies, excise tax cuts or subsidies, or public sector investment.

A recent review by Davies and Metcalf reports estimates of the differences in employment impact of various measures which add £1 billion to the Public Sector Borrowing Requirement (PSBR) (an increase which represents about one-third of a per cent of GDP). Table 2.2 shows a summary of the detailed findings they report.[10]

Table 2.2 Employment effects of £1 bn increase in PSBR (cut in thousands unemployed)

Tax cuts	*Public infrastructure investment*	*Public current expenditure*	*Employment programmes*
17–21	38	65	488

Note: The figure for public infrastructure investment is an overall average. Many individual categories of such expenditure have much larger effects on unemployment.

Special employment programmes are so much more cost effective *in generating employment* than any other measure because of two features: they involve direct expenditure on labour, and the cost is merely the extra cost of employment above unemployment benefits. Any other fiscal measure will involve a significantly larger non-labour component, will involve higher-paid labour and may imply leakages into saving or import spending. The staggering differences in the employment impact of different programmes would appear to make special employment programmes the obvious candidate except for this: they are not clearly preferable once longer-term objectives of growth and the valuation of output are taken into consideration. Here is how Davis and Metcalf pose the problem:

> It is clear that macroeconomic measures to reduce taxation (income tax, VAT or employers' NICs) are by far the most expensive way of cutting unemployment, at least over a 2-year period. However, income tax cuts may pay off in the longer term through their supply-side benefits. General public spending measures are much cheaper in the short term, but it should be noted that infrastructure investment costs more, in terms of jobs created, than

current spending. On the other hand, most of the jobs created through public investment are in the private sector, rather than in direct public employment. Special employment measures are *by far* the most cost effective way of cutting unemployment – the next cheapest method is five times as expensive. However, there are serious problems in valuing the output produced under such schemes.

The choices to be made are primarily political, except for the following considerations. Public sector infrastructure investment cannot be neglected merely because there is a budget problem. In fact a recession as deep as the present one is the best time to use the otherwise idle labour to upgrade the national capital stock. Surely the biggest mistake would be to wait for a cylical recovery of revenue to heap increased public sector spending on top of a strong economy? The other point is that public and private sector investment cannot be neglected because of the risk of bottlenecks. Basing an expansion entirely on investment might generate little employment, at least within reasonable budget costs, but investment should definitely be part of an expansion programme. The crowding out issue raised above calls for special attention in this context.

The next observation is that the fiscal expansion programme must be forward-looking. We have to ask how, sooner or later, the budget stance can return to consolidation without at that time risking a renewed slide into recession and record unemployment. That perspective suggests that employment programmes may be less effective as a measure of sustained expansion unless they represent reasonably permanent job creation in the private sector or investment in skill and mobility that offers the prospect of increased employability.

The most difficult question is what size of fiscal programme would offer the prospect of much increased growth without the outright threat of inflation escalation. A short-lived programme that is too small is lost like water in the sand, simply because there is no momentum of demand growth and employment expectations. The momentum is essential to lead firms to hire more labour and to invest in expanding capacity, rather than working overtime while charging higher prices. Too large a programme might be inflationary, because bottlenecks build up faster than firms can expand jobs and capacity. The spill-over into imports might be large, and the inflation and exchange rate consequences would be difficult to contain. Fiscal stimulus of the order of an extra 1.5 per cent of GDP for this year and up to a further 1.5 per cent the following year, with an eventual phasing out, would be the kind of programme that strikes a rough balance between objectives.

International Considerations

All of Europe faces the choices Britain is considering, with as little enthusiasm and confidence, and with much the same urgency. At the same time the United States faces the problem of unwinding the excessively large deficits, and the overvalued dollar, without sacrificing the gains in disinflation and strong growth. The choices abroad will, of course, influence the opportunities that present themselves to British policy makers. A collapse of world growth would call for a much more expansionary policy, as would a collapse of the dollar. But, whereas the former is just bad news, the latter at least carries the bonus of making room for non-inflationary growth.

The international interdependence emerges especially in two respects. Any country that moves fiscal policy towards expansion in fact subsidises employment abroad. Import leakages spread the expansionary effects abroad and thus dissipate the domestic cost-effectiveness of a deficit policy. It is clear that joint expansion in Europe would make every country more willing, and more able, to contribute their own fiscal resources to the venture. Exchange markets would be calmer, and growth would be stronger by a very significant margin. Joint expansion has been poo-poohed in the aftermath of the experiment of encouraging economies to act as 'locomotives' in the late 1970s, but none of the case for it is lost. Just as the world descended into recession jointly in 1980–2, we can get out of the hole by giving each other a hand. There is no need for elaborate targeting or co-ordination. The point is simply to stop pretending to one another that fiscal consolidation has been a success story and to agree that fiscal expansion should take place now rather than being exactly timed to satisfy election-cycle criteria. In Europe, that means that Germany, the United Kingdom and France should now take the lead in restoring confidence.

From the US side of the Atlantic it is increasingly obvious that fiscal adjustment must take place on both sides: contraction in the United States and vigorous expansion in Europe. Only in that manner can the recovery be strengthened and given extra impetus to run another few years. If fiscal correction does take place here and abroad, extra room exists for a joint effort to talk down real interest rates. The dollar might fall less and growth everywhere would be more balanced, with higher investment, than on the current beggar-thy-neighbour pattern. Clearly, lower real interest rates would help the budget problem immensely, to the point that extra fiscal programmes could be afforded more easily.

OTHER POSSIBLE CHANGES

The case for fiscal expansion is obvious and uncontroversial. The only problem is to persuade policy makers that there is so big a need, and so little harm, that they can do something now with another helping in time for their re-election. But there are also some more fundamental reforms that are attracting attention. The two most striking ideas are in the area of labour compensation and government employment programmes. These ideas are new and immensely controversial. More thought, discussion and analysis is needed about the details. But these ideas do address in drastic ways the problem of unemployment.

A government employment guarantee for the long-term unemployed has been advocated by, among others, Charter for Jobs.[11] The proposal is that the government should undertake to employ at a living wage all such people who cannot find market employment. The saving on benefits now paid to these people might contribute a good part of the extra cost of the public employment programme. Once this major reform has been achieved, another one can follow. There ceases to be a case for giving benefit to the unemployed for an indefinite duration. Where work is guaranteed, we need not offer the alternative of paid leisure. The Swedish government (but not, I see, Charter for Jobs) accepts this logic and it is a major reason why unemployment there is so low.

Massive public employment programmes as a permanent feature are a hard dose to swallow for almost any economist. Even with a hardy disposition for interventionism, few people believe that the government is the best employer of idle labour for ever. In fact, what would the government do on a permanent basis with a million people in an employment programme? Against this argument we must hold the following reflection: anyone who objects to mass employment programmes must, by much the same logic, object to mass *un*employment programmes. Without a work test, unemployment benefits may be just that. Moreover, from a supply-side perspective we can go even further. The fact that some people choose to be on unemployment benefits rather than working (and paying taxes) means that others have to work harder to pay the taxes that finance the unemployment benefits. Clearly a more even-handed approach is worth thinking about before the unemployment culture makes a reversal even more difficult.

The second drastic reform is to change compensation principles in one form or another. A proposal by Professor Martin Weitzman has attracted attention to the idea of profit sharing as a means of shifting the demand for labour and increasing and stabilising employment.[12] The practice of profit sharing in Japan is worth noting in view of that country's ability to sustain growth and employment so much better than any other industrialised country.

A different idea has already found its way into the labour market: the two-tier system. To the extent that labour market problems involve excessively high real wages and too much rigidity in employment terms, there is a common social interest in relaxing these obstacles to employment. But workers who hold jobs do not have that same interest; they would in fact be paying for other people to get jobs. The obvious answer is to create a system where extra employment attracts lower wages and fewer privileges than are being enjoyed by workers who already hold jobs. The system is unfair, but less so than the present arrangements whereby some people have a job, high real wages and security and other people do not even have a chance of finding a job. It is interesting to note that in the aftermath of deregulation the two-tier system is already catching on in the United States. When everything is said and done a job is better than no job.

PRIORITIES

Whatever the merits of these innovatory ideas – and they offer valuable guides for the future – there are some things that simply must be done now. The top priority is to undo the budget cuts and let prosperity return.

Notes

1. An extended version of an Employment Institute lecture delivered on 29 May 1985 in King's College, London. Rudiger Dornbusch is Ford International Professor of Economics at Massachusetts Institute of Technology.
2. See Keynes, J. M., 'Can Lloyd George Do It? (General Election May 1929)', in *Keynes* (1978) Vol. IX.
3. See Layard, P. R. G. and Nickell, S. (1985).
4. A detailed account is offered in Davies, G. 'The Macroeconomic Record of the Conservatives', paper presented to a conference on 'The Thatcher Government and British Political Economy', Harvard University, April 1985.
5. Quoted from his essay, 'The Right Stuff', *The Economist*, 4 May 1985, p. 23.
6. Quoted from IMF Survey, 3 September 1984.
7. See also the discussion in Blanchard, O., R. Dornbusch, J. Drèze, H. Giersch, P. R. G. Layard and M. Monti (1985).
8. Quoted from his essay, 'Stopping Moderate Inflation: The Methods of Poincaré and Thatcher', Dornbusch, R. and Simonsen, M., *Inflation, Debt and Indexation* (Cambridge, Mass.: MIT Press) p. 58.
9. For an assessment in the British context see the essay by Beckerman, W. 'How the Battle Against Inflation Was Really Won', *Lloyds Bank Review*, January 1985. See also the discussion by Sachs, J. in *Brookings Papers on Economic Activity*, 1, 1983.
10. See Davies, G. and Metcalf, D., 'Generating Jobs', *The Economics Analyst*, Simon and Coates, April 1985.
11. Charter for Jobs (1985). See also Layard, P. R. G. 'Cutting Unemployment Using Both Blades of the Scissors', *Catalyst*, Spring 1985.
12. See Weitzman, M. L. 'The Case for Profit-Sharing' *Making the Economy Work* (Employment Institute, 1989) or Weitzman (1984).

3 Governments Can Affect Employment: A Critique of Monetarism, Old and New

Gavyn Davies[1]

'Let us be quite clear. Let us be absolutely clear. You will not reduce unemployment by increasing what governments spend or borrow.' — Nigel Lawson, Chancellor of the Exchequer, Conservative Party Conference, 10 October 1984

I INTRODUCTION

One of the distinguishing features of the present British government is the extremely strong position it has taken on questions which have taxed and puzzled economic theorists for decades. Indeed, it is often remarked within the Conservative Party that a long tradition of Tory pragmatism has been overthrown by the Thatcherite fundamentalists. Nowhere is this clearer than in the realm of employment policy, where the government contends:

'The one thing clearly not responsible for unemployment is the lack of demand.' — *Employment: The Challenge for the Nation*
Department of Employment (1985)

Note that this is stated without qualification. There is no attempt to distinguish between the short and long term, nor to distinguish real from nominal demand. In this area, the government has always been absolutist.

The belief that the level of cash spending on goods and services does not under any circumstances affect how much is actually produced in the economy is an unusually rigid proposition for practising politicians to hold. So is the notion that changes in budgetary policy have no effect on the real level of *either* demand *or* output. But these beliefs are certainly not original to Mrs Thatcher's administration. In recognisably similar form, they can be traced back throughout the history of classical economic thought.

The origin of these propositions lies in the so-called 'classical dichotomy'. This states quite simply that output growth and employment are determined by real variables in the economic system (notably the capital stock, technical change and the real supply and demand for labour) while the price level is determined by monetary variables (and in particular by the supply of money itself). This was the dominant belief in economics through the nineteenth century and up to the time of Pigou and Wicksell. After the events of the 1930s, and the frontal assault on classical economics led by Keynes and Kalecki, belief in the classical dichotomy began to fade, and the consensus of the 1950s and 1960s (known somewhat confusingly as the 'neo-classical synthesis') took it for granted that government manipulation of the level of demand could have a considerable effect on the behaviour of real variables, including of course the unemployment rate.

The breakdown of this consensus, and the shift back towards classical thinking in some quarters, received its major boost when Milton Friedman's Presidential Address to the American Economics Association, published in 1968, asserted that policy aimed at regulating the level of money demand could not permanently depress unemployment below its 'natural' rate, and predicted that attempts to do this would simply result in accelerating inflation. The simple power of Friedman's argument was enough to fire the imagination of many of the best American economists of the 1960s, and his ideas were elevated from the universities to the mainstream of the policy-making process when his warnings appeared to be borne out by the rise in inflation of the early 1970s. But those economists whose imaginations had been stirred were not content to let matters rest. Friedman's generation – let us call them the 'Old Fogey' monetarists – had accepted that government manipulation of nominal demand could affect employment for short periods, but only at the expense of accelerating inflation. By contrast, the 'Young Fogey' monetarists – Robert Lucas, Thomas Sargent, Neil Wallace and (later) Robert Barro – argued that even this limited role for policy was not soundly based. Because the private sector would adjust its expectations in a rational way to changes in government policy, and because markets would tend to clear through rapid price movements, systematic attempts to manage demand would not affect employment even for short periods. They would instead succeed only in changing the inflation rate – and this would happen immediately. In keeping with their intellectual antecedents, these Young Fogeys became known as the new classicists. They could just as well be called 'new monetarists', and we use the two terms interchangeably in the remainder of this text. In academic circles, the crucial debate is now between the Keynesians and the new monetarists, whose particular strain of monetarist thinking has became increasingly dominant.

However the degree of difference between the Friedman-style 'old monetarists' and the Lucas-style 'new monetarists' can be overstated. Both schools believe that inflation is determined solely by monetary growth (at least over periods longer than a year or two) and that output and employment will be quickly restored to their equilibrium levels after changes in the rate of monetary growth or other types of nominal demand 'shock'. The main differences between old and new monetarists lie not so much in their long-term propositions, but in their views about the speed at which the economy converges on its long-term equilibrium after a change in nominal demand policy. The new monetarists believe that the price level will adjust immediately and completely to any systematic attempt to manage demand, and that real variables such as output and employment will not be affected at all, even in the shortest of short terms. The 'old monetarists', in contrast, tend to believe that the full price adjustment will take about two years to achieve, and that in the meantime output and employment can be affected by macroeconomic demand policy. As we shall see later, the main reasons for these differences lie in the varying assumptions made about how expectations are formed in the economy, and about the degree of price flexibility which typically exists in labour and goods markets.

The Present UK Administration and the Monetarist Approach

The present UK government has always been unashamedly monetarist in its approach. In its first term, from 1979 to 1983, its language and actions were dominated by Friedman-style thinking. Reliance on a single monetary target, confidence that this would succeed in bringing down inflation without causing a prolonged recession, and belief that unemployment would eventually decline without any need for a more expansionary fiscal stance – all these were typical of the old monetarist approach. More recently, there has been a subtle change of tack. Whether he knows it or not, Mr Lawson's theoretical approach often appears more closely related to the Young Fogey monetarists than to the Friedman generation. But one thing is certain – Mr Lawson is no less of a monetarist than his immediate predecessor. In the major statement of his economic philosophy – the intellectually assured Mais Lecture delivered in June 1984 – the Chancellor expressed his belief in several of the basic tenets of monetarism, albeit with a 'new classical' tinge:

1. He denied that macroeconomic policy could affect the level of employment, arguing that 'it is the conquest of inflation, and not the pursuit of growth and employment, which should be the objective of macro-economic policy'.
2. The particular wing of macro policy which determined inflation was monetary rather than fiscal: 'Inflation is above all a monetary phenomenon in anything other than the short run'.
3. Fiscal policy was subordinate to the needs of monetary control: 'Each version of the MTFS has included projections of a path for the PSBR which is considered to be consistent with monetary objectives at acceptable interest rate levels'.
4. Expectations were formed rationally, at least in the financial markets: 'The long-term consequences (of increased budget deficits) would tend to be foreseen by the financial markets, and the effects on interest rates brought forward as a result of changes in expectations. In a market economy, the private sector is bound to take into account its expectations of the behaviour of the government when deciding its own behaviour'.
5. Government measures to reduce unemployment should steer totally clear of demand management, and concentrate instead on measures to facilitate price flexibility, and the functioning of markets: 'It is the rediscovery of the enterprise culture, operating within the framework of markets progressively liberated from rigidities and distortions, that will provide the only answer to the curse of unemployment'.

Some may consider it unfair to make judgements about practising politicians on the basis of the strengths or weaknesses of the theoretical underpinnings on which their actions must rest. Yet in the same way that all governments before 1976 depended ultimately on Keynesian thinking, the present administration in the end must rely on the validity of the monetarist case for its legitimacy. The observations quoted above from the present British Chancellor could certainly have been penned by any of the new classical theorists, and for that reason alone it is important to analyse the ideas of the Young Fogeys. However the importance of these new monetarists ranges much wider than any influence (whether direct or indirect) they may have on the existing UK government. Their work is the culmination of a trend away from active demand management (or 'policy activism') which has been running for at least ten years, not only in Britain but in most European countries, and their arguments in favour of the 'policy ineffectiveness proposition' (PIP) represent a formidable barrier in the way of those who believe that governments have been responsible in their fiscal policies for much of the recent rise in unemployment.

The New Classical Approach

The new classical (NC) approach is a refinement and extension of Friedmanite monetarism. Yet it produces conclusions which are so startling in their implications, and so different from those of the postwar macroeconomic synthesis, that it should come as no surprise to learn that the debate on their theoretical and empirical validity dominates the macroeconomics of the 1980s. The writings of the NC school have all the ingredients – intellectual brilliance, logical rigour and apparent policy relevance – which are necessary to stimulate the interest of the best of the current crop of young economists. In the United States, the academic journals are crammed with contributions examining the ramifications of NC thinking. Furthermore, the NC conclusions are sufficiently simple and compelling to have a chance of seeping still further out of the seminar rooms into the political process. Only two comparable upheavals have occurred in macroeconomics this century: the Keynesian revolution, when the world came to believe it could spend its way out of recession; and the first monetarist, or Friedmanite, revolution, when the world convinced itself that it could spend its way into inflation. Both of these upheavals combined a novel theoretical approach with disarmingly simple policy recommendations and direct relevance to the most pressing economic problem of the day. The policy ineffectiveness proposition (PIP) has extended the work of Friedman to achieve a similar combination, and threatens eventually to take a similar grip on policy. Already the territory of economics is increasingly being shifted onto ground defined by the NC school.

But none of this should be taken as a *fait accompli*. Unlike either the Keynesians or the Friedmanites, who were willing on occasions to compromise with their opponents and (at least in their academic writings) were guarded in their claims for generality, the new classicists often seem in danger of overreaching themselves. For they are not content with claiming that, in perfectly competitive models, the economic system will *tend* to eliminate involuntary unemployment through eventual changes in price levels, or that governments should be careful to take account of the expectations of the private sector when contemplating policy changes. They go much further, advancing the infinitely stronger propositions that markets are *always* in equilibrium, that recorded unemployment is therefore always voluntary, and that any government attempts to reduce unemployment must inevitably result *only* in higher inflation. It is the uncompromising nature of these propositions which makes them vulnerable to attack, since exceptions to the NC rules, both empirical and theoretical, are easy to find. In fact, the 'exceptions' are so numerous that NC economics should perhaps be seen as a special theoretical case which exists in the textbooks, but which has little relevance for the applied economist.

This chapter will in fact argue that the work of the new classicists may be rigorous and logically appealing, but that it happens to be a rather poor description of the world in which we live. The unbending application of a laboratory model based on perfect competition principles to a modern industrial economy characterised by oligopoly and imperfect competition does not seem intrinsically sensible and it should be no surprise that this can lead to costly policy mistakes.[2] Markets in the real world are not normally perfect. Prices do not adjust instantly to changes in aggregate demand. Taking account of these facts leads to the conclusion that governments have a vital role in promoting full employment – if not in the *very* long term (when supply considerations are dominant) then certainly over time spans which are highly relevant to five-year governments and their electorates.

2 ECONOMIC THEORY AND THE OLD AND NEW MONETARIST PROPOSITIONS – OVERVIEW

The next five sections will cover a large part of the battleground over which the macroeconomic debate is currently being fought. Since they are primarily about economic theory, rather than about day-to-day economic policy issues, the subject matter is necessarily complex, and the language may be difficult for the non-specialist reader. For this reason, a short summary appears in bold italics at the beginning of each section, and the main points can be grasped just by reading these summaries.

Before setting out, it will be useful to lay out a brief map of where we are going. The thrust of the argument will be designed to explain and evaluate the theoretical case against using demand management policy to bring down unemployment in the United Kingdom. (The main effort will be to dispute the case *against*, rather than to establish the case *in favour of* demand management.) The case against is broken down into 3 main blocs:

1. We consider the proposition that changes in the budget deficit will fail even to alter the level of demand in the economy. This is the subject matter of Section 3.
2. In Sections 4 and 5, we accept that an appropriate combination of fiscal and monetary policy *can* affect demand, and examine the separate proposition that this cannot affect the level of output or employment, even in the short term.
3. In Section 6 we accept that demand can affect output and employment in the short term, and proceed to question whether it can also do so in the long term, or whether the economy will naturally tend to return to full employment (if left to its own devices) from virtually any starting point.

The strict new classical case is that fiscal policy cannot affect demand, and that demand cannot systematically affect output or employment even in the short run. (The long-run question is therefore uninteresting.) Since this is where the frontiers of the monetarist argument lie today, it is the natural focus for much of this chapter. The alternative Keynesian case – which will be supported – is (i) that fiscal policy can affect demand in both the short and long run; (ii) that demand can affect output and employment in the 'short run' of macroeconomic models (which may last many years); and (iii) that any automatic tendency for the economy to restore full employment in the very long run can all too easily get blocked without government support. The key differences between these two approaches will turn out to be the way in which expectations are formed and – much more important – the degree of price flexibility assumed.

Many different models and approaches will be interwoven into the discussion: Section 3 will discuss the so-called 'Ricardian Equivalence Theorem', which contends that private sector individuals will automatically offset changes in government borrowing by equal and opposite changes in their own spending. This proposition depends on perfect rationality and altruism, and perfect capital markets.

Section 4 will lay out the case for short-term policy ineffectiveness, as propounded by new classicists such as Lucas and Sargent. This will be found to rest on full rationality and perfectly flexible prices. The close affinity between this approach and that of traditional classical economists will be emphasised, as will the differences of detail between the new and old monetarists. The latter tend to assume slightly less flexible prices and expectations based on an error-learning process.

Section 5 assesses the new monetarist approach. The practical and theoretical problems of formulating rational expectations will be considered first. Next, we look at continuous market clearing through perfectly flexible prices, and this approach is contrasted with Keynesian models in which prices and wages are totally fixed. The latter models stem from the work of Barro and Grossman, and Malinvaud. Keynesian demand management is effective in such models, even where expectations are rational. This is demonstrated, among others, by Neary and Stiglitz. We then consider the question of *why* prices may be 'sticky'. This involves the 'invisible handshake' between buyers and sellers introduced by Okun. It also involves implicit contract theory and staggered contract theory. Next, we examine the consequences of breaching other assumptions of perfect competition, on which the strict new monetarist case is based. Models mentioned here are those developed by Weitzman, Blanchard, and Layard and Nickell. The section ends by looking at the empirical evidence, concluding that both formal econometric and less formal 'casual' evidence conflicts with the short-run policy ineffectiveness proposition.

Section 6 focuses on the long-run conclusions from models based on imperfect competition. It becomes clear that most of these models, which are rapidly becoming the bed-rock of modern mainstream Keynesianism, incorporate sufficient price flexibility in the long run to produce steady state solutions in which output and employment are not affected by demand. Concentrating on the empirical work of Layard and Nickell, it is shown that variations in the inflation rate may tend to restore the economy to the NAIRU –

the one unemployment level consistent with constant inflation – in the long run. However this process can easily get stuck for long periods and there is a strong case for assisting the shift back to full employment by government action. The government should also accept a responsibility to influence and reduce the NAIRU itself, since its level is certainly not set by 'natural' economic laws.

3 FISCAL POLICY AND DEMAND

This section is concerned with the link between fiscal policy and demand. It starts with the Ricardian belief that changes in government borrowing have no effect on aggregate demand because they are automatically offset by equal and opposite changes in private sector spending. We argue that this proposition is unlikely to be true: even if people are infinitely rational, they are unlikely to be infinitely altruistic, or to have access to perfect capital markets.

We need not be detained too long on the Ricardian theorem, since the stringency of the assumptions required to make it true has already been widely recognised among economists to be extremely implausible. The theorem states the following. For any given level of public expenditure, it makes no difference to the level of nominal demand whether the government chooses to finance that level of spending wholly through taxation, or through a mix of taxation and public borrowing.[3] Hence variations in the budget deficit do not alter the spending decisions of the private sector, even for a temporary period, and even if they make large differences to the disposable income of individuals and companies.

How can this be so? According to the Ricardians, the secret is that the private sector is rational enough to realise that the act of running a government budget deficit, financed by the sale of bonds, is nothing more than a *postponement* of the need to raise tax. When bonds eventually mature they can either be redeemed through the issue of more bonds (which will themselves eventually mature), or by increasing tax receipts. Holders of bonds will not be willing to lend indefinitely large amounts to the government, so taxes will eventually have to be raised to redeem or service bonds. Since people will instantly realise this, they will react to a rise in the budget deficit (and the bond issue) by increasing their savings to pay the expected higher level of taxes as the bonds are serviced. Total private spending therefore does not change.

At this point, some readers may feel that this sounds so absurd that I must be caricaturing the Ricardian argument. I assure them I am not. Others will have realised that there are serious objections to the Ricardians, the first of which is that individuals do not live forever. If people expect bonds to be serviced by increased taxation not on themselves but on some future generation, then they are much less likely to increase their savings in anticipation of higher taxes. In fact, they will only do this if they fulfil two separate criteria. First, they must be infinitely rational, and able to see immediately the ultra long-term tax implications of any change in the budget deficit. Second, they must be infinitely altruistic, just as worried about the well-being of their children and future grandchildren as they are about their own. In these circumstances, they will increase bequests to future generations to help them pay the eventual increase in taxation, therefore reducing their own spending fully to offset an increase in the budget deficit. Ricardians actually assume that this will happen.

On the other hand, non-Ricardians[4] point out that many individuals have no children, or care nothing for their welfare, and that it is a little implausible to suggest that the proverbial old lady who leaves her estate to the Battersea Dogs Home will raise her bequest to pay for a possible future increase in the dog licence. In addition, some individuals who may wish to increase their net borrowing to adjust their bequests will find that capital market imperfections will prevent them from doing so. They will not in fact be able to plan their saving in an optimal fashion spread over many generations, and will instead react to a bond-financed tax cut by increasing their current spending. (The government is actually making a loan to them at a rate of interest equal to the bond yield, and this may represent an extension of credit on terms which would otherwise be unavailable to them.)

Even if everyone is *rational* enough to take infinite time horizons into account, there is no reason therefore to assume in general that they will all be sufficiently *altruistic* to increase bequests fully in line with a perceived rise in the future tax burden. Furthermore, in the imperfect capital markets which characterise the real world, many individuals may be constrained to consume less than they would optimally wish by a lack of borrowing opportunities. They will therefore react to a tax cut at least in part by raising their current expenditure, so private savings will not rise fully to offset the impact of higher public borrowing, and the Ricardian theorem falls. This will happen even if all markets are continuously cleared by flexible prices;

but if some markets are not cleared, then a rise in the budget deficit (as we shall see later) will ease effective demand constraints and create an increased flow of actual and expected future incomes for the personal sector. There is then all the more reason to expect an increase in household spending when taxes are cut, even if households know for sure that they will have to pay the eventual debt servicing charges themselves. (See Tobin, 1980 p. 61.)

The Ricardian hypothesis therefore seems most unlikely to be *generally* true, though it is hard to deny that, beyond a certain point *part* of the impact of any increase in the budget deficit may be offset by an increase in private savings. For the purposes of the present argument we merely need the savings offset to be less than 100 per cent of the change in the budget deficit, and virtually all UK empirical evidence – from consumption studies to complete models of the economy – confirms that this is the case.

Other Forms of 'Crowding Out'

Even if the Ricardian theorem is rejected as rather extreme, fiscal policy may fail to effect demand because its impact is 'crowded out' by higher interest rates, or by a rise in imports. These effects can, however, be avoided by following an accommodatory monetary policy. The important question is whether this combination of fiscal and monetary policy will lead to an unacceptable increase in inflation. This is something we will return to in Section 6.

Although there are many academic and City economists who have emphasised the Ricardian theorem in recent years, the government itself has tended to argue that fiscal policy will be ineffective in influencing demand because its effects will be 'crowded out' by the impact of higher interest rates and (possibly) by a higher sterling exchange rate. This argument, of course, makes the implicit assumption that monetary policy (defined as the growth rate of the money stock) will be left unchanged as fiscal policy is eased.

The question of whether fiscal policy can have long-term effects on demand in the context of unchanged monetary policy can only be settled empirically, and the complex interactions involved really need a full econometric model to sort them out. A few years ago, simulations on all the main econometric models of the UK economy showed unequivocally that such a policy mix did indeed result in significant permanent additions to aggregate demand, but more recently such results have become less clear-cut, with most models beginning to incorporate larger interest rate effects on private spending. Nevertheless, the latest set of common simulations run by the Warwick University Macroeconomic Modelling Bureau (Wallis, 1984) still show demand and output increasing after an expansionary shift in fiscal policy on the Treasury, London Business School and National Institute models, even with a fixed money supply target. The output effects are fairly small, but they are all positive.

More important for our present purposes, all the models continue to show a large increase in demand and output if monetary policy is allowed to accommodate the shift in fiscal policy (by fixing interest rates and allowing the money supply to grow more rapidly). Under these conditions, there seem no serious grounds for doubting that an easing in overall macro-economic policy can affect demand. What is much more doubtful, of course, is whether this combination will have unacceptable consequences for inflation. All the models suggest that the inflationary impact of an expansionary shift in fiscal policy will be greater if monetary policy is allowed to accommodate the fiscal injection. This is a subject to which we will return in Section 6. For the moment, it is sufficient to note that fiscal policy can unambiguously affect demand, provided that monetary policy is set in an accommodating fashion. With a non-accommodating monetary policy, aggregate demand still responds to a fiscal injection in most model simulations, but by smaller amounts.

4 SHORT-RUN POLICY INEFFECTIVENESS – THE PROPOSITIONS EXPLAINED AND RATIONAL EXPECTATIONS EXPLORED

Having established that macroeconomic policy can affect aggregate demand, we now need to examine the argument that changes in nominal demand will affect only the price level, and will – despite the evidence of the models in the previous section – have no systematic role in determining employment even in the short term. As noted above, this proposition stems from the so-called classical dichotomy. While some (but not all) Friedman-type monetarists, and most new classicists, believe in the Ricardian theorem, *all* believe in a modern version of the classical dichotomy, differing only in the time scale to which the dichotomy should be applied. This branch of economic theory has been around for over a century but, with one modern twist, it remains the heart of the 1980s theoretical case against policy activism, and it therefore merits careful examination.

Much of the rest of this chapter will be devoted to a discussion of this modern case against policy activism. In the present section, we explain the basic under-pinnings of the classical dichotomy, and then show how the assumption of rational expectations has added a new twist to this familiar story. Readers who are familiar with the basic new classical approach should perhaps skip to Section 5, where our evaluation begins.

The Classical Dichotomy – Old Style

The first step it to review the simple logic which lies behind the classical dichotomy, as it was originally developed by the classical economists and general equilibrium theorists. In an imaginary economy characterised by perfect competition, and in which no trades are permitted except at equilibrium prices, nominal demand (proxied by the money stock) affects only the price level, while output and employment are determined only by real variables.

It is useful to start at the highest level of abstraction, which is the Walrasian system of general equilibrium. This system, first formalised by Walras in the 1870s, relates to an imaginary economy where all the postulates of perfect competition are assumed to hold. In particular, no individual economic agent can affect the price level, which is determined by the interplay of supply and demand for each of the traded commodities, including labour itself. Nothing is actually traded at 'false' or non-equilibrium prices.[5] A Walrasian 'auctioneer' continues to take bids and offers for each commodity until demand and supply is equated in each market, at which point trades are permitted. If there is an initial excess demand for any product, the auctioneer simply increases the price until this is eliminated. In the case of initial excess supply, the price is reduced. The auctioneer's process of groping towards equilibrium prices by trial and error is called *tâtonnement*.

What does this process imply for the determination of output and employment? First, consider an economy where money has not been invented, so barter is the only means of exchange, and prices are expressed as the number of units of one commodity which can be exchanged for a single unit of any other commodity, one of which is arbitrarily chosen as the standard 'measuring stick' or numeraire.[6] Prices for goods and labour are then expressed as x units of the numeraire commodity. For a given set of tastes and preferences, the *demand* for any commodity will decline continuously as its price rises. With a given set of production methods, the *supply* of each commodity responds positively to its price, also on a continuous basis. Labour is again treated like any other commodity.

With these assumptions, it should be obvious that the level of production for each commodity will be determined by the intersection of these real supply and demand curves, which will also determine the price. In this system, real output, sales and prices will all be simultaneously determined by the exogenous variables (notably technology and consumer tastes) which set the positions of the supply and demand curves. In the case of labour, the quantity demanded will be equated with the quantity supplied because the price of labour (that is, the real wage, or the amount of the numeraire commodity which is earned for every unit of labour supplied) is assumed to be completely flexible.

Involuntary unemployment – an excess of labour supply over labour demand at a given price – therefore cannot occur in this system. If labour supply exceeds demand when the process of *tâtonnement* starts, the auctioneer simply drops the real wage continuously until the excess disappears. No trades are permitted unless labour supply equals labour demand. Employment is then at its equilibrium or 'natural' level. The 'natural' level of output of each commodity is similarly determined in the various goods markets. Neither output nor employment ever budge from equilibrium, and will only change when equilibrium itself changes because the real supply and demand curves shift.

Now add to this system a new commodity called money which has the useful properties that it is exchangeable for other commodities, is widely acceptable in the community and is easily stored and carried. Furthermore its supply is not freely available, but is controlled by the imprimatur of monarchs or the accident of gold mining discoveries. It will take on the role of numeraire in the system already described, so prices are expressed in money units; but it also has a use value of its own (since it prevents the wastages involved in barter and acts as a store of value), and there is consequently a separate need and demand for it as a commodity. Its supply is taken as given, but is liable to change if the monarch wishes to create some to buy a new palace, or if a new gold mine is discovered.

In this imaginary economy, the price level must be determined by the supply of money. To see this, we need to invoke a further relationship known as Walras' Law, which stems from the fact that individuals are constrained to purchase only those commodities which can be financed by the sale of other commodities (notably their own labour) and by a run-down in money balances. Across the whole economy, these budget constraints mean that the sum total of demands for all commodities must equal the sum total of supplies, both before and after the auctioneer has reached the equilibrium prices at which trades are permitted. Any breach of this economy-wide equality between supplies and demands would mean that some traders were breaching their budget constraints, which cannot occur. So excess demand across the whole economy must always equal zero, and excess demand for any one commodity must always be matched by excess supply elsewhere.

This rule applies to money as to any other commodity. In equilibrium, the equality is trivial, since prices have been set in money units such that all excess demands and supplies are zero anyway. But what happens if the monarch now decides to pay a Christmas bonus of 10 extra units of money to all the realm's contented subjects? Before the next period of trading is permitted by the auctioneer, it will become apparent from the first round of bids and offers that the contented subjects are attempting to swap some of this money for extra goods: there will be excess supply of money and (by Walras' Law) excess demand for goods. This can only be eliminated by raising the price of goods in terms of money, so goods become more expensive; or (to put this in a different way) money becomes cheaper in terms of goods. Equilibrium trades are permitted only when goods prices have risen in the same proportion as the stock of money. Any rise or fall in the supply of money relative to its demand must create an opposite imbalance in the goods market which will require a general move in the price level to sort out. Hence money determines prices.

We have now established both parts of the classical dichotomy in this highly abstract system. The brilliant work of the auctioneer in changing *relative* prices (such as the real wage) will ensure that the real variables in the system, notably output and employment, will always be at their equilibrium levels; meanwhile the absolute price level in money units will be set by the arbitrary decisions of the monarch in deciding how much money to create. What remains true throughout is that changes in the supply of money will have no effect on the level of output or employment.

Modern Twists to the Classical Dichotomy

Modern monetarists have adjusted the account of a classical economy outlined above to produce models which they believe are applicable to the real world. The substantive change they introduce is that the assumption of perfect certainty is removed from the models of the previous section. This results in temporary deviations in output from its natural level if prices are misperceived. Output can therefore be affected by nominal demand policy if this produces unanticipated changes in the price level.

We have spent some time looking at the classical dichotomy because its basic characteristics are reproduced almost in full in the work of the new classicists.[7] In particular, markets are assumed to clear on a virtually continuous basis by price adjustments, and the postulates of perfect competition are assumed to hold for both firms and individuals. In fact, the way in which macroeconomic postulates are constructed from the optimising behaviour of rational microeconomic agents is often held to be a particular advantage of new classical (NC) economics, especially in contrast to the supposedly '*ad hoc*'[8] Keynesian relationships. As we shall see later, however, acceptance of the classical postulates of microeconomics also carries the substantial disadvantage of creating a macro-system which lacks application to the real world.

Only in one major respect do the modern new classicists differ from the description of the classical dichotomy just given. This concerns the role of the Walrasian auctioneer, who was originally invented not only to equate supply and demand but also to ensure that the general equilibrium system behaved as if all agents had perfect certainty about the bids and offers being made for all commodities (including labour) across the whole economy. With such perfect certainty, false trading at non-equilibrium prices could never occur, since this would imply that some bids or offers were being frustrated at the trading prices, and this is precisely what the auctioneer's process prevents. Not even the most unworldly NC economist could actually believe that such an auctioneer in fact exists (or that the real world even approximates to one of perfect certainty). On page one of the NC creed, the auctioneer loses the magic gavel. What is surprising is that, on their analysis, this concession to realism makes relatively little difference to the effectiveness of nominal demand policy in the economy.

To see this, we need to start with a closer examination of the labour market in the classical system. The key point is that both labour demand and labour supply should be related to the *real* wage (as well as to other exogenous variables), and not to the nominal wage. After all, neither workers nor firms should be interested in what labour earns in arbitrary nominal units. However, when wage offers are made, they are actually quoted in nominal units, so workers and firms have to divide these by the price level to obtain estimates of the real wage. The price level concerned will not simply be that which applies on the first day of the wage offer, but will be that which is *expected* to apply on average for the duration of the wage contract. The relevant real wage which determines the supply and demand for labour is therefore the nominal wage divided by the expected price level.

In a full Walrasian system this would present no problem, since knowledge of existing prices across the whole economy would be held by all agents with perfect certainty, and since markets would exist in *all* future prices (rather as they actually exist in the real world for primary commodities and a few financial assets). If an individual anticipates a demand for a motor car in ten years' time, this and all other future demands are assumed to be tradeable now at prices which will relate to the date at which the trade will occur. The 'auctioneer' assumption therefore ensures perfect knowledge of all present prices, while existence of future markets make uncertainty about tomorrow a tradeable commodity, thus eliminating the possibility that expectations will be unfulfilled. In modern NC economics, the assumption of perfect certainty is removed, both about the present and about the future.

The New Classical 'Island Parable'

The removal of perfect knowledge about economy-wide prices and wages has interesting effects on the behaviour of firms and workers. Firms will of course still know the price they are receiving at any time for their own products, but they will not have perfect knowledge about *all* other prices in the whole economy. It is as if each producer lives on a small island (or enclosed market) within which prices can be perfectly observed, but which is cut off from knowledge of what is happening on other islands during the same period. Although knowledge becomes available at the end of each period, information on economy-wide prices can only be inferred *at the time* by observing what is happening within each market.

Now assume that an increase in the supply of money results in prices being bid up in each of the islands that make up the overall economy. Within any island, producers may simply believe that demand has shifted in favour of their particular product, causing an increase in its relative price. Since other commodities will be used as inputs in any production process, each firm will believe that the relative price shift has increased its selling price relative to its input prices, and will therefore be willing to increase production, offering higher wages to attract more workers. Since the same process is happening simultaneously on every 'island', production in the whole economy rises.(There are no inventory adjustments in such models.) However, at the end of any period, all firms will realise that *relative* prices have not moved in their favour after all, but that the *general* price level has risen. There will therefore have been no improvement in selling prices relative to input prices, and the perceived incentive to increase output will have disappeared. Firms will therefore restore output to its original level. All that the episode will have achieved is an increase in the general price level, an equal increase in nominal wages (leaving the real wage unchanged) and a strictly temporary rise in output.

An extra twist to this story occurs if producers are willing to change the pattern of their output from period to period in response to changes in relative prices which they perceive to be *temporary*. Let us return to the stage at which producers believe that relative prices have moved in their favour. If they believe that this is wholly or partly a temporary phenomenon, they will have a clear incentive to bring forward their production plans to take advantage of the period when prices are high. Farmers will, for example, do their best to miximise beef production at a time when they believe that the selling price for beef is unusually high, and will risk a drop-off in their output when prices have subsided. That way, they will be better off on average than if they maintained a constant level of output through time. This form of inter-temporal substitution has two effects. First, it results in potentially large output adjustments to quite small changes in relative prices, provided that the latter are seen in part as temporary. Second, it produces periodic variations in output which take on the appearance of a business cycle.

We have now seen how incorrect price expectations can lead to temporary deviations in real variables from their natural levels when nominal demand changes. The supply of output (Y_s) is therefore equal to its natural level (Y_n), which is determined by real variables as before,[9] plus a variable term which represents the difference between actual and expected prices (P and P_e respectively). This produces the 'surprise supply equation' which is fundamental to the NC results:

$$Y_s = Y_n + b(P - P_e) \quad \text{(all variables in logs)} \tag{3.1}$$

Obviously, if prices never deviate from their expected level, output will be fixed at its natural rate, and the classical dichotomy will always hold. On the other hand, if the price level permanently deviates from its expected level, then the supply of output can also deviate from its natural level in response to change in nominal variables such as the money supply. (Often the inflation *rate* replaces the price level in such equations.) Clearly, the way in which expectations are formed is a matter of crucial importance, and this is where the NC school have made their most distinctive contribution to economic theory.

Rational Expectations

The new classicists believe that output (and employment) will be equal to their 'natural' levels unless there is a deviation between actual and expected prices. We now look at the way in which price expectations are formed. The old monetarists believed that they are formed by an adaptive (or learning) process based on past price behaviour. But the new monetarists argue that this process is irrational, since it can lead to systematic errors in expectations which should be eradicated by rational agents. As an alternative, they propose forward-looking or 'rational' expectations, which take account of all available information at the time they are formed. Such expectations will not always prove accurate, since some events are non-forecastable, but they will not be systematically inaccurate at the time they are made.

Until the 1970s, there was relatively little interest among economic theoreticians in the process by which expectations are formed, partly because *price* expectations did not seem to be a major problem in an environment where inflation was low and stable, and partly because the Keynesian tradition had been to view *output* and *profits* expectations (which are vital for investment spending) as too volatile to be properly analysed. Furthermore, since expectations were not actually observable, they did not seem particularly useful for econometric estimation. However the work of the old and new monetarists has changed all that.

Adaptive or Error-Correcting Mechanisms

Friedman's work after 1968 initially supposed that price expectations would be formed mainly by extrapolating previous experience of price changes through an error-correcting mechanism. This mechanism is called the 'adaptive expectations' process. It suggests that the expected price level (or the inflation rate) in any period will be equal to the out-turn in the previous period plus some fraction of the error made in predicting prices in the previous period. Provided that the error-correction mechanism is constant, the process produces an expected level of prices (or inflation rate) equal to a weighted average of the price level in all previous periods, with the weights declining geometrically over time.[10]

This formulation at first appeared to have two great merits. First, it enabled expectations to be 'measured' simply by reference to actual past data, which made it possible to incorporate them into econometric estimation. Second, if the economy moved from one long-run inflation rate to another, the adaptive formulation resulted in inflation expectations slowly 'homing in' on the new inflation rate. It seemed appealing that economic agents might take time to adjust to new circumstances, but that they would eventually catch up with the changed reality.

If expectations are formed adaptively, then demand management can work for a time in affecting output and employment in the economy by driving a wedge between actual and expected prices. Consider, for example, what would happen if prices and the money supply had both been rising by 5 per cent per annum for a long period of time, and that adaptive price expectations had fully adjusted to this inflation rate. According to the NC supply function, output and employment would then be fixed at their natural levels, determined by real variables, and the classical dichotomy would hold. Associated with the 'natural' levels of employment and output, the monetarists (both old and new) believe that there is also a 'natural' level of *unemployment*. This exists because there will always be a residue of people who are temporarily unemployed as they switch jobs. Such frictional or search unemployment is not symptomatic of a situation in which the economy is out of equilibrium, since there is an optimum quantity of search unemployment which is necessary for the efficient functioning of the labour market.[11]

Imagine now that the government becomes impatient with the

natural level of unemployment associated with this equilibrium, and attempts to reduce it by increasing nominal demand, for example by boosting the rate of monetary growth. The rise in monetary demand will tend to put upward pressure on price inflation and – given the adaptive expectations formation system – actual prices will start to run ahead of expected prices. This will lead to an increase in the supply of output and the level of employment compared with their natural rates, and the government may believe for a time that its nominal demand management policy has been successful.

However, if it now holds monetary growth constant at a new higher rate (say 7 per cent), price expectations will eventually 'home in' on this new rate, the gap between actual and expected prices will be eliminated, and both output and employment will return to their original levels. The problem is that price expectations are now fixed at 7 per cent per annum, and the government will need to maintain this rate of monetary growth simply to allow employment and output to stay at their original levels, which had previously been consistent with 5 per cent inflation. Alternatively, if the authorities wished to continue holding employment above its natural rate, they would need to create another 'surprise' by boosting inflation above the 7 per cent rate, say to 9 per cent. This would again have a temporary effect on output and employment, but eventually price expectations would adjust to the new rate, and output would again return to normal. In order to keep output permanently above the equilibrium level, price inflation would not simply need to be held at a higher level than in the original case, but would need to be continuously increased to produce the required surprises in labour and commodity markets.

Consistent with this analysis is a formulation of the Phillips Curve which explicitly allows for changes in price expectations. This implies that the apparent trade-off between unemployment and inflation is only stable in the short term, while price expectations are out of line with actual prices. In the longer run, this trade-off disappears, since the short-run Phillips curve moves upwards as price expectations rise. Only one level of unemployment – the natural rate – is consistent with constant inflation in the long run. Note that in this formulation of the Phillips Curve, it is changes in the rate of inflation relative to the expected rate which produce temporary movements in the level of output and unemployment. It is very important to realise that in this analysis the direction of causation runs from prices to unemployment, rather than vice versa. Later we shall see that an apparently identical formulation can be derived in which the direction of causation runs from unemployment to prices. These two different approaches have quite distinct implications for policy.

Friedman's old monetarist approach therefore permits unemployment to be affected by active government policy only for the 'short-run' periods during which actual prices diverge from their expected level (though with adaptive expectations this period may actually run in calendar terms for rather a long time). Some governments might therefore choose to incur somewhat increased inflation in the long run in order to enjoy a period of reduced unemployment in the short run. This might become especially attractive if they believe that price expectations will never quite adjust fully to an increase in the actual inflation rate, so that a permanent gap might be engineered between actual and expected prices, leading to some permanent employment gains. By the mid-1970s, some degree of consensus had developed between monetarist and Keynesian economists (at least in the United States) that this type of analysis broadly described the policy choice facing the authorities. But then any semblance of consensus was shattered by the increasingly influential writings of the new monetarist school, which was applying the radical new concept of rational expectations.

The Concept of 'Rationality'

The revolt against adaptive expectations began when economists realised that this hypothesis required economic agents, under certain circumstances, to make systematic mistakes. For example, if the price level is always rising, then any weighted moving average of previous prices will always under-predict the future price level. Similarly, if economic agents form expectations about the inflation *rate* according to a moving average of past inflation rates, then they will always under-predict the rate of change of prices in an environment of generally rising inflation, and will always over-predict it in a general environment of decreasing inflation. It seems hard to believe that rational agents will persist with an expectations formation mechanism which makes such consistent errors. In addition, it is difficult to see why rational agents will form expectations simply by looking at the past movements of a single variable. Often there might be alternative sources of information about future movements in prices which will enable private sector agents systematically to out-perform expectations made in an adaptive framework. For example, if rational agents know that price inflation is determined by the rate of change in the money stock, and they know that the government intends to change the rate of monetary growth, they will surely adjust their price expectations accordingly, whatever the recent history of price expectations has shown. Rational economic agents should therefore form expectations which do not make avoidable mistakes on a systematic basis and, up to a limit imposed by marginal cost effectiveness, should incorporate all available sources of information into their expectations formation system.

If rational agents form their expectations in this way, they should have the following characteristics:

1. They should be derived from the best available economic model which can be used to predict the variable in question. (In the case of price expectations, the usual NC proposition is that present and past rates of monetary growth should be used to predict future price levels.)
2. No information which is available when the expectations are formed should be omitted from the process of forming the expectations in question. Technically, this means that the errors made by the expectations process should not be correlated with any information available when the expectations are formed. If such a correlation exists, it implies that agents are failing to use all available information in forming their expectations, and this (allowing for cost constraints) is clearly not optimal. In fact, the errors made by a rational expectations process should on average be zero, and should be free of any discernible patterns.
3. Rational expectations will turn out to be the most accurate available, since if any superior process were available, optimising agents would adopt it. *This does not mean that rational expectations will always prove completely accurate*, since any process is subject to random disturbance, which by definition cannot be predicted in advance. However, the essence is that the disturbance term (that is, the forecast error) should be truly random, and not related to any information which is available when the forecast is made.

While these features may not seem revolutionary at first sight, the application of rational expectations theory has had profound implications throughout economics. For example, when applied in a microeconomic framework to a financial variable such as the exchange rate, it implies that it should be impossible to make systematic (super-normal) profits by trading the market, since all known information is incorporated into the price at any given moment. Future moves in the price will either be random, or will reflect the announcement of new information. Either way, they will be wholly unpredictable. In macroeconomics, the application of rational expectations has results which are just as startling. When combined with the other NC propositions (notably the assumption of continuous market clearing), they eliminate any role for government stabilisation policy, whether in the short or long term.

Price Expectations and Stabilisation Policy

We now show how important the price expectations mechanism is for macroeconomic policy. If the private sector 'rationally' takes account of the known impact of macroeconomic policy on economic variables such as the price level, it becomes impossible for the predictable component of demand management policy to produce deviations between actual and expected prices. Consequently the anticipated element of monetary or fiscal policy cannot affect output, even for short periods, in the new monetarist system.

In the discussion of adaptive expections above, it was shown that the government could produce deviations from the natural level of output by altering nominal demand policy in such a way that it temporarily creates a divergence between actual and expected prices. But, with rational expectations, such a divergence can never be systematically induced by the government, since the government's actions themselves will be predicted by the private sector. In particular, the link between monetary growth and future price inflation will be fully understood by the private sector, and this will be used to form price expectations. Hence, when the government increases the rate of monetary growth with the intention of driving output above its natural rate, this will be immediately built into price expectations, and the divergence between actual and expected prices which is needed to change the level of output will never occur. The economy will therefore stay stuck at its long-run real equilibrium, and the government's attempt to increase output above its natural rate will fail.

This very strong result depends of course on the private sector having knowledge not only of the money stock during *previous* periods, but also in the period under review. Even to NC theorists, it seems somewhat implausible to assume that monetary variables are known within any given time period, since economy-wide prices are assumed *not* to be known until the end of any time period. If we make the slightly more realistic assumption that the evolution of the money stock (and other variables influencing nominal demand) is also discovered only at the end of each time period, then at the beginning of each period its level needs to be forecast from information known at that date. In accordance with rational expectations, the money stock will be forecast using all known information available when the expectations are formed, including any patterns of behaviour which have been displayed by the government in the past. For example, if the government has habitually increased the rate of monetary growth when the level of output falls for several successive quarters, or when a general election is approaching, this will be built into the private sector's expectation of the money supply at the beginning of any period. If the government then follows its previous pattern of behaviour, increasing the money supply as predicted, this will be fully discounted by firms and individuals, and their behaviour in the real labour and commodity markets will not alter.

It is only if the government departs from its previous behaviour pattern, introducing a new element into its monetary policy, that an unexpected deviation in the money stock (and therefore the price level) can be engineered. Such an unanticipated change in monetary policy *can* then produce a temporary change in output, but the government's new mode of behaviour will soon be incorporated into the private sector's expectation mechanism. The government must continue to change its behaviour on a *random* basis in order to maintain its influence over the level of output. But then, far from contributing to greater stability in output, these random changes actually lead to greater variability in output than that which would occur if the government did not vary its monetary policy at all.

The Catch 22 is therefore this. If the government varies its monetary policy in a predictable fashion, its actions will be entirely foreseen by the private sector, and will induce no changes in output or unemployment. If, on the other hand, the government varies its monetary policy unpredictably, it will succeed only in destabilising the economy, actually increasing the variability of output and employment around their natural levels. (These conclusions, which we have couched in terms of monetary policy, apply in full to any form of government intervention which affects the growth of nominal demand in the economy, including of course changes in fiscal variables.)

The observation that only random changes in government policy can affect real aggregates leads naturally on to the proposition that nominal demand management policy should be set in the most predictable fashion possible. Within any given period, the private sector's labour supply and output decisions will depend on attempting to distinguish a general increase in demand across the whole economy from a relative increase in demand for a particular product or type of labour. In the former case, rational agents will not change their real supply behaviour, since they will recognise it to be simply an economy-wide inflationary shock, but in the latter case output changes will need to be made. The more volatile is the random component of aggregate demand, the more likely is a rational agent to decide that a given shift in demand represents a change in economy-wide nominal demand, rather than in the relative demand for an individual product. This means that, in an economy where the random element in government demand policy is very substantial, agents may become inefficient in responding to relative demand changes with required alterations in production plans, simply because they mistake such relative changes for a generalised inflationary shock. By contrast, in an economy where demand shocks are very few, most observed changes in demand are likely to be correctly recognised as *relative* rather than *general* changes. The lesson from this is that the government should adopt a perfectly predictable demand management policy, involving for example a constant rate of growth in the money supply, and should avoid any attempts to shock the system by altering demand policy on a random basis.

We have now finally arrived at the standard results of new monetarist macroeconomics – the 'state of the art' among the now-dominant subset of monetarist economists. The main conclusions are:

1. In an economy where prices are continuously flexible, employment and output will tend rapidly to settle at their equilibrium or natural levels.
2. The rate of inflation in such an economy will be determined by monetary growth.
3. Except for periods in which prices deviate from their expected levels, changes in nominal demand policy will affect only the price level, and will have no real effects on output or jobs.
4. Price expectations will be formed 'rationally', and this will prevent the government from engineering differences between actual and

expected prices by changing its demand policy in a predictable fashion.

5. Random changes in demand policy will succeed in affecting real variables, but only by increasing the *variability* of output, without altering its natural level.
6. Therefore the government should adopt a simple and predictable demand management policy aimed only at controlling inflation. This should involve setting targets for monetary growth for as far ahead as possible. These targets should then be hit to ensure the credibility of policy.

Although the new monetarists have rationalised these conclusions rather more tightly than their Friedmanite predecessors, and have added a vital new ingredient in rational expectations, the similarity between the basic conclusions of old and new monetarism should be obvious. In the monetarist view, the best advice that macroeconomists can give to politicians is therefore simple enough:

'Don't just do something – sit there!'

5 EVALUATION OF SHORT-RUN POLICY INEFFECTIVENESS

In this section, we evaluate the monetarist arguments which lie behind the belief that systematic government policy is ineffective in both the short and long run. Our conclusion will be that real world deviations from the assumptions that lie behind new monetarism are sufficiently likely to restore a role for policy activism, at least in periods other than the very long run.

The structure of this section is as follows:

(a) We discuss the plausibility and applicability of the rational expectations assumption.
(b) We look at the assumption of continuous market clearing.
(c) We examine the other assumptions of perfect competition.
(d) We look at the empirical and econometric evidence on the subject.
(e) We summarise the main theoretical conclusions relating to short-run policy ineffectiveness.

In reviewing the literature in each of these areas, it will become clear that attacks on the new monetarist school have been so numerous that it is surprising that they have barely succeeded in slowing the momentum of Lucas and his followers. This is perhaps for two reasons. First, some of the academic work in this area has been of a somewhat nit-picking variety, accepting the basic framework of the new classicists, and then showing that exceptions to their propositions can be produced by relaxing some of their assumptions. This has almost had the perverse effect of strengthening the basic message. Second, where more fundamental objections have been raised, many of the academic articles have been disparate and technically demanding and have too rarely been gathered under a single umbrella. The next few pages of this chapter attempt to provide such an umbrella.

The Plausibility of the Rational Expectations Assumption

Although the assumption of rationality has probably come to stay as an indispensable modelling tool in theoretical work, it raises many problems which have yet to be solved. For both theoretical and empirical reasons, it may be difficult for economic agents, however rational they may wish to be, to identify a unique model structure and solution on which to base their expectations. Hence, in the short term they may resort to simple 'rule of thumb', one of which may involve adaptive expectations, especially in the labour market. This of course would allow active demand policy to be effective for the duration that these rules of thumb are in use. Some econometric evidence suggests that price expectations are not in fact formed rationally, even by professional economists.

In response to the introduction of the novel concept of rational expectations, Keynesians have frequently argued that the idea that economic agents rationally formulate their expectations by reference to the best available economic model is inherently absurd. After all, most ordinary people – and perhaps the people reading this chapter – could not even define the money stock, still less explain its relationship to the inflation rate, or write a discourse on the differences between monetarist and non-monetarist views of the inflation mechanism. Even if two professors of economics are given exactly the same set of information, they are quite likely to produce two entirely different inflation projections, which could be viewed as equally rational.

The rational expectationists have now largely accepted these arguments, but have come back with a strong counter-attack of their own. They are willing to concede that individuals do not as a rule spend much time solving economic models, but they point out that the results of such models – especially on important variables like inflation – are frequently published in the newspapers and broadcast on television. In addition, individuals club together in groups which make it possible for them jointly to acquire an information-filtering process (such as a trade union research officer). Expectations may therefore be rational at one or two removes; and it is not necessary for everyone to hold the same expectations for them to be rational *on average*. Individual peculiarities should cancel out, leaving the population as a whole making no systematic errors.

These new classical points are difficult to refute. It certainly seems objectionable for economists, who base so much of their work on a belief in optimising behaviour by individuals, to make the quite arbitrary assumption that agents will suspend optimality in the single area of information processing, while retaining it everywhere else. Any sane individual would surely learn from an expectations mechanism which made persistent mistakes, and would amend it until it could be improved no further. Nor is it theoretically acceptable to propose economic models which incorporate expectational mechanisms which in the long run flatly contradict the processes embedded in the models themselves. For example, on what basis is it defensible for Friedman to assert that price expectations are formed adaptively in a monetarist model of inflation? This carries the implication that only Friedman himself can understand the true link between money and prices embodied in his models, while the rest of the world fails to spot the money/prices relationship, and instead fumbles around in the dark. This may happen for a time, but it is scarcely an equilibrium condition, or a permanent basis for policy activism.

The rational expectations hypothesis (like the profit maximisation hypothesis before it) has almost certainly come to stay as an indispensable tool of long-term economic modelling, if only because all alternative assumptions seem less logical in the optimising structures of most theoretical work. Not everyone agrees with this. Hahn (1983) objects to the term rational expectations 'revolution', saying that 'Portentous terms like "revolution" applied to economics suggest not only unseemly enthusiasm but perhaps a certain coarseness. . . . In ten years' time the "revolution" will be seen to have been a little local disturbance'. This seems likely to prove a rare misjudgement by a great economist. However an acceptance of rational expectations as a vital and permanent tool of long-term equilibrium analysis does not mean that all its analytic problems have been solved, or that it need always be empirically valid in the short as well as the long term. The development of rational expectations theory is, it must be admitted, still in its infancy, and there are significant unsolved problems in at least three crucial areas. These are:

1. *Multiple equilibrium paths*. Where models generate more than one steady-state path to long-run equilibrium, how can rational individuals choose between them?
2. *Interdependent expectations*. What happens when economic outturns depend on one person's expectation of someone else's expectations?
3. *Empirical identification and testing of relevant models*. Can economic models in fact be identified statistically?

Taken together, problems in these areas mean that the assumption of rational expectations is not yet ready for automatic inclusion in the policy maker's tool-kit.

Multiple Equilibrium Paths

The frequent existence of multiple equilibrium paths is probably the main theoretical problem which the rational expectationists need to solve. The problem is this. Many economic variables are dependent, not on expectations of contemporaneous variables where data have not yet been published, but on expectations about *future* variables. Investment is dependent on expected future output, and consumption on expected future income, to name only two. If the economy starts (or is moved by a random shock) away from equilibrium in many such models, there will be an infinite number of possible paths back to equilibrium, since each trajectory for expected income or expected output will generate a different path for consumption and investment. If the system is globally stable, *all* such paths will lead back to equilibrium, and all (if followed) will eventually be consistent with the original set of expectations being fulfilled. But this means that, after a disturbance from equilibrium, there is no obvious basis for rational agents, even if they are in full possession of all the details of the equations which make up the economic system, to expect any *particular* trajectory to occur. They cannot therefore formulate a single set of rational expectations, and there will be no unique solution to the system. This is very worrying for many theorists, though it turns out that in systems which are *not* globally stable (or globally unstable) the problem is admittedly much less severe.[12]

Interdependent Expectations

A somewhat similar problem exists if expectations are interdependent. This difficulty has a particular tendency to arise in financial markets where, as Keynes observed, people will buy securities if they expect other people to buy them. Since everyone is in the same boat, the whole system becomes a multidimensional guessing game where almost any set of expectations, once determined, will be fulfilled, but where any set of expectations initially appears as good as any other. Keynes held that similar considerations applied to the investment decision undertaken by entrepreneurs: provided all expected *others* to expand investment out of a recession, all would do so and would make profits; but if none expected others to expand, none would do so themselves. Again, there is no obvious basis on which to formulate a single set of expectations from the outset.

Empirical Identification

So far we have assumed that full knowledge of the underlying structure of the economy is available to rational agents, but this of course may be totally unrealistic. Apart from the inherent unlikelihood of individuals or firms having the technical expertise to understand such models (which is a practical rather than a theoretical problem), there is a real theoretical problem involved with identifying the correct model structure. It is quite often the case that new classical economic models incorporating rational expectations turn out to be observationally identical to models which are based on Keynesian propositions. Although econometricians are beginning to develop ways of distinguishing between Keynesian and NC models by observing what happens when the policy regime changes,[13] it may take years after the regime switch to sort out the competing claims of different models, so there will be some periods where the correct models cannot be distinguished even by the best econometricians. In such cases, it surely becomes theoretically invalid to assume that rational economic agents are able to identify the correct economic model from which to formulate expectations about the future. Furthermore, on many occasions, complete knowledge of the model may be of little or no help. If the government decides to change its policy regime – for example by adopting an explicit set of domestic monetary targets for the first time – even the most rational agent will have little basis on which to judge how rigidly the government will stick to its new targets. This is in a way an example of 'Keynesian' unpredictability, where uncertainty cannot be handled by looking at probability distributions based on past data. It is then not clear how rational expectations can be formed, or indeed how expectations can be modelled at all.

Problems such as these undoubtedly mean that the rational expectations school has a long way to go before it can claim to have a product which is ready to be absorbed wholesale into policy making. Nor would it be surprising if, faced with these difficulties, people resorted to simple 'rules of thumb' to formulate their price expectations. One such rule of thumb may involve an error-learning process such as that suggested by the adaptive expectations hypothesis. As we noted above, this would restore a role for policy activism for the duration that such rules are in use. But in the long-term equilibrium solutions of *theoretical* models, it does seem reasonable to suppose that expectations will be fulfilled, and will be formed rationally.

Testing the Assumption of 'Rationality'

The empirical evidence on expectations formation has certainly not established beyond dispute that all economic agents *do* form their expectations rationally in the world which is relevant to policy makers. There are two approaches to testing the rational expectations hypothesis: indirect and direct. Where expectations are not directly observable, it is usual to make the assumption that expectations are rational, to incorporate this assumption into a model structure, and then indirectly to test the *joint* proposition that expectations are rational *and* that the model structure is valid. However, if the data reject this joint proposition, it is impossible to tell whether this is because expectations are not rational, or because the model structure is invalid, so such tests are rarely conclusive. Second, where expectations have been directly collected by survey data, it is possible to test whether they conform to the predictions of rationality, and in particular whether expectational errors are uncorrelated with any information which is available when the expectations are formed.

A vast literature has been spawned testing the rationality hypothesis, and there are now several excellent surveys of the literature readily available.[14] There is certainly no consensus, but on the (far more common) *indirect* tests, it is probably fair to conclude that expectations tend more to rationality in financial markets than in labour or goods markets.[15] On the direct tests, the macroeconomic evidence most relevant to our main theme has concentrated particularly heavily on a single set of price expectations data which is available for the United States on a continuous basis since 1947. This series, known as the Livingston series, is almost unique in macroeconomics, and results relating to it are of particular interest. It consists of a twice-yearly series of price forecasts made by a sample of professional economists in the United States. Early work was again ambiguous, but the most rigorous testing of the data by Figlewski and Wachtel (1981) has concluded that price expectations are *not* formed rationally, even by this group of professional economists. The series exhibits a significant downward bias with forecast errors being positively serially correlated, both of which results imply that the forecasters fail to incorporate all the available information into their projection systems. Furthermore the adaptive expectations hypothesis seems to fit the series of price forecasts much better than the 'rational' hypothesis. (This, incidentally, does not mean that adaptive forecasts are more accurate than rational forecasts. It means that the agents sampled in the Livingston series tended to use adaptive rather than rational methods to derive price expectations.)

Assessment

Many Keynesian economists may therefore be persuaded that the rational expectations hypothesis can be safely discarded, since it does not explain actual data, and since it raises theoretical problems which have yet to be solved. To raise doubts is valid, but Keynesians must be careful not to discard the baby with the bath water. Many of the problems faced by the rational expectationists are faced by *all* economic models in which expectations are important; and, to say the very least, the assumption of rationality fits easily into the mainstream of theoretical economic work, whereas the assumption of almost capricious irrationality does not. If we are to incorporate expectations into equilibrium models without assuming capricious irrationality, it may be the route which future theoreticians will increasingly follow. Practising macroeconomists will, on the other hand, remain understandably loath to accept the assumption of rational expectations for short-term policy advice. Despite this, it should have taught them that it would be unwise to set policy in the belief that individuals and firms can be systematically fooled, or that policy makers can rely on having access to information which is clearly superior to that processed by the private sector.[16] In ramming home these lessons, the NC economists have probably done a service to the whole profession.

Continuous Market Clearing

We now turn to the important question of price flexibility. The new classicists' proposition that policy is ineffective in the short run depends on continuous market clearing, as well as on rational expectations. This effectively rules out involuntary unemployment from the outset. Empirical evidence, however, suggests that prices and wages are not sufficiently flexible to ensure continuous market clearing. This raises the possibility that Keynesian or involuntary unemployment can exist. For the duration of time that prices and wages are sticky, nominal demand policy can affect employment, and this process is helped rather than hindered by rational expectations. The microeconomic explanations of why prices are sticky are still somewhat shaky, but are beginning to make progress. Nevertheless most models allow sufficient price flexibility following a decline in demand to restore equilibrium in the long run through automatic price adjustments. If the authorities use demand management to short-circuit these long-run equilibrium processes, they will lock in a higher price level (or inflation rate) than would otherwise have occurred on the restoration of equilibrium. Against this, they will make considerable savings in output in the meantime and will arrive more rapidly at the natural rates of employment and output that the long-run price adjustments are groping towards.

The new monetarists assume that prices and wages are so flexible in response to excess supply or demand for goods and labour that all markets clear on a continuous basis. This assumption – and it is an assumption which the NC school considers so self-evident that it is hardly worthy of further rationalisation – carries with it several direct implications. Most important, since the supply of labour is always equal to the demand for labour, involuntary unemployment can never be a problem.

Under these conditions, variations in recorded unemployment can be due only to changes in the equilibrium level of 'search' unemployment, or to temporary misperceptions between actual and expected prices. It is therefore scarcely surprising that the assumption of perfectly flexible prices leads directly to non-Keynesian conclusions, since below-equilibrium levels of output and employment are assumed never to emerge in the first place. It also turns out that the market clearing assumption is much more important for the NC propositions than a belief in rational expectations. Even if expectations are formed adaptively instead of rationally, the time period during which prices are misperceived must, as Friedman realised, be only 'temporary' (though it might go on for years). The difference between adaptive and rational expectations governs how temporary these temporary deviations may be. It is the assumption that prices will eventually move to clear markets which is crucial in ruling out the possibility of *permanent* deviations from the natural level of unemployment.

A second consequence of market clearing is that all economic agents, whether individuals or firms, are permanently on the supply and demand curves which are relevant for the full equilibrium of the economic system as a whole. In particular, there are no quantity constraints in any market, since firms are assumed to be able to sell all the output they choose to produce at the given price level, and individuals are assumed to be able to sell as much of their own labour as they wish at the ruling real wage. This means that (with a given capital stock) the demand for labour, and hence the level of employment, will be determined only by the real wage, and not by the level of output. Output will instead be an endogenous variable, determined simultaneously with the level of employment by the free choice of firms faced with a given set of wages and prices (which are outside their direct control). Similarly the level of consumption will be determined by tastes and preferences, the wage rate and the interest rate, but not by the level of household income, since this too is an endogenous variable determined simultaneously with consumption by the free choice of households. This means that the familiar Keynesian relationships in which output changes 'cause' employment changes or income 'determines' consumption, do not exist in a world of full market clearing. Instead, these variables are simultaneously chosen by the free choice of individuals and firms.

The problem with this line of reasoning is that there is a vast body of empirical research in Britain and other economies which in general suggests that output is the most important (often the only) determinant of employment,[17] and that household income is closely related to the level of consumption. Furthermore it appears obvious from observing the real world that the prices of most goods are not continuously flexible, and that money wages are in the main set by collective bargaining which occurs at intervals of one year and upwards. The only markets which clearly do appear to resemble those of the NC world are the auction markets in primary commodities, and the foreign exchange and other financial markets. Elsewhere, it is very difficult to see how firms can generally be labelled as price takers: at the crudest level, if all firms are price takers, then who is setting the price?

Non-Market Clearing Models – The Consequences of Fixed Prices

Once we accept the possibility that markets are not continuously cleared by infinitely flexible prices, the NC proposition of short-run policy ineffectiveness immediately falls. (This is true whether we permit price inflexibility in goods markets, or money wage inflexibility in the labour market.) It is certainly not surprising that this turns out to be crucial, since it has long been recognised that one of the key distinctions between Keynesian and classical economics concerned the flexibility of prices and wages. However, it was not until quite recently that the consequences of price inflexibility in one market for *other* markets in the economic system were worked out within a general equilibrium framework. The formalisation of this work was mainly due to Barro and Grossman (1971, 1976) and Malinvaud (1977).

Real Wages Fixed – The Classical Case

For our present purposes, two particular forms of disequilibrium are worth considering. The first exists when the real wage is fixed above the equilibrium level in the labour market. Clearly labour supply will now exceed labour demand (provided that the supply and demand curves are conventionally-sloping), and the emergence of unemployment will be observed. Workers will find that they are unable to sell all the labour they would wish (at given wages and prices) to firms, who find it unprofitable to employ all the labour offered at such high real wages. Consequently individuals are constrained by a lack of income, and they respond by reducing their consumption in the goods markets. Firms discover that they are able to sell all of the output they produce, but, compared with full equilibrium at market clearing prices, the labour market is in a situation of excess supply, and the goods market in one of disguised excess demand (since workers would like to purchase more goods if they could sell all the labour they wished in the labour markets). This situation is known as classical unemployment, and it will continue to exist until the real wage is reduced sufficiently to clear the labour market.

Prices Fixed – The Keynesian Case

A quite distinct situation, though with many of the same superficial characteristics, occurs if prices are too high to clear the goods market. This situation produces 'Keynesian' unemployment. Because prices are above their equilibrium level, firms would theoretically find it profitable to produce and sell more goods than are actually demanded at the ruling price level, but they are prevented from doing this by lack of aggregate demand. The level of real wages and selling prices means that firms would like to produce additional output if only they could sell it. Unfortunately, however, they find that a shortage of effective demand prevents them from actually *selling* some output which would otherwise be profitable to produce at existing wages and prices. Firms are therefore *quantity*-constrained – by the level of effective demand in the goods market, rather than by the real wage in the labour market. As a result, they are forced to reduce output below the general equilibrium level. This has feedback effects in the labour market. Because firms cannot sell all the output they would otherwise like to produce, they cut back the number of jobs they offer. Employment consequently falls below its full equilibrium level and, over a potentially wide range, the effective demand curve for labour in fact becomes totally inelastic with regard to the real wage. It can *never* be profitable, at any real wage, to produce output which cannot be sold because of a lack of demand. Hence, in this Keynesian situation, employment is no longer related to real wage movements, but is related instead to the severity of the quantity constraints in the goods market.

The existence of price inflexibility in the goods market can accordingly lead to the emergence of unemployment regardless of the real wage, and variations in the real wage are powerless to restore the economy to full employment. Consider what happens in a situation of Keynesian unemployment if the real wage is forced downwards, say by an increase in the price level relative to the money wage level. The rise in the price level actually worsens the situation of excess supply in the goods market, increasing the severity of the quantity constraints faced by firms, and reducing their demand for labour compared with the initial situation. Meanwhile, since the economy is operating on the totally inelastic portion of the labour demand curve, the reduction in the real wage fails to generate any additional employment, even if the real wage is driven well below that which would be observed in full general equilibrium. It is possible that a reduction in the real wage may choke off the *supply* of labour sufficiently to hold down any consequent increase in recorded unemployment, but employment simply moves further below the full equilibrium level.

Assuming price stickiness, the correct policy response is not to reduce the real wage, which can only make matters worse, but to take measures to restore equilibrium in the goods market by boosting aggregate demand. Since the initial price level was too high for equilibrium in the goods market, a rise in the demand for goods (generated for example by increased government expenditure, reduced taxation or an easing in monetary policy) brings forth the previously frustrated excess supply *with no increase in prices*. (Remember that firms would always *like* to have sold more at existing prices and wages. Profitability was not a problem, provided the goods could be sold.) With the government intervening to increase demand, firms now find they are able to sell everything they wish at ruling prices, and they are therefore no longer quantity-constrained in the labour market. Employment is increased to its full equilibrium level, and unemployment is reduced to its 'natural' rate, without any reduction in the real wage proving necessary or desirable.

Rational Expectations with Sticky Prices

So, for the duration that price stickiness exists, the economy can be characterised by Keynesian unemployment, and none of the new classical propositions apply. If the government acts to alleviate a shortage of demand, output rises and prices do not. Furthermore the effectiveness of demand management policy in boosting real output without increasing the rate of inflation is helped, rather than hindered, by the existence of rational expectations. Imagine that prices are fixed in the short run and that the economy is in a situation of Keynesian unemployment. Imagine also that rational economic agents perceive this to be the case. One way of restoring the system to full equilibrium, which rational agents may be expected to recognise, would be to reduce the price level in the goods market (and simultaneously to reduce the money wage level to leave real wages unchanged), thus eliminating excess supply through price changes.

But now let us assume that, for reasons we shall discuss below, it is in no-one's *private* interest to reduce prices immediately. The system is then stuck with Keynesian unemployment and, under rational expectations, everyone realises this to be the case. They therefore also know that, if the government steps in with an increase in aggregate demand, then the system will eventually respond by releasing a surge of additional output with no increase in price inflation. Rational agents will consequently have no reason to expect any increase in prices as a result of expansionary demand management policy and will have every reason to expect the full increase in nominal demand to be reflected in higher output. Firms will have a strong incentive to react to this knowledge by increasing their output levels immediately, taking on additional labour in anticipation of extra sales. This will, in itself, bring forward the process of equilibrating the economy under rational expectations. Under adaptive expectations, on the other hand, firms will be more likely to wait until they perceive an increase in the demand for their products before they formulate plans to increase output and employment. This will result in a less rapid, and possibly smaller, output response to any announced expansion in government policy.

For time periods in which prices are sticky, resulting in conditions of Keynesian unemployment, the standard results of new monetarism are therefore neatly reversed, with expansionary demand management policy being wholly justified to create employment, nominal demand being reflected in output changes rather than price changes, and demand management policy being helped, rather than hindered, by the assumption of rational expectations.

All of these results have now been formalised in an important article by Neary and Stiglitz (1983). This adopts a two-period model, in which Keynesian unemployment can exist in either the first or the second period. Among other results, Neary and Stiglitz demonstrate that the mere expectation that Keynesian unemployment will exist in the second period makes it more likely to exist in the first: if households expect to be constrained by a shortage of employment opportunities in period two, they will respond by reducing their current consumption in order to save more for the future. In addition, if firms expect their level of sales to be constrained during period two, they will cut back on their investment expenditure during period one. For both of these reasons, the expectation of sales constraints during period two will increase the probability of Keynesian unemployment developing in period one, and for each set of expectations there will be a different outcome in period one, even without any change in the prices and wages ruling during the first period. Neary and Stiglitz go on to demonstrate that, under these conditions, the Keynesian policy multiplier (the responsiveness of output to a change in exogenous demand) is actually *increased* when rational expectations are assumed to exist, compared to other expectations mechanisms.

By now it should be clear that the NC propositions do not hold for periods during which prices are less than fully flexible. It is also true that, if the money wage level is fixed for any period of time, then this also removes the self-equilibrating properties from the entire system, and there is once again scope for active government policy to eliminate the resulting unemployment. (This applies unless a fixed money wage leads to a real wage level which is above equilibrium in the labour market, thus making it unprofitable for firms to take on labour up to the full employment equilibrium.)

Faced with this attack on the proposition of short-term policy ineffectiveness, the new classicists have hit back in two ways. First, they have argued that fixed prices are not empirically important, since in practice they believe that prices actually do move to clear markets over very short time periods. Second, they have attacked the assumption of sticky prices on the grounds that it is '*ad hoc*', arguing that there are no convincing microeconomic reasons for believing that rational agents will fix their prices or wages in non-contingent contracts. (These are contracts which do not permit renegotiation in the case of surprise events occurring during the contract period.)

Do Prices Clear Markets?

On the empirical question, the evidence certainly does not seem to support the NC school. A test of price sluggishness in the United Kingdom from 1950 to 1980, conducted by Alogoskoufis and Pissarides (1983) concluded that, after a demand or supply shock which takes the economy away from equilibrium, only 21 per cent of the gap between actual prices and equilibrium prices is closed within one year. Since only about one-fifth of any *remaining* gap is closed in any year, this actually means that it takes about ten years for the price level to move within 10 per cent of its equilibrium level, following a once-and-for-all change in the latter. Obviously this offers massive scope for active fiscal and monetary policy to assist the process of moving back to equilibrium. In the United States, Rosen and Quandt

(1978) and Fair (1979) both find that the data reject the hypothesis that the labour market is in continuous equilibrium, while Gordon (1983) finds varying but persistent evidence of wage and price inflexibility in the United States, the United Kingdom and Japan throughout this century. Interestingly, he finds particular evidence of wage and price stickiness in both the United Kingdom and the United States in the 1930s, which of course confirms the widespread impression that high unemployment in these episodes did not lead to the required downward adjustment of wages and prices. Gordon speculates that the adjustment process may be asymmetric in extreme cases. If true, this would carry interesting implications for the United Kingdom today, since it would mean that the further the economy moves from full employment equilibrium, the longer (proportionately) it takes for price flexibility to restore equilibrium.

Why are Prices Sticky?

Quite apart from the 'evidence' to be derived simply by looking at real world behaviour, there therefore appear strong econometric grounds for believing that wage and price stickiness are frequently observed in modern economies. But this still leaves the NC question of *why* such stickiness occurs, given that rational individuals and firms may not be expected to involve themselves in non-contingent contracts in an uncertain world. This is a point which has been taken to heart by Keynesian advocates of sticky price models, and some progress has been made in the past few years in explaining how price stickiness can be consistent with optimising behaviour by microeconomic agents.

Perhaps the most important work in this area so far is that by Okun (1981). This takes as its basic theme the proposition that economic agents will seek to economise on their transactions costs by trading repeatedly with the same people, so that trust develops between buyers and sellers. In the context of the labour market, a career-long attachment is set up between workers and firms, in which the concept of 'fairness' is paramount. Before an individual is willing to agree to build up firm-specific human capital with one employer rather than another, clear evidence is needed that the firm will not in future cut wage rates without due cause, or at least without a clear signal that new conditions have arisen which require wage cuts to be implemented. Since all firms and workers think the same, wages become 'sticky' in the face of demand shocks, and changes are possible only after quantity adjustments have occurred which signal that a new set of trading relations is now necessary. In Okun's now-famous phrase, the 'invisible hand' of Adam Smith is replaced by an 'invisible handshake' between firms and their workers.

Implicit Contracts

Related ideas have been developed in what is called 'implicit contract theory', in which firms and workers agree to unwritten obligations which are deemed to be in the long-term best interests of both. Such implicit contracts may occur for many reasons, but the one most often cited in the literature concerns cases where firms are more willing to undertake risk than workers (perhaps because of superior access to capital markets), and are therefore willing to offer workers insurance against fluctuations in real wages as economic conditions alter. The consequence is that firms agree to hold real wages steady (or at least steadier than they otherwise would) across 'states of nature' which are both favourable and unfavourable for the firm. In exchange for this, workers agree to accept lower real wages *on average* as economic conditions change. This kind of approach can explain why the private maximising behaviour of individual economic agents can result in sticky real wages which fail to clear the labour market during adverse 'states of nature'.

There are, however, severe problems still present in Okun's work, and in the implicit contracting approach. For example, it is by no means clear why *nominal* wage rigidity should follow from long-term career relationships, or from implicit contracting. In both cases, it would seem to be more rational to express the implicit contracts in terms of real wages, where a flexible money wage is deflated by an appropriate price index. This would certainly not seem likely to involve prohibitive transactions costs. In order to explain nominal wage rigidity, it seems that we still need to fall back on Keynes's suggestion that workers are more interested in their relative money wages than in their real wages in absolute terms. A second problem for Keynesians is that it can be argued that the unemployment which emerges when implicit contracts are in operation is in fact *voluntary*, since individual agents know about the risk of unemployment when acceding to the contracts in the first place. The resulting unemployment, the argument goes, stems simply from the existence of efficient insurance contracts, and it cannot therefore be taken as evidence of a deviation from Walrasian equilibrium, requiring government intervention to sort out. While this point is strongly emphasised by most free market adherents to implicit contract theory, others have denied its force. Baily (1979), for example, points out that, if a miner is insured against accidents at work, it is absurd to claim that any future injury suffered is voluntary. Similarly, if workers know that their jobs are unstable, and firms set wages with this in mind, this does not mean that the resulting unemployment is intentional, or that public policy has no responsibility to mitigate the ensuing fluctuations in employment.

Despite these objections, implicit contract theory is still developing rapidly, and there are now areas where clear-cut involuntary unemployment is shown to be produced by the profit-maximising behaviour of rational agents. The most important of these is where asymmetric information exists between workers and firms, and in particular the case in which firms are able to recognise the 'state of nature' (that is, their own trading conditions), but workers are not. Firms would obviously like their workers to take wage cuts when trading conditions are bad; but, if only the firm itself knows that this is the case, implementable contracts cannot easily be written which adjust the wage in line with trading conditions. This is because it is *always* in the interests of the firm to claim that trading conditions are bad, whether or not this is really the case. In such circumstances, wages must be made to depend on 'signal' variables such as total employment within the firm, which are observable both to the firm and to its workers. Optimal contracts under such conditions specify that the firm can reduce total wages only if it simultaneously gives the correct 'signal' by reducing its total employment. As a result, when trading conditions are bad the total number of jobs will fall by more than they otherwise would: this is the only way that firms can get wages down at all. The overall level of employment across the cycle is then less than in a full Walrasian equilibrium, and there is scope for successful macroeconomic policy management. (Optimal contract theory under asymmetric information is surveyed in Azariadis and Stiglitz (1983) and Hart (1983).)[18]

Staggered Contracts

A completely different way of producing wage stickiness in a model incorporating rational agents is to assume that the dates of wage contracts are staggered. A negative demand shock then cannot produce an immediate adjustment in wages across the whole economy, since some contracts will come up for renewal earlier than others. When the first contract does come up for renewal, it will be in the interests of the bargaining group concerned to make only a partial downward adjustment in wages towards the eventual equilibrium level, since it can temporarily 'take advantage' of other bargaining groups who are trapped into even higher wages by their outstanding contracts. When these latter groups come to renegotiate their contracts, they will also make only a partial downward adjustment towards the full equilibrium wage level, since they can now take advantage of the relatively high wages set by the initial group. Provided that wage contracts are staggered, therefore, rational bargaining groups may decide to adjust wage levels downwards in a series of 'leap-frogs' towards the new equilibrium level; and the full adjustment will take much longer than the contract period, since each new contract involves only a partial move towards the eventual equilibrium. Models in this spirit have been presented by Begg (1982b), Taylor (1979) and Jackman (1984).

Sticky Prices and Wages – Summary

It would be wrong to pretend that a consensus has yet emerged on the question of how sticky wages and prices may be in the interests of optimising agents. However, this section has established that some cases do exist where stickiness, either in nominal or real terms, can be the result of individual optimising behaviour. Given the overwhelming empirical evidence that such stickiness does exist, it seems foolish to ignore it in macroeconomic models, just because the microeconomics have not yet been fully worked through. The alternative new classical approach – which is to accept propositions just because they have clear microeconomic foundations, even if they appear empirically invalid – seems far more dangerous.

On the other hand, there is a legitimate question concerning the length of time for which prices and wages will be sticky in modern economies. For the duration that they *are* sticky, government demand policy can be expected to affect employment and output. Hence a negative demand shock can be offset by an expansionary shift in policy over these time periods. But the government always has an alternative to policy intervention, which is to wait until prices eventually do move to equilibrate markets, however long that may be. Such a strategy has one clear advantage: the price level (or, in many model specifications, the rate of inflation) will be lower when equilibrium is eventually restored by price flexibility than when it is restored more rapidly by government action. Offsetting this is an equally obvious disadvantage: the interim loss of output which is incurred in waiting for price flexibility to work. Provided that governments are willing to wait long enough, most models are likely to incorporate sufficient price flexibility to restore full employment eventually. Over these very long runs, demand policy will have no impact on the level of employment and output, which will be determined entirely by long-term considerations, such as supply factors and the exercise of monopoly power in labour and goods markets. But, over periods shorter than this unspecified long run, demand management has a role to play.

It is true that, if the authorities choose to short-circuit the 'automatic' recovery process after a negative demand shock, they will lock in a higher price level, or inflation rate, than would have occurred if price flexibility had been allowed to run its full course. However, since they are simply returning the economy more rapidly to the same natural levels of output and employment which full price flexibility would achieve over long periods, it is not clear that the higher price level (or inflation rate) is having any damaging effect on real variables. It often seems ironic that those monetarist economists who most emphasise the need to control inflation are those whose models most clearly divorce the inflation rate from the determination of the variables which ultimately matter – output and jobs.

The question of long-term policy effectiveness, and its relationship to the inflation rate, will be discussed in more detail in Section 6.6 onwards.

Other Assumptions of Perfect Competition

These final paragraphs on new classical theory consider models in which imperfect or oligopolistic competition replaces perfect competition as the basis for macroeconomic models. Not surprisingly, price stickiness is much easier to justify in such models, and demand will have short-run effects on real variables. The long-run impact of demand is less clear and will be discussed further in later sections.

We spent a large part of the last section discussing *wage* stickiness, since price stickiness is very difficult to justify in the price-taking world of perfect competition. Once we admit the possibility of imperfect competition or oligopoly, then price stickiness becomes easier to rationalise. Firms are not able to assume that they can make unlimited sales at the ruling price level, and are forced to consider both prices and quantities simultaneously. Okun (1981) argues that, in a world which encompasses product differentiation, customer loyalty will be vital for any firm, and will lead to the same kind of 'invisible handshake' which exists between firms and their workers. By pledging to maintain fair and competitive prices, the firm prevents the customer from having to engage in time-consuming comparative shopping. Again, however, it is admittedly difficult to see why this should lead to stickiness in absolute prices, rather than in relative prices.

It is rather easier to see how this may happen in oligopolistic markets, where the price response of any firm to a demand shock will depend on the expected response of other producers. In circumstances where any individual price cut could trigger a generalised price war, with all firms losing out simultaneously, it is not difficult to believe that the overall price level may remain invariant to aggregate demand shocks for very long periods of time. Certainly, the empirical evidence that large corporations set their prices primarily through cost mark-ups, rather than through any direct relationship with market conditions, seems overwhelming.[19]

While a departure from the assumptions of perfect competition undoubtedly helps to explain the phenomenon of price stickiness, it may have wider and more damaging implications for the NC propositions. Recall from an earlier section that the short-run classical dichotomy rests on a version of general equilibrium theory which incorporates *all* the perfect competition assumptions, including the assumption that economic agents can sell all they wish at the ruling price level. A major deviation from this, or any other, of the building blocks of perfect competition leads to models which differ totally in spirit from those of the new monetarists, and which can again produce different policy conclusions, at least in anything other than the long run.

The macroeconomics of imperfect competition are developing rapidly. Weitzman (1982) gave the process a major push by arguing that two, apparently separate, developments which occurred simultaneously in the 1930s – the macroeconomics of Keynes and the microeconomics of Chamberlin – should be seen as highly complementary. He attempted to show that perfect competition with constant returns to scale is almost wholly incompatible with the emergence of involuntary unemployment. However, once increasing returns to scale are permitted, and once we move into a world of

Chamberlin-type imperfect competition, the emergence of involuntary unemployment becomes possible in his model.

Assuming constant returns and perfect competition, the concept of the firm is essentially arbitrary, since existing firms can be split up without limit, and without incurring any increases in average costs. Because all firms can sell as much as they wish without altering the price, all will produce at the minimum point on the average cost curve. Imagine now that workers are declared 'unemployed' by an existing firm. All they have to do is set up new firms, start to produce at the minimum cost level of production, and sell their produce on the open market. Unless capital market constraints intervene (and these are assumed away under perfect competition), involuntary unemployment is automatically eliminated, since constant returns to scale imply that new firms can be set up without cost penalty relative to existing firms. Say's Law – that supply creates its own demand – works under these circumstances almost by definition. As Weitzman puts it:

> In effect, the unemployed are induced to create on their own scale an exact replica of the full employment economy from which they are excluded. . . . Say's Law means that an exact scale replication by the unemployed of the production pattern of the employed economy will take place in a linearly homogenous production system and that it is self-supporting because it generates an equiproportionate increase in demand.

The situation is not as simple in an economy characterised by imperfect competition, product differentiation and increasing returns to scale. In such an economy, which might be thought to approximate rather more closely to the real world, firms are faced with downward-sloping demand curves under which an increase in production will lead to a drop in price. The possibility therefore exists that an increase in output can glut markets, forcing a decline in prices which more than offsets the favourable impact on profits of increased sales. When unemployment arises under these conditions, Weitzman claims that in his system there is no spontaneous route back to full employment. If potential new firms are small enough not to affect the ruling price level for any particular product, the existence of economies of scale will mean that their unit costs will be too high for them to compete with existing firms. On the other hand, if new firms are large enough to take advantage of scale economies, they will glut existing markets, driving down prices and profits for all firms.

Weitzman establishes mathematically that (given his particular assumptions, which include exogenous money wages), the existence of increasing returns allows economies to become permanently locked into involuntary unemployment conditions, with it being in no-one's *private* interests to break the log-jam. All firms are constrained by demand shortages and they know that if they expand alone they will glut their own markets, but will have no effect on aggregate demand. It is only if all firms can be certain of a joint expansion that any of them will undertake plans to expand at all. With this kind of externality preventing the economy from returning to full employment, a case for government action to expand demand arises. Greater buoyancy in demand will be met by higher output (not higher prices) as unemployed workers are re-employed, and the classical dichotomy will fail to hold. The assumption of rational expectations will again help rather than hinder this process, since firms and workers will base their plans on the correct belief that a rise in demand will call forth an output response, not a price response.

Although the Weitzman model has frequently been cited by Keynesians as offering proof that demand management policy is justified and effective in the long as well as the short run, more recent work suggests that the macroeconomics of imperfect competition are much more complex than Weitzman's early article indicated. In order to focus exclusively on the operation of the firm under imperfect competition, Weitzman excluded any serious reference to wage formation or to the determination of aggregate demand in his model. Allowing for wage responses and for real balance effects on demand, there *may* be a long-run route to equilibrium after negative demand shocks in imperfect competition models. This is a subject to which we will return in detail in Section 6.

Whatever the long-run position, the existence of imperfect competition restores a role for policy intervention *at least* in the short-run. Imperfect capital markets can do the same by making it difficult for the unemployed to produce for themselves even under strictly constant returns, Shortages of futures markets can have a similar effect, as can the absence of completely perfect information. Startz (1984), for example, shows that one common speck of misinformation can undermine the deceptive simplicity of the new classical structure. If firms are unable to observe the precise marginal productivity of each of their individual workers (which is surely impossible in any integrated operation), they are unable to equate marginal product with the real wage. Startz establishes that this relatively minor deviation from the strictest code of perfect competition confuses the market system sufficiently to prevent it from ensuring the maintenance of permanent full employment, and allows public policy to play a role in eliminating unemployment. Diamond (1982) explores the consequences of a different type of information failure. He argues that, in the absence of a Walrasian auctioneer, markets can only clear by means of a search process involving repeated 'meetings' between buyers and sellers. These meetings will never exhaust all the possibilities for mutually advantageous exchange, so the full general equilibrium will not be attained. Again, the government has a role in helping the system to function (though in this case the government's responsibility is more complex than basic demand management).

It should not be surprising that the assumptions of perfect competition and perfect capital markets are highly relevant to the derivation of short-run policy ineffectiveness by the new monetarists since, under these assumptions, involuntary unemployment can never be a meaningful concept. As Hahn[20] has emphasised for years, the macroeconomics of monetarism, and the microeconomics of perfect competition, are natural bedfellows. Yet, microeconomists have become accustomed to regarding perfect competition only as a useful benchmark, and not as a system which is frequently observed in the real world. The new classical structure, built on perfect competition, rational expectations and perfect price flexibility, should perhaps also be seen as an intellectual curiosity, rather than as a model on which governments can act.

Empirical Evidence on the New Classical Propositions – General

The next two sections comment on how well real world evidence fits the new monetarist propositions. First, we consider some 'stylised facts' of modern economies, showing that they do not fit easily with the predictions of the NC model. Nor does the behaviour of the US economy in the Great Depression appear explicable by these models. More formal econometric evidence is then examined.

It will become clear in the econometric section below that it can be extremely difficult to test in the real world which of the Keynesian and NC models is superior, since they may often suggest relationships which are observationally identical. But some economists (see, for example, Tobin (1980)) have claimed that the new monetarists fall at a rather simpler hurdle – their inability even to begin to explain the basic facts of the trade cycle and the attendant rises and falls in unemployment. For example, if variations in employment and unemployment are always voluntarily supply-determined, why do we find that so many people in recessions actually describe themselves as *involuntarily* unemployed? Similarly, if changes in employment rely only on misperceptions between actual and expected prices, why do recessions last so long, and why is there a fairly regular trade cycle in most developed economies? Misperceptions about prices should surely be wiped away in the time it takes to publish official price statistics (a matter of a few weeks), and changes in output should be random, rather than exhibiting the regularity of a cycle. The very existence of a political business cycle, in which variations in output and employment appear to coincide with election timing also seems to constitute prima facie evidence against short-run policy ineffectiveness.

Many other 'stylised' facts contradict the NC propositions, at least in their purest form. Tobin lists the following:

1. Voluntary leaving of jobs is high when reported unemployment is low, while lay-offs move the other way. If variations in unemployment were entirely voluntary, the opposite pattern should apply.
2. Cyclical movements into and out of labour force (which are very important in determining changes in the recorded supply of labour) appear much more sensitive to the output cycle than to variations in the real wage or the price level, This suggests that quantity constraints are in general more important than price movements in determining the recorded willingness to work. The new classicists require the opposite.
3. Most voluntary job switches are accomplished without any intervening period of unemployment, which appears unnecessary for the 'search' process. But if the new classicists are right to suggest that all unemployment is of the 'search' variety, there should be clear-cut advantages to be gained by becoming unemployed before looking for a new job. These do not seem to exist.
4. Firms typically report capacity utilisation below their preferred level during recessions, and say they are constrained by demand shortages. Under the new classical system, firms should be voluntarily choosing to vary their output, and should not feel frustrated by low demand and idle capacity.
5. The number and duration of job vacancies fall sharply when

unemployment increases, suggesting a rise in the excess supply facing firms.

All of these 'facts' appear much easier to reconcile with a Keynesian system in which firms and workers are sometimes constrained by lack of demand at the ruling price level than with a NC system in which prices always clear markets, thus ensuring the absence of quantity or income constraints on individual decision, and where intertemporal substitution generates the business cycle. However, the new classicists have been quick to amend their basic models in ways which make them more compatible with real world experience. For example, they often explain the persistence of output fluctuations by variations in stocks and capital expenditure plans which may initially occur while prices are misperceived, but will then take some time to wash out of the system. If demand and prices are unexpectedly low for one period, output will fall and stocks will build up to undesired levels. Firms will then hold output below equilibrium levels for several more periods until stocks have been reduced to intended levels once more. Hence a one-period shock to demand can cause a multi-period disturbance to output, and similar results can be generated from alterations in fixed capital investment.

Some of these amendments may be valid, but they are no less *ad hoc* than Keynesian attempts to offer microeconomic explanations for inflexible prices, which are a favourite subject for NC attack. Nor is it clear that they fully solve the new classicists' problem on this front. As Hahn (1982) points out, once it is accepted that stocks or capital investment can deviate from their full-equilibrium paths 'it is by no means the case that on these errant cyclical paths monetary policy fully anticipated must be ineffective'. Since the economy is not in full rational expectations equilibrium in such instances (and, even in the NC world, they must crop up all the time), Hahn argues that it is quite possible for nominal demand policy to affect real outcomes, provided that firms expect them to do so.

On the question of why mistakes ever happen at all when price statistics are published so frequently, the new classicists retort that the price indices published by governments relate to economy-wide averages, and not to the specific basket of goods relevant to any one producer. Hence they are not a perfect source of price information. Again, this may be partially true, but if a lack of relevant price information is such a serious problem for economic agents, it seems astonishing that more effort has not been expended by the private sector to remedy this deficiency. According to the NC school, temporary mistakes about relative prices lead to vastly expensive errors being made on output, stocks and capital investment. Surely it would be sensible under these conditions for producers to pay a relatively small fee for the production of daily price indices, weighted as necessary according to the needs of each individual firm, so that these costly errors could be eradicated altogether? The absence of such action suggests either that agents are not rational, or that output changes are not primarily caused by erroneous price expectations. Either way, the NC tenets are breached.

None of this means that expectational mistakes can *never* account for small deviations of output from equilibrium. What it does mean is that the fundamental predictions of equilibrium economics are either at variance with many of the most frequently observed behavioural characteristics of real economies, or are made compatible with them only by making *ad hoc* additions to the theory which can create theoretical inconsistencies in the overall approach. Some of the more realistic of the new classicists have recognised this problem, and have reacted by limiting the area of applicability of NC theory. For example, Barro (1984) argues that expectational errors may be able to explain short and relatively shallow recessions, but cannot explain very prolonged downturns in activity, such as that which occurred in the United States after 1929. Barro concludes:

> . . . it seems reasonable that ignorance about the general price level and quantity of money can account for small and short-lived confusions about relative prices. That's because people would find it too costly to monitor continuously and interpret the behaviour of general prices and the quantity of money. But it is unlikely that large or long-lasting confusions would arise. The costs of being misinformed about relative prices . . . seem excessive relative to the costs of gathering the necessary information. . . . In particular, the confusion between general and relative prices probably played only a minor part in the Great Depression of 1929–33.

Since NC economists originally argued that the increase in unemployment in the 1930s was due to an upsurge in the preference for leisure in response to real wage changes, this balanced appraisal from Barro is most welcome – and is highly relevant to present British conditions, which (as we shall see below) bear more than a passing resemblance to those of the Great Depression. Baily (1983) examines in detail the power of NC theory to explain the behaviour of the main economic aggregates in the United States from 1929 to 1941, and concludes that it is found wanting. For the market-clearing model to be valid, the decline of 28 per cent in labour input between 1929 and 1932 must be explained by a simultaneous drop in labour demand *and supply* of the same amount. The drop in labour supply must, in turn, be explained by a drop in the actual real wage relative to the expected 'normal' level. Lucas and Rapping (1970) calculate that the actual/expected real wage ratio fell by 11.8 per cent from 1929 to 1932, which could explain a 28 per cent fall in labour supply only if the supply elasticity were around 2 1/2. But this is completely implausible – virtually all micro-economic studies suggest a long-run labour supply elasticity of well under unity, and often close to zero. (The short-run elasticity could admittedly be somewhat higher if intertemporal substitution is important.) Furthermore the behaviour of consumers' expenditure after 1929 fails to support the market-clearing approach. If the whole of the change in employment really had resulted from a temporary rise in leisure preference, then households' permanent income would not have needed reassessing, and a large decline in consumers' expenditure would not have resulted. But consumption *did* fall substantially, suggesting that households had revised downwards their estimates of permanent income. The most likely explanation is that involuntary unemployment imposed unwelcome constraints on their income levels.

Hence it is difficult for the NC approach to explain more than a small proportion of the decline in *employment* in the United States after 1929, and even more difficult for a theory based on voluntary market-clearing behaviour to explain an eight-fold rise in the *unemployment* rate, much of it apparently involuntary, over four years. And if NC economics fails this important test, why should it pass the test of the 1980s, when conditions in Britain seem different only in degree, and not in nature, from those of the 1930s?

Empirical Evidence on the New Classical Propositions – Econometric Studies

We now take a more formal look at the empirical evidence on the question of short-run policy ineffectiveness, concentrating on econometric studies. Although this section has been written as simply as possible, readers who are completely unfamiliar with this area may wish to skip to the next section. Designing tests which are capable of dis-

tinguishing between Keynesian and new monetarist propositions is not straightforward, which partly explains why many results have been inconclusive. However, much of the recent econometric evidence for the United Kingdom seems to conflict with the policy ineffectiveness proposition.[21]

The econometric evidence on the short-run policy ineffectiveness issue, as on many others, is not fully decisive. This is partly because expectations are not directly measurable and partly because Keynesian and NC models may frequently be 'observationally equivalent' – which is to say that they are indistinguishable from each other by econometric methods. Nevertheless the weight of the more recent econometric evidence for the UK seems to conflict with the new monetarist predictions.

To understand the problem of 'observational equivalence', we need to look at a highly simplified version of the NC model which is normally used as the basis for tests in this area. It consists of two basic equations, the first relating output to its natural rate and to monetary 'surprises' in the usual manner, and the second explaining how the rate of monetary growth is determined. This model was first tested in a famous article by Barro (1977):

$$Y_t = aN_t + b\,(DM_t - E_{t-1}\,DM_t) + v_t \qquad (3.2)$$

$$DM_t = cX_{t-1} + u_t \qquad (3.3)$$

where Y_t = the actual level of national output.
N_t = the natural level of output.
DM_t = the rate of monetary growth.
$E_{t-1}DM_t$ = the expected rate of monetary growth (expectations formed in period $t-1$).
X_t = exogenous determinants of monetary growth.
u_t, v_t = random errors.
t = time subscript.

Under rational expectations, the private sector will recognise that the authorities are setting their monetary policy according to the rule shown in equation (3.3) – the government may, for example, relate monetary growth to the level of unemployment – and rational expectations will be formed accordingly. Hence the expected rate of monetary growth will be given by:

$$E_{t-1}DM_t = cX_{t-1} \qquad (3.4)$$

(Note that the random error term disappears from (3.3) since it cannot be forecast.)
Substituting (3.4) and (3.3) into (3.2), we obtain the familiar result:

$$Y_t = aN_t + bu_t + v_t \tag{3.5}$$

or $$Y_t = aN_t + bDM_t - bcX_{t-1} + v_t \tag{3.6}$$

Equation (3.5) shows as usual that output is equal to its natural level (provided that $a=1$), except where random deviations occur. This is known as 'structural neutrality', since anticipated monetary policy cannot affect output. Equation (3.6) is essentially the same, but it clearly shows that the assumption of rational expectations imposes a constraint on the coefficient on X_{t-1}: it must be equal to b, the coefficient on DM_t in equation (3.6), multiplied by c, the coefficient on X_{t-1} in equation (3.3).

This system has been used to test the joint hypotheses of structural neutrality and rational expectations in two different ways. The method employed by Barro (1977) was first to estimate a version of equation (3.3), relating monetary growth to such variables as previous rates of monetary growth, unemployment and federal government expenditure – and then to make the assumption that the estimated equation would be used by rational agents to determine expected monetary growth in each period.[22] This produces a series for anticipated money growth and (by subtraction from actual monetary growth) a separate series for unanticipated money. It is then possible to test whether anticipated policy variables have any effect on output.

Barro's approach involved estimating versions of equation (3.3) and (3.5) separately by ordinary least squares. However this is not a fully efficient estimating procedure, since it does not take account of the cross-equation restrictions imposed by the assumption of rational expectations. An alternative approach is to estimate equations like (3.3) and (3.6) simultaneously, imposing the relevant cross-equation restrictions, and then to test whether such restrictions are supported by the data.

However both of these approaches suffer from one major problem. They assume that equations (3.3) and (3.5) can be statistically identified, which requires that at least one of the variables which determines monetary growth does *not* have any independent effect on output. In the examples we have used so far, this presents no problem, since the variable determining the natural level of output

(N_t) is different from that determining money growth (X_t). But what happens if X_t also has a direct influence on output growth? Equation (3.2) is now amended to:

$$Y_t = aN_t + dX_{t\text{-}1} + b(DM_t - E_{t\text{-}1}\,DM_t) + \mathrm{v}_t \qquad (3.7)$$

Substitution of (3.4) into (3.7) now yields:

$$Y_t = aN_t + dX_{t\text{-}1} + bu_t + v_t \qquad (3.8)$$

or $$Y_t = aN_t + (d\text{-}bc)X_{t\text{-}1} + bDM_t + v_t \qquad (3.9)$$

Neither of the methods so far described to test the NC propositions works under these conditions. Because of the appearance of the extra coefficient (d) on the $X_{t\text{-}1}$ variable in equation (3.9), it is not possible to test cross-equation restrictions implied by the rational expectations hypothesis. Essentially, the coefficient on $X_{t\text{-}1}$ in (3.9) can now take on any number, depending on the value of d; the NC model is therefore not observationally distinct from a model which does not incorporate rational expectations and which therefore *does* include a role for policy activism. In general, if the same variables which determine monetary growth are also correlated with output, then the problem of observational equivalence can arise.[23]

The most common way round this problem has been simply to make the assumption that at least one of the variables which appears in the money growth equation does not appear in the output equation. For example, Barro's original work in this area[24] related money growth in the United States over the period 1941–73 to the lagged unemployment rate and the deviation of federal government expenditure from trend, and he simply assumed that neither of these variables would be correlated with output or unemployment. He then derived a series for anticipated money growth from his money equation, and subtracted this from actual money growth to derive unanticipated money. Regressing this on output and unemployment, he found that his unanticipated money series was positively correlated with output (and unemployment), but that the anticipated series had no effect on real variables. The procedure was extended to the United Kingdom by Attfield *et al.* (1981a, b) who used the real value of the government borrowing requirement and the lagged current account balance in their money growth equation. Using a simultaneous equation technique to estimate the money and output equations with all the cross-equation restrictions imposed, they too concluded that only unanticipated money growth had any significant effect on output.

In this initial work, there was therefore some support for the NC propositions. More recently, however, the balance has swung decisively in the other direction. One reason for this was that neither Barro nor Attfield *et al.* really dealt satisfactorily with the observational equivalence problem. In the process of explaining anticipated money growth through relationships with unemployment, government expenditure, government borrowing and the current account balance, their derived series for unanticipated money (that is, the residual series derived by subtracting anticipated from actual money) are automatically related to these variable. These unanticipated money series are then used to explain output, which of course means that unemployment and so on are in effect being correlated with output. But it is not difficult to find Keynesian relationships which would produce identical correlations, so the Barro/Attfield tests can be said to have proved nothing. For example, in the Barro procedure (lagged) unemployment is positively related to money growth, and is therefore *negatively* related to unanticipated money, which in turn is positively related to output. Hence output and unemployment are negatively related – which is scarcely a surprise under any model of the economy. Similarly, in the Attfield work, the upshot is that government borrowing and the current account balance are negatively related to output, which would certainly not astonish Keynesian economists.

The more that the Barro/Attfield approach has been studied, the less watertight it has seemed. Mishkin (1982 a,b) extends the lag structures used by Barro on the money equations and finds (on US data from 1954 to 1976) that anticipated money growth calculated with these new lag structures *does* have a significant effect on output. He therefore rejects policy neutrality but (interestingly) discovers that his results *do* support the separate proposition that expectations are formed rationally. This of course emphasises our earlier conclusion that rationality is an entirely separate issue from policy neutrality: one does not necessarily imply the other.

A further body-blow to the NC propositions has been delivered in the work of Gordon (1982) and Demery (1984) using identical analytic techniques on US and UK data respectively.[25] The main innovation in their work is to allow for influences on nominal demand in addition to the rather restrictive use of money growth alone by Barro and other early researchers in this field. Specifically, they use nominal national income as the relevant measure of demand. Under conditions of policy neutrality, the anticipated component of nominal income should not affect real output. Both Gordon and Demery show that, on the contrary, the anticipated component of nominal income does have a significant effect on output, thus invalidating the neutrality propositions. They reconcile this result with previous work by arguing that the lack of a relationship between anticipated money and output is explained by the fact that money does not affect nominal demand, rather than by the fact that nominal demand does not affect output.[26] This, of course, is a super-Keynesian result.

Two final pieces of recent work should be mentioned, both unfavourable to the NC school. Pesaran (1982) argues that it is insufficient for Barro and others to claim that an economic model is supported by the data simply because it is not rejected by the standard econometric tests; instead, it has to be systematically compared with at least one genuine alternative. He then proceeds to compare Barro's results for the United States with those derived from a simple Keynesian model, in which output is explained by money growth and government expenditure without making any attempt to distinguish between anticipated and unanticipated components. Pesaran finds that testing the two models in isolation results in neither being rejected – a common econometric problem. However, when appropriate testing procedures for non-nested models are employed (comparing one hypothesis directly against another), Pesaran finds that at least some versions of the Barro model are now clearly rejected, while the Keynesian model is unambiguously supported.[27]

Finally, Bean (1983) takes advantage of changes in the UK policy regime to overcome the observational equivalence problem mentioned earlier. If the policy rule determining monetary growth is suddenly altered, then, under rational expectations, the private sector would be expected to notice that equation (3.3) was no longer applicable. The adoption of a new policy rule would then be built into expectations, and this would change the coefficients in the output equation in a predictable fashion. Bean conducts a search for policy regime switches in postwar British data, and finds that switches did occur in monetary policy (at least as measured by interest rate policy and M1 growth) when the exchange rate was floated in 1972 and when formal monetary targets were adopted in 1976. (Interestingly, no major policy break is identified with the election of Mrs Thatcher in 1979.) Using these policy switches to identify the model, Bean discovers that fully anticipated changes in monetary policy *do* have sizeable effects on UK output, though these are not generally as large as those of unanticipated policy changes.

In summary, then, it seems that the NC propositions initially got off to a strong start in the econometric literature, but subsequent work has steadily chipped away at this position, and the bulk of the evidence – at least in the United Kingdom – now seems unfavourable to the new monetarist view of the economy. In a sense, this mirrors the way in which the theoretical debate has proceeded. The spectacular early claims of the new classicists, both on the theoretical and the econometric front, seem less solidly based with every year that passes.

Short-Run Policy Ineffectiveness – Conclusions

We have now concluded our discussion of whether nominal demand policy, either fiscal or monetary, will succeed in influencing output and employment in periods other than the very long run. The main conclusions are:

1. The new monetarist case rests on very strict assumptions relating to rational expectations, totally flexible prices and perfect competition. Deviations from these assumptions are almost certain to occur in the real world.
2. The assumption of rational expectations seems legitimate in long-run equilibrium models. However, the problems in formulating such expectations, both theoretical and practical, are severe, and there is some evidence that real world agents resort to simpler rules of thumb in formulating expectations. Even if prices are perfectly flexible, this offers scope for policy to influence real variables for the duration that expectations are unfulfilled.
3. It is, anyway, not realistic to assume that prices are perfectly flexible. For the duration that they are 'sticky', nominal demand policy can affect real variables, even under rational expectations. (Indeed rational expectations can then prove a help rather than a hindrance to 'Keynesian' policy.) Involuntary unemployment can exist for those periods in which prices are less than perfectly flexible.
4. Obviously, price and wage stickiness is easier to justify in models built on oligopolistic or imperfect competition underpinnings than under conditions of perfect competition. Such models typically allow demand to affect output, in the short run at least.

5. The likelihood is therefore overwhelming that nominal demand policy can affect output and employment. After a negative demand shock which leads to the emergence of involuntary unemployment, the government can act through demand policy to restore the economy to equilibrium. This will short-circuit the process of price adjustment which could otherwise take much longer to work, if indeed it works at all.
6. In deciding to short-circuit the elimination of unemployment in this way, the government will force the economy to an 'equilibrium' in which the price level (or inflation rate) will be higher than that which would have occurred if the price adjustment process had been allowed to work in the long run. However, the equilibrium levels reached for output and employment will be the same in both cases and will be attained more rapidly if government policy is active.
7. These conclusions are obviously a far cry from the belief that governments are completely powerless to affect employment through demand management.

6 EVALUATION OF LONG-RUN POLICY INEFFECTIVENESS

We ended the last section by arguing that governments could affect employment 'in the short run' by sidestepping the processes of long-term price adjustment which are present in many macromodels, whether they are built on foundations of perfect or imperfect competition. This section will consider whether demand management can also affect employment in the long run. It will not be able to do so if, in the end, there is only one level of demand, output and employment which is consistent with a stable rate of inflation. If this is the case, then any attempt to choose another level of demand will, in the long run, be doomed to failure, since this will generate either permanently falling or rising inflation.

Models which exhibit these long-run characteristics are said to incorporate a NAIRU – a non-accelerating inflation rate of unemployment. *It is important to realise that models which allow for any price adjustment in the long run will produce a NAIRU as their steady-state solution*. This can be seen intuitively as follows. Imagine that a negative demand shock – such as a sudden decline in world trade – leads to a recession and to the emergence of involuntary unemployment. In what we have called 'the short term' there may be little or no price adjustment, so the economy will not rapidly be able to restore equilibrium if left to its own devices. But, if the government does not step in to help the process of restoring equilibrium by increasing demand, the existence of excess supply will ensure that there will *at some point* be downward adjustments in the price level (or the inflation rate). These will tend to increase demand via a rise in the real value of money balances, which will induce extra private spending in real terms. As demand rises for this reason, output and employment will increase. This process will stop when employment has been restored to the NAIRU, the one level of unemployment which is consistent with calling a halt to the process of price adjustment. Hence, in the long-run, demand and employment levels associated with the NAIRU become endogenous variables and are therefore determined by the overall properties of the economic structure. It is only if the government can alter these overall properties that it can change the long-run level of unemployment in such models.

This section starts by outlining a model based on imperfect competition which incorporates a long-run NAIRU. It then explains how this is related to the real wage debate and the inflation 'constraint' on active demand management in the long run.

Imperfect Competition Models With a Long-Run NAIRU

In section 5, we briefly considered the consequences for short-run policy activism of departing from the assumption of perfect competition. This section expands on recent work based on imperfect competition assumptions, and looks at the consequences of such work for long-run policy effectiveness. Although there will be a tendency for the economy to revert to a single long-run NAIRU in such models, this can be a long and painful process which can too easily get blocked. Furthermore the government has a responsibility to reduce the NAIRU itself.

The new monetarist models which we have been discussing up to now make little important distinction between short- and long-run propositions regarding policy effectiveness, since they suggest that policy is never effective over any interesting time period. There is therefore little point in considering the long-run policy effectiveness proposition in the context of such models; this will add very little to what we already know about them. On the other hand, we have also seen that several deviations from the new monetarist assumptions permit demand policy to be effective over 'short-run' periods. The question now is whether this also extends to steady-state solutions of Keynesian models. The answer to this question seems much less clear-cut. But the whole issue raises another, equally important, question: what determines the long-run NAIRU, and is this itself subject to policy influence?

The macroeconomic approach which seems most closely related to the real world problems of the British economy at present is exemplified in the imperfect competition or oligopoly models of Layard and Nickell (1985), Snower (1983), Hart (1982) and Blanchard (1985). In the following paragraphs, we describe the Blanchard model, which has extremely clear short- and long-run policy implications. The Blanchard model leaves open the possibility of complete price flexibility in the long-run, and this makes it very easy to distinguish its policy implications over different time periods. The Snower and Hart models reach different (and rather more Keynesian-flavoured) long-run policy conclusions because they permit less price flexibility over most time periods. It is worth noting that the Keynesian-inclined results of these models are consistent with the assumption of full rationality by both firms and workers. It is the degree of price flexibility, not of rationality, which is under the microscope.

The first step in these models is to specify the behaviour of firms and individuals under imperfect competition. The key feature of imperfect competition is that firms sell differentiated products, so that they face downward-sloping demand curves and (unlike perfect competitors) cannot sell all they would like to at the ruling market price. However, none of them is assumed to be large enough to exert a dominating impact over the market for its product. Similarly, workers are assumed to sell differentiated types of labour, but not to have a monopoly of any labour type. Under these conditions, the actions of both firms and workers will need to take account of quantities as well as prices, since they would in general like to sell more at the ruling price. If they attempt to do so, however, they find the price will be forced down. This generally seems a more satisfactory way of introducing quantity-type constraints into macro models than the apparently arbitrary assumption of totally fixed prices against a perfectly competitive background (which was the approach used in the Barro and Grossman models discussed in Section 5.

With the normal assumptions of profit and utility maximisation respectively, Blanchard establishes that the output of each commodity under imperfect competition will be related to real money balances and relative prices, while the demand for each type of labour will be related to real money balances and relative wages. Hence (in the short term) both output and employment will be affected by real demand (proxied by real money balances) as well as by relative prices. This leads to short-run Keynesian results similar in type to those outlined earlier, since government-induced changes in real money will affect both output and employment. However, imperfect competitors (both firms and workers) will sooner or later respond to changes in aggregate demand by adjusting their wage and price demands. For firms, the mark-up they desire over costs will be positively related to demand (given the state of technology and the utility functions of individuals), while workers will require a real wage which is also positively related to aggregate demand. So far so good – but the key additional point to grasp is that *the mark-up charged by firms (P/W, where P is the average price level and W is the average wage level) is in fact the inverse of the real wage (W/P) demanded by workers.* Only one level of aggregate demand is capable in the long run of producing a mark-up (P/W) which is consistent with the real wage demands of workers (W/P).

This point can be grasped best with the aid of Figure 3.1 which should be understood as follows. The curve describing labour market equilibrium under imperfect competition is shown by LL. The higher is the level of real money balances (and therefore the higher is aggregate demand), the greater will be the real wage desired by workers, so this curve will be upward sloping. The curve CC describes the conditions for equilibrium in the commodity market. It will be downward sloping because firms will require a higher mark-up (which is the inverse of the real wage) as real money balances increase. There will only be one level of demand (M*) which will produce a real wage in the labour market which is consistent with the mark-up generated in the commodity market. This level of demand will generate the real wage (W/P)*.

What happens if a negative demand shock reduces real money balances below the level represented by M*? Because of a shortage of demand, an increase in the level of unemployment will immediately occur, but the real wage generated in the labour market will now be lower than the inverse of the mark-up generated in the commodity market. Whether or not there is any route back to M* (which is associated with 'equilibrium' levels of output and employment) will depend on the degree of wage and price flexibility in the economy. If both are perfectly flexible, then prices will decline as

***Figure* 3.1 The macroeconomic 'settlement' under imperfect competition**

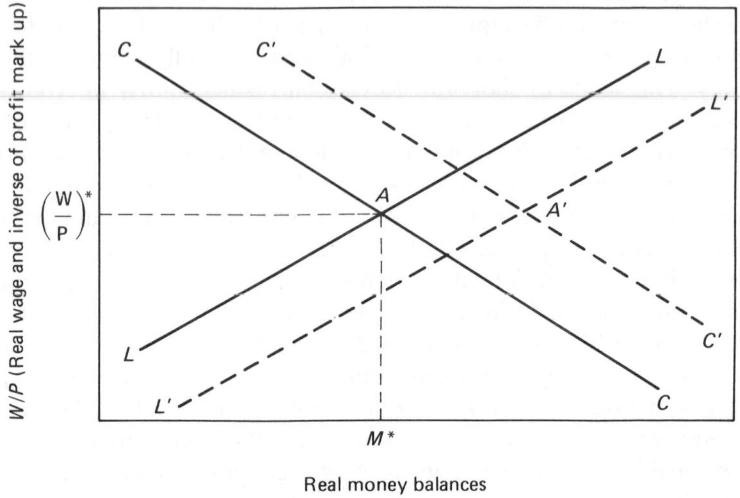

firms drop their mark-up, and wages will fall as workers reduce their real wage requirements. This will have the effect of boosting the real value of money holdings, which will slowly increase aggregate demand. The process will stop only when demand has been restored to M*, which is the one level of demand, output and employment which is consistent with steady prices and wages (or, in more complex formulations, with steady inflation). The essence is that, after any disturbance to demand, price and wage changes will eventually adjust the level of real money balances until the original level is restored. The unemployment rate associated with real demand at M* will be the long-run NAIRU.

This has the consequences for policy effectiveness which were summarised at the start of this section. If prices and wages are fully flexible at all times, disturbances to demand can create only very temporary deviations from M*. On the other hand, if price adjustments work only slowly, then deviations from M* (causing higher or lower unemployment) can be long-lasting, and there is every justification for the government stepping in to restore equilibrium more rapidly by adjusting the nominal money stock (or other determinants of nominal demand). This will reduce the cumulative output and employment losses which follow a negative demand shock, but will restore equilibrium at a higher price level (or inflation rate) than would have occurred if the price adjustment process had worked in full.

This higher price level (or inflation rate) will then be built into the model until another deviation from M* occurs. One reason for such a deviation occurring could be that the authorities become dissatisfied (as they did in 1979) with the inflation rate built into the system at M*, so they decide to cut nominal money balances to run the economy for a period with employment lower than is implied by M*. This should eventually produce a downward adjustment in prices and wages which restores the economy to its original level of employment but with a lower steady state inflation rate. 'Temporary' (but perhaps very long-lasting) costs in terms of output/employment are therefore incurred in achieving permanent inflation gains.

Problems, arise however, if the downward adjustment to prices somehow gets stuck. Blanchard suggests that this might happen because, after any demand shock, the private advantages which any firm or worker can derive from adjusting prices are shown to be extremely small, and these could easily be outweighed by the private costs associated with price changes. (In a world of differentiated products, the largest of such private costs could of course be the breaching of Okun's 'invisible handshake' between firms and their customers.) In such circumstances, prices may become stuck for long periods, since it is in no-one's private interests to change them. This would have two consequences. First, the only way to restore equilibrium employment after a negative demand shock would be through government action. Second, any government programme to cut the core inflation rate through demand reduction would not work, or would work only extremely slowly and with great cost. Even if the private costs and benefits from adjusting prices are such that some flexibility is forthcoming, it is likely to be extremely slow in a world where wage contracts and price revisions are staggered rather than all negotiated simultaneously.

The consequence in these modern 'Keynesian' models is that, while demand and employment will both be determined in the long-run steady state by the positions of the curves CC and LL (and in this sense demand policy is incapable of influencing the steady state employment level), lack of price flexibility may mean that the economy gets blocked in a 'short-run' position away from equilibrium. Alternatively, the process of restoring equilibrium through extremely slow price adjustments takes so long that there is an overwhelming case for the government to step in to shorten the process.

The long-run NAIRU in such models is the unemployment level produced when effective demand is at M*. How will this be determined? In Figure 3.1, the dotted lines show the positions of the equilibrium curves for the commodity and labour markets which would (notionally) occur under conditions of *perfect competition*. The commodity market curve (C′C′) is to the right of CC, since at any given level of demand the mark-up would be lower under perfect competition than under imperfect competition; the labour market curve (L′L′) will also be to the right of LL, because under perfect competition the real wage will be lower at any level of demand. The exercise of monopoly power by workers and firms will therefore shift the 'equilibrium' level of demand from the perfectly competitive position A′ to another level such as A, which will involve a lower level of 'equilibrium' employment and output than that which would occur under conditions of perfect competition. The extent of the gap between curves CC and C′C′ (and between LL and L′L′) will be determined by the extent of the monopoly power exercised in product and labour markets. The greater this is, the lower will be equilibrium employment. Employment will therefore be connected in the long run with the degree to which monopoly power is exercised anywhere in the economy, but there will not necessarily be a negative relationship between real wages and employment. *In fact, it is unclear whether real wages will be higher or lower at point A than at the perfect competition equilibrium point A′*. This depends on whether the monopoly elements in the labour market are more successful at increasing real wages than firms are at depressing them.

In models which incorporate trade union activity and/or oligopoly elements in the goods market, the position of point A (and therefore the long-run NAIRU) will be determined by the degree to which such power is exercised. Furthermore, as we shall see (below) in discussing the empirical work of Layard and Nickell, other factors can affect the position of the curves, including, for example, the intensity of search activity in the labour market (which affects the relationship between unemployment and vacancies). There is therefore very little that is 'natural' about the NAIRU in these models, and it seems absurd to call it a 'natural rate'. It could change for entirely institutional reasons, such as an increased or reduced desire by unions and management to co-operate with a government incomes policy. It is therefore quite likely to be a will-o'-the-wisp, affected by the political climate and institutional factors as well as by economic considerations (and it could change so frequently that it may not be sensible even to talk of stable long-term properties in such models). It contrasts sharply with the 'natural rate' of monetarist models, which emerges from the equilibrium behaviour of atomistic agents in the labour market. Although they may *appear* to generate similar relationships between inflation and unemployment, the policy conclusions to be derived from the two approaches are entirely different. The monetarist model suggests that deviations from the natural rate will be temporary (and not subject to influence by demand policy) while the natural rate itself is a full equilibrium phenomenon which does not need to be changed. The NAIRU, by contrast, is not a full equilibrium phenomenon but just happens to be that level of unemployment which, at any given time, reconciles the competing claims of firms and workers for profit mark-ups and real wages.

With regard to government policy and employment, the Keynesian-type models described in this section therefore suggest that there are two different factors to consider:

1. When the economy is away from its long-run NAIRU, it may get stuck in a 'short-term' state of involuntary unemployment because of insufficient price flexibility. Alternatively, it may move back towards the NAIRU only very slowly. The government can then choose to accelerate the move back to the NAIRU through active demand policy.
2. The NAIRU itself can and should be shifted by government attempts to control or reduce the exercise of monopoly power in the economy.

The government's responsibility is therefore both to ensure that the economy does not get stuck at unemployment rates above the NAIRU *and* to ensure that the NAIRU itself is reduced as far as possible.

Some Comments on the Real Wage Debate

The model outlined above, possibly amended to include more specific allowance for oligopolistic elements (rather than imperfect competition), comes as close as we are likely to get at present to a theoretical description of how the UK economy actually works. It is also useful because it sheds light on two practical issues often used by the government as arguments against reflation. The first is that real wages are 'too high' to permit expansion; the second is that inflation would take off if

unemployment were brought down. In fact, the model shows that both these 'problems' are reflections of the same phenomenon: the struggle to reconcile the competing claims of firms and workers relating to the profits mark-up and the real wage. This section argues that it is a mistake to view real wages as if they descend exogenously from the skies, or to claim that there need necessarily be a negative relationship between observed real wages and employment. Nor is it justified to measure the extent of any real wage problem by calculating the gap between real wages and productivity, which is commonly done.

The real wage debate has been reawakened in the past year or two, after many years lying dormant. Essentially, the argument – which has now been picked up by the UK government – is that the general level of real wages is in some sense 'too high' to clear the labour market. Increases in demand will therefore fail to be met by higher output (which is unprofitable at the going wage levels), and will instead feed straight into prices. At first sight, this seems very similar to the new classical propositions, but in fact it is quite different. While the new classicists require continuous market clearing, the real wage argument is based on the pre-supposition that markets do *not* clear – otherwise the real wage could never be 'too high'. In fact, the argument assumes that monopolistic or oligopolistic elements in the labour market can exert control over the real wage, which immediately distinguishes this case from the new classical assumption of perfect competition.

A full evaluation of the real wage argument would require a chapter of its own, and it will not be attempted here. However, a few comments are in order. First, the relationship between real wages and employment is not a straightforward matter since both variables are endogenous to the entire economic system. Whether the relationship will be positive or negative depends on the full set of relationships within the economy. For example, if we backtrack a few pages to the fixed-price macro models of Barro and Grossman explained in Section 5 – models in which it might make sense to speak in terms of exogenously given wages and prices – it is useful to recall that there is *no* necessary correlation between observed employment and real wages. If the price level is too high in these models to clear the commodity market, variations in the real wage will not be sufficient to restore full employment, since the number of jobs is constrained by the level of demand, not the price of labour. Hence there is no correlation between the observed level of wages and employment. Nor, as we saw in the previous section, do the latest imperfect competition models suggest that there will be any necessary correlation between the two variables. It is therefore quite wrong for anyone to claim that the existence of large-scale unemployment *necessarily* proves a priori that the real wage is too high: this makes the error of applying single-market supply and demand analysis to a macroeconomic situation in which disequilibrium can spread like a disease from one market to another. In most large economies we might expect the real wage to be the binding constraint in some sections of the labour market, while a lack of demand might be the binding constraint elsewhere. As aggregate demand and the *average* level of the real wage vary, the dividing line between these two conditions may alter, but both may be present in varying degrees at all times. Making judgements about appropriate policies at any given moment will then involve careful empirical analysis.

On the empirical question, the standard approach has been to compare changes in the real wage with the growth rate of productivity. If the former is higher than the latter, this is taken as evidence of a real wage problem which may be putting downward pressure on employment, since employers might under these conditions find that the price they are paying for labour is rising more rapidly than its marginal product. (This makes the implicit assumption that changes in the marginal product of labour can be proxied by changes in its average product, which may be far from the case.) But there are several problems with this approach. First, as Gordon (1985) has pointed out, many forms of production function would predict that real wages *should* rise relative to productivity as the natural counterpart of capital accumulation. The Cobb-Douglas form of the production function admittedly suggests that this will cause problems for employment, but most other forms do not. Second, Blanchard *et al* (1985) show that, even given capital and other relative factor prices, the relationship between real wages and employment also depends on international competitiveness changes, which in the UK experience from 1979 onwards clearly swamped changes in domestic real wages. Third, and most important, observation of *ex post* data on real wages and productivity does not give any indication of when (or whether) real wages are proving an *ex ante* problem for the level of employment. For example, if high labour costs are inducing firms to conserve labour (perhaps by tilting capital investment in a labour-saving direction), this will show up as an increase in labour productivity. Comparisons between real wages and productivity will then suggest that there is no real wage 'problem', despite the fact that the decline in employment has been caused by the high cost of labour.

There may be some readers who remain unconvinced that the

***Figure* 3.2 The 'wage gap' in the UK and other OECD economies**

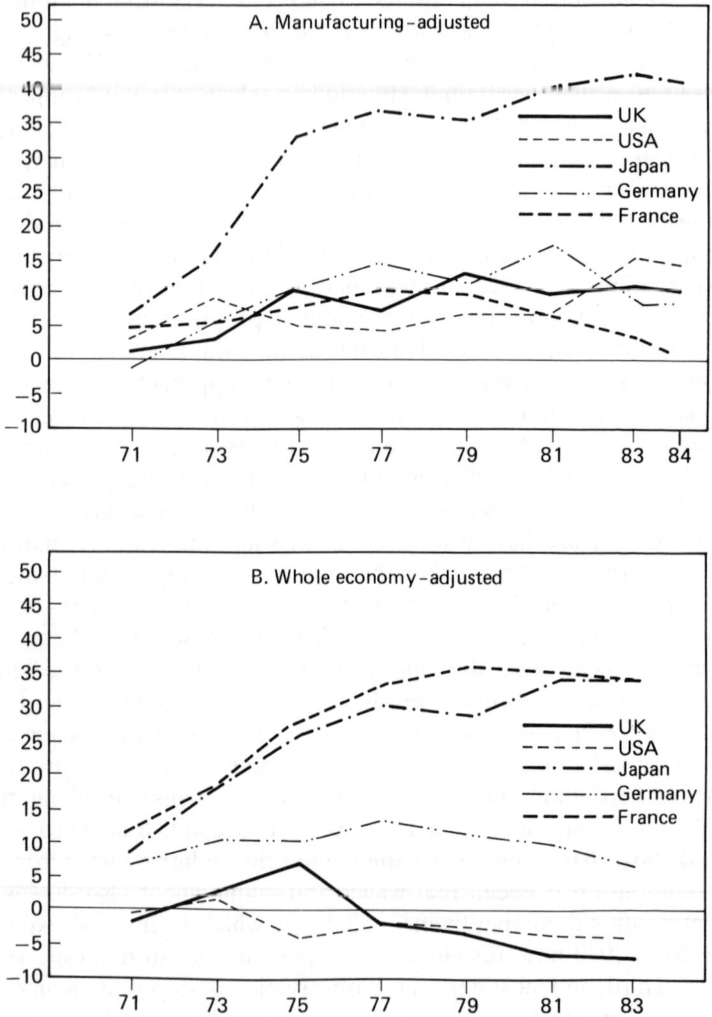

Note: See text for variable definitions and source.

standard empirical approach is flawed. For them, Figure 3.2 presents data on the 'wage gap' which do not suggest (for what they are worth) that the United Kingdom has a particular problem in this regard compared to other nations with much lower levels of unemployment, including the United States and Japan. The diagram shows calcula-

Figure 3.2 cont.

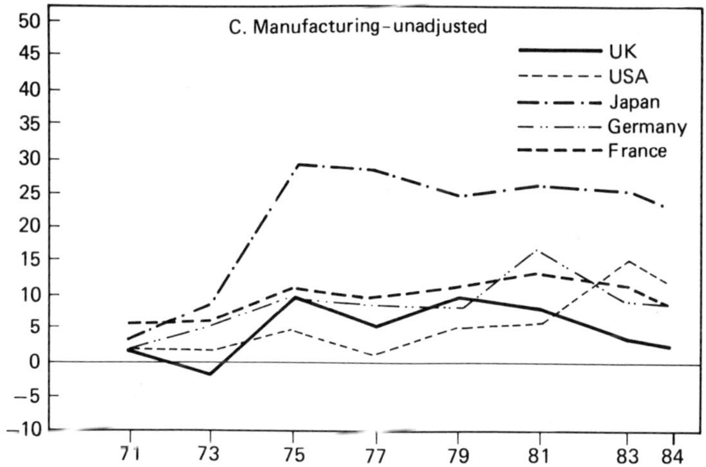

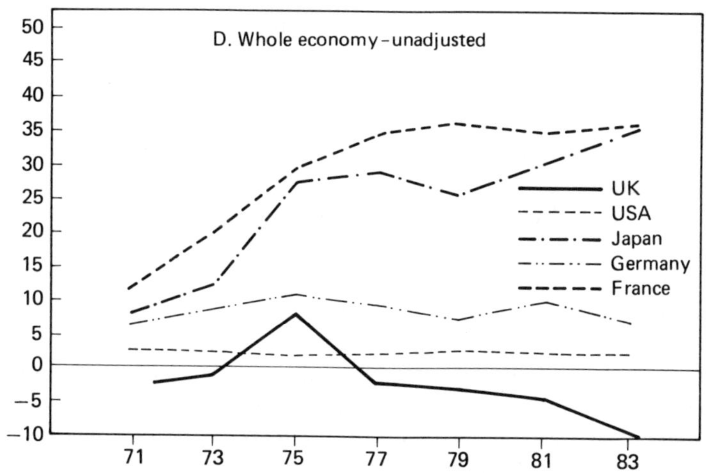

tions made by Gordon (1985) on the 'wage gap' for five major OECD economies from 1971 onwards. Data are shown for both the manufacturing sectors and the entire economies, and the wage gap is defined as the difference between the log of the real product wage and the log of the average product of labour, expressed on a base of 1965–9 = 0. (Presumably this was chosen because it was the last period of generalised 'full' employment.) The unadjusted figures use the average product as actually recorded, while the adjusted figures are based on productivity *trends* calculated for each country (with trend breaks at 1972–4). The adjusted figures therefore abstract from cyclical variations in productivity.

It is immediately clear from the diagram that, on all four measures shown, Japan appears to have a much more severe real wage 'problem' than the three major European economies, including the United Kingdom. Yet it is the European economies which have ended up with by far the more serious unemployment problem. Even compared with the USA – supposedly the real wage success story – Britain compares very favourably on these figures. In fact, Gordon finds 'no strong relationship between the extent of the increase in unemployment rates . . . and the level or extent of the increase in the wage gap'. The polar extremes represented by the employment records of high wage-gap Japan and low wage-gap Britain are surely warning enough to avoid simple conclusions about real wages and unemployment. Another reason for caution is the fact that the real wage gap in the United Kingdom has actually *fallen* since 1979 on all Gordon's measures. Even allowing for potentially long time lags, this would not seem consistent with a trebling in unemployment in the last six years.[28]

A further difficulty with much of the recent discussion on real wages is that it is a mistake to discuss the 'problem' as if it exists in isolation from the level of demand. In fact, the level of real wages which is consistent with full employment can be greatly affected in the longer term by demand management policy, via the effect of the latter on capital investment. Blanchard *et al.* (1985) remind us of the standard result that, *for any given level of the capital stock*, there will be an inverse relationship between the real wage and output. Hence, the real wage will need to take on a specific value to achieve the full employment level of output. But if the government now allows a recession to develop through a shortage of demand, the resulting drop in net investment can cause the capital stock to decline (as it has in some sectors of the UK economy since 1979). As a result, a *lower* real wage level is needed to support the 'full employment' level of output. If real wages fail to drop, this may be seen by some as evidence of a 'real wage' problem. But it could equally be seen as the long-term consequence of a demand shortage. In fact, it would emphasise the dangers which governments are courting when they allow recessions to develop, since the decline in the capital stock initially caused by a demand shortage may subsequently become a constraint on future expansion.[29] Recessions can then become much longer-lasting than the government originally bargained for.

In the last few paragraphs, we have fallen into line with the normal practice of the 'real wage' school and made the implicit assumption that the real wage problem is confined to the labour market. As should be clear by now, this too is wrong. In fact, real variables cannot be determined in the labour market alone. Real wages are equal to nominal wages (W) divided by the price level (P). As Keynes pointed out, this means that workers cannot reduce the real wage simply by accepting cuts in the level or rate of change in nominal wages, since these can be offset by price changes. In fact, ignoring differences between various wage and price indices, we have seen that the real wage (W/P) is simply the inverse of firms' mark-up on the main element of their variable costs (P/W). Instead of asking why real wages are too high in the labour market, we might as well ask why mark-ups are too low in the commodity market.

All this suggests that the government's emphasis in the early 1980s on excessive real wages as the main source of unemployment in the United Kingdom is misleading. On 30 October 1984, the Chancellor of the Exchequer stated in the House of Commons:

> The evidence suggests that, in Britain, a 1 per cent change in the average level of real earnings will, in time, make a difference of between 0.5 per cent and 1 per cent to the level of employment. That will mean, in all probability, between 150,000 and 200,000 jobs.

The way this statement is worded suggests that the Chancellor believes that there is a clear-cut relationship between *exogenous* real wages and the *consequent* level of employment. In choosing to use this formulation, Mr Lawson has fallen into line with the practice of previous Chancellors, who have repeatedly emphasised that wage restraint is one key prerequisite for the return to full employment. But Mr Lawson's emphasis on the level of real wages, as distinct from the rate of change of nominal wages, represents a new slant. Interestingly, however, the Treasury evidence on this question (HM Treasury, 1985) placed much more weight on the rate of change of nominal wages than the Chancellor himself has done. This seems sensible, since the models outlined in the last section suggest that the basic long-run constraint on active government policy to cut unemployment is not the level of real wages but the implications for the rate of inflation of a mark up/real wage battle between firms and workers. This raises again the twin questions discussed earlier: can the government bring unemployment down to the NAIRU, and can the NAIRU itself be reduced? These are the subjects to which we now turn.

The Inflation Constraint

We have seen that, in an oligopolistic economy, a conflict over real wages and profit mark-ups between firms and workers may result in increased inflation, rather than any rise in real wages. This may then induce the government to cut demand in order to hold inflation down. In this sense, the inflation constraint may be closely related to real wage conflict. In this section, we outline the standard approach to estimating the inflation/unemployment relationship in the United Kingdom, based on an augmented Phillips Curve with a long-run NAIRU. The 'Keynesian' imperfect competition models discussed earlier can produce such a relationship. Recent empirical work suggests that the long-run NAIRU has substantially increased in the last three decades, but some doubts must be raised about the implications of this work. In particular, there exists an awkward possibility that the NAIRU is simply trending upwards with the actual rate of unemployment. Appendix 1 spells out the simple algebra of the Phillips Curve, on which this section is based.

The relationship between unemployment and inflation in the United Kingdom and elsewhere is usually studied in the context of an expectations-augmented Phillips Curve, relating inflation to unemployment, price expectations and to other exogenous variables. As was explained earlier, it is possible to derive such an empirical relationship from a monetarist model with adaptive expectations, in which the direction of causation runs from prices to unemployment, and in which markets always clear. (Price 'surprises' then cause temporary shifts in the level of *voluntary* unemployment.) A quite separate theoretical approach, with entirely different policy conclusions, is more frequently applied in UK work. This stems from the kind of monopolistic competition model discussed in the last two sections. Although this can also produce an empirical relationship which looks like an expectations-augmented Phillips Curve, the direction of causation runs from unemployment to prices, and changes in unemployment are largely *involuntary*.

To understand this, we need to take a brief look at the Phillips curve relationship. Stripped to its bare essentials, the most common form of this relationship as applied in the United Kingdom is:

$$\dot{w} = a_1 + a_2U + a_3\dot{p}_e + a_4X \tag{3.10}$$

$$\dot{p} = a_5 + a_6\dot{w} + a_7Z \tag{3.11}$$

$$\dot{p}_e = a_8\dot{p} \tag{3.12}$$

Equation (3.10) states that (ignoring error terms) wage inflation ($\dot{w}$) will be negatively related to the level of unemployment (U), positively related to expected price inflation ($\dot{p}_e$) and a vector of other variables. Equation (3.11) relates price inflation ($\dot{p}$) to wage inflation ($\dot{w}$), via a mark-up relationship, and to other variables (Z). Equation (3.12) states that expected price inflation is related to (past or present) rates of actual inflation. This system is normally taken to be representative of a bargaining/mark-up inflation sector, where markets do not automatically clear. The wage equation (3.10) is obviously related to the real wage curve in Figure 3.1, while the price equation (3.11) is related to the mark-up curve, where demand variables are included in the group of other variables (Z). Hence, the Keynesian imperfect competition models discussed earlier are capable of generating the familiar Phillips Curve relationships, which can be seen as explaining what happens to inflation when demand and unemployment move away from the equilibrium levels generated in such models.

If $a_8 = 1$, then equation (3.11) can be substituted directly into equation (3.10) to produce:

$$\dot{w} = a_1 + a_2U + a_3(a_5 + a_6\dot{w} + a_7Z) + a_4X \tag{3.13}$$

Now assume that wages respond fully to expected prices (so that $a_3 = 1$), and that prices respond fully to increases in wage costs (so that $a_6 = 1$). On all of these assumptions, some of which are more reasonable than others, $\dot{w}$ can be eliminated from equation (3.13), so there is no long-run relationship between inflation and unemployment. (See Appendix 1, part (i)). Furthermore unemployment can be expressed as a function of the structural coefficients a_1 to a_7 and the exogenous variables included in vectors Z and X. This unemployment rate, which is independent of the inflation rate, is the long-run

NAIRU, which should now be familiar. It changes when the structural coefficients change or, more likely, when the components of vectors X and Z alter.[30] Normally included in these vectors are: trade union power, productivity, the ratio of unemployment benefits to earnings, and the terms of trade.

It is now possible to distinguish between two different *types* of change in unemployment. If the recorded level alters relative to the NAIRU, this will cause a permanent acceleration or deceleration in price inflation, which will continue until the unemployment rate returns to its NAIRU level, at which point a new steady-state rate of inflation will be built into the system. For example, if a tightening in policy leads to a rise in unemployment, wage inflation will drop (via equation (3.10)), and this will bring down price inflation. This, in turn, will bring down expected inflation, which will feed back into equation (3.10) and lead to another cut in wage inflation. The process will continue indefinitely until unemployment returns to the NAIRU. (This process is clearly the same as the price/wage 'equilibration' described in the imperfect competition models above.)

The NAIRU is therefore the single rate of unemployment which is consistent with a steady rate of inflation. It may change if any of the items in vectors X or Z in equations (3.10) and (3.11) alter. For example, consider what would happen if trade unions became more aggressive in their wage bargaining behaviour at any given level of unemployment. (In the context of Figure 3.1, the LL curve would shift to the left, reducing the equilibrium level of demand and employment or, equivalently, increasing the NAIRU.) At the initial level of demand, wage and price inflation would start to increase, and the government might eventually choose to stop the process of accelerating inflation by allowing aggregate demand to fall, permitting a rise in unemployment. (An alternative would be to try to act directly on other factors which influence the NAIRU, or on trade union power itself.) The level of unemployment would then increase until it had succeeded in dampening wage/price bargaining pressure sufficiently to stabilise the inflation rate. In other words, the exogenous rise in trade union aggressiveness would need to be offset by a permanently higher rate of unemployment if inflation were to be held constant. The NAIRU would consequently have increased.

Several other factors can similarly cause changes in the NAIRU. They include changes in taxation, social security benefits, import prices, the degree of search intensity or structural mismatch in the labour market, and the operation of incomes policies. If the sum total

Table 3.1 Recent attempts to measure the NAIRU

(% of labour force)	Actual unemployment rate	NAIRU estimate: OECD[1]	NAIRU estimate: Layard et al[2]
1967–70	2.2	2.1	2.4
1971–75	3.0	4.2	4.0
1976–80	5.4	7.6	4.7
1981–83	10.6	9.4	9.2

	Actual unemployment rate (male only)	NAIRU estimate: Layard and Nickell[3] (male only)
1955–66	2.0	2.0
1967–74	3.8	4.1
1975–79	6.8	7.8
1980–83	13.8	10.7

Sources: [1]Coe D.T. and F. Gagliardi, *Nominal Wage Determination in Ten OECD Economies* OECD Working Papers, March 1985.
[2] Basevi, G., O. Blanchard, W. Buiter, R. Dornbusch and Layard, P.R.G. (1984).
[3] Layard, P.R.G. and S Nickell (1985).

of these factors has changed in a net detrimental direction since 1979, then part of the rise in unemployment might represent an increase in the NAIRU, and should perhaps be seen as the sacrifice made to hold down the steady-state rate of inflation.

Recent Estimates of the NAIRU

Table 3.1 shows three attempts to measure the NAIRU in the United Kingdom. While the figures may differ in detail, they have two common links. First, they show a continuing upward trend in the NAIRU ever since the late 1960s, running almost parallel with the rise in unemployment itself. Second, they show a jump of 2–3 per cent in the NAIRU between the late 1970s and the early 1980s, taking the current NAIRU up to around 9 per cent of the labour force (or 11 per cent for males only). If these figures are right, then some 2–3 per cent of the rise in unemployment since the late 1970s should be seen as necessary to hold inflation constant, while the rest should be seen as a temporary cost of reducing the rate of inflation.

Why should the NAIRU have increased by 2–3 per cent since the

Table 3.2 Causes of the suggested rise in the NAIRU (Layard and Nickell estimates)

	Change in the NAIRU (percentage points)		
	1956–66 to 1967–74	*1967–74 to 1975–79*	*1975–79 to 1980–83*
Cause			
Employers' labour taxes	0.6	1.1	1.6
Unemployment benefits	0.7	−0.1	−0.2
Union power	1.2	1.4	1.2
Real import prices	−0.5	1.6	−1.4
Labour market mismatch	0.2	0.3	0.9
Incomes policy	–	−0.5	0.9
Total change in NAIRU	2.2	3.8	3.0
Total change in actual unemployment	1.8	3.0	7.0
Other causes (mainly demand)[1]	−0.4	−0.8	4.0

[1] This is mainly the impact of demand *in addition* to any change which is necessary to offset shifts in the NAIRU.

Source: Author's calculations from Layard P.R.G. and S. Nickel (1985).

late 1970s? The most detailed study of this question is that recently published by Layard and Nickell (1985). Although their approach is slightly different from that shown in the equations above, they essentially derive their estimates of the NAIRU by attempting to measure each of the exogenous items contained in vectors X and Z of our equation system. They then use these measures in their own estimated equations, and proceed to calculate the impact of each of the exogenous factors on the NAIRU since the 1950s. The results are shown in the top half of Table 3.2. Taking the most recent period (which compares the early 1980s with the late 1970s), the rise in NAIRU of 3 per cent is explained mainly by the increase in employers' labour taxes (national insurance contributions), in union aggressiveness, and in the mismatch between unemployment and vacancies in the labour market. Against this, declines in the real level of import prices, and in unemployment benefits relative to average earnings, have tended slightly to reduce the NAIRU.

The total effect of these independent factors is calculated to have caused a rise of 3 per cent in the NAIRU, compared with the actual rise of 7 per cent in recorded unemployment between the late 1970s and early 1980s. Consequently, unemployment on these calculations has risen by about 4 per cent more than would have been necessary to stabilise inflation, and this can be interpreted as the temporary unemployment cost of bringing inflation down. On all the measures shown in Table 3.1, there is now a substantial excess margin on unemployment above the NAIRU, suggesting that an expansion in demand could safely bring down unemployment without putting up the rate of inflation (though any further *downward* pressure on the inflation rate should disappear as soon as the actual unemployment rate has fallen to the NAIRU). This observation lies behind the case in favour of expansion now being put forward by many Keynesian-inclined economists. However, the problem with this case is that, if unemployment really is above the NAIRU, then inflation should still be falling. Unfortunately, it rose steadily between 1983 and 1985. Although much of the rise in retail price inflation in the first half of 1985 was caused by the effect of the exchange rate depreciation on import costs, the *trend* in pay settlements and labour costs has definitely been rising rather than falling.

This discrepancy between actual evidence from the recent behaviour in inflation, and evidence from econometric estimates of the NAIRU could be explained if the NAIRU had shown a *further* increase after 1983,. in which case a still higher level of unemployment (perhaps 13 per cent?) is now necessary to hold inflation constant. However it seems difficult to substantiate this from looking at recent moves in the causative factors shown in Table 3.2; employers' labour taxes have come down; unemployment benefits have continued to drop relative to average earnings; union power has been attacked by government legislation; and there has been no significant change in the application of public sector incomes policy. On the analysis discussed so far, it would therefore be surprising if the NAIRU had increased substantially in the last two or three years. *Why, then, is core inflation not now falling?* There are two possibilities. The first is that the *trend* in inflation will, in fact, continue downwards after a temporary pause, and therefore that the actual behaviour of inflation in the past year or two has simply been a temporary aberration. As labour costs continue to rise, however, this belief is becoming harder to sustain. The alternative possibility is far more radical. It is that the whole concept of a single NAIRU is misconceived, and that it is a mistake to view any stable level of unemployment as being the only one consistent with constant inflation at any given moment.

There are in fact two main lines of attack on the NAIRU concept. The first is that inflation is related, not to the level of unemployment, but to its rate of change. The second is that increases in unemployment, perhaps initially caused by inadequate demand, cause a deterioration in the quality of the labour force which automatically drags up the NAIRU. This might explain why unemployment seems to affect inflation only up to a certain level, after which further increases in the level of unemployment produce no additional gains on the inflation rate.

Criticisms of the NAIRU Concept

(i) Hysteresis – the change versus the level of unemployment It has been suggested by many authors that the *rate of change* of unemployment may have a larger effect on price inflation than the *level* of unemployment, presumably on the basis that a rising jobless total has more impact on wage/price bargaining than a steady high level. Appendix 1 explains in algebraic form how the concept of the NAIRU is affected by adding the rate of change of unemployment into the Phillips Curve relationship. This involves examining equations of the form:

$$\dot{p} = b_1 - b_2U - b_3(U - U_1) + \dot{p}_e \quad \text{(see Appendix 1)}$$

Essentially, the conclusion is as follows. If inflation is not related at all to the level of unemployment (that is $b_2 = 0$), but *only* to its rate of change, there will be no long-run NAIRU, and the inflation rate will stay constant at whatever level it happens to have attained unless unemployment changes. When unemployment rises, inflation will fall; when it stops rising, inflation will get stuck at a constant rate, with no tendency to continue dropping. There is therefore no constant NAIRU, and no tendency for price and wage adjustments to restore the economy to any particular level of unemployment, even in the very long term. In fact, the appendix establishes that the NAIRU under this system simply trends up or down in line with actual unemployment – a process that has become known to economists as 'hysteresis'.

However it in fact seems unlikely that the level of unemployment, as distinct from its rate of change, has *no* effect on the inflation rate. If both the level and the change have some effect, then there will exist a long-run NAIRU (consistent with constant inflation and unemployment in steady state) which will exert a gravitational pull on the inflation rate whenever unemployment stops rising or falling. In a long-run steady state, the level of unemployment must be constant (otherwise the position would not, by definition, be a steady state). With the level constant, the rate of change in unemployment is obviously zero, so the change term disappears from the inflation equation, and inflation is determined solely by the level term. This is why the addition of a change term makes no difference to the long-run properties of the equation, and does not negate the existence of a long-run NAIRU (as long as the level term has a non-zero coefficient). However, outside the steady state, unemployment can change from one period to another, and the rate of inflation in the short run is then determined by a combination of the level and change in unemployment. If unemployment is falling, inflation will be higher than the level term alone would have produced, and vice versa. For inflation to be constant from one period to another, the impact of the change term has to be offset by the level term. This produces a short-run NAIRU which will exist for only one period, and which will differ from the long-run steady-state NAIRU. In fact, as the appendix demonstrates, it turns out that this short-run NAIRU will always lie between the long-run NAIRU and the actual unemployment rate recorded in the previous period. The change term will then be exactly offset by the impact of the level term, leaving inflation constant for one period. Provided that the level of unemployment has *some* effect on inflation, hysteresis will not occur in the long run, since both the short-run NAIRU and the actual unemployment rate will eventually move, however slowly, towards the long-run NAIRU.

The empirical evidence on the question of whether the level or rate of change of unemployment should be included in the inflation equation has tended to find that the level does have some significant effect, so that a long-run NAIRU does exist at any time. On many occasions, the rate of change has also shown to be significant. For example, Grubb (1984) finds that the change in unemployment is significant in his wage inflation equations, and that the coefficient on the level of unemployment is roughly halved when unemployment changes are added to the explanatory variables. But only one recent study has found that the level of unemployment has no effect on inflation (which would negate the NAIRU concept in the long run).

This study – Beckerman and Jenkinson (1985) – reports that unemployment has no stable impact on inflation, which is in fact determined in the main by import prices. Indeed, Beckerman claims that the relationship between wages and import prices is so large that it is capable of explaining the whole of the increase in inflation up to 1980, and the deceleration in inflation thereafter. According to this view, neither the government's fiscal/monetary policy, nor the increase in unemployment, has had anything to do with the deceleration in inflation. Beckerman suggests that the following events have occurred in the past few years. The commodity price explosion up to 1980 caused a sharp increase in price inflation, which the authorities believed (erroneously) that they could combat through reducing demand and allowing unemployment to rise. The jobless total consequently went up, but this had no beneficial effect on inflation, so the government concluded that the NAIRU must have risen, and deflated demand further. Inflation eventually began to improve only after import prices dropped. While this is one of the most radical attacks yet made on the government's approach, it certainly cannot be said to have yet been established. Beckerman's full econometric results have not so far been published in detail, and other authors (for example, Grubb) have not found such large effects of import prices on wage behaviour.

The balance of evidence on the hysteresis hypothesis is therefore still tilted in favour of the proposition that the level of unemployment has *some* effect on inflation, so that a long-run NAIRU exists. But is it likely that the level of unemployment has a uniform effect on inflation? Or will its impact depend on the composition of the unemployed? And will the impact of the level term in the inflation equation decline as unemployment rises, possibly falling to zero above two and a half or three million?

(ii) The composition of unemployment – long-term versus short-term On the composition of the unemployed, the most important concern is on the split between short- and long-term unemployment. It seems possible that only the short-term unemployed (say up to six months' duration) have any effect on the inflation rate, since the long-term unemployed have become so discouraged that they have ceased to compete for work. Because of this, they no longer have any dampening effect on wage bargaining behaviour. It is almost as if the long-term unemployed have emigrated from the country, but are still

counted in the United Kingdom unemployment figures. They have no impact on any UK economic variables except the recorded unemployment rate. This in fact makes the NAIRU no longer a constant; instead it becomes a variable which changes with the ratio of long- to short-term unemployment. As unemployment begins to rise from a level at which it has been steady for some time, much of the initial increase is in the short-term category. These people effectively compete for work, so they drive down wage settlements. After a time, however, with unemployment continuing to rise, they become discouraged and stop looking actively for work. A new supply of short-term unemployed workers is needed to keep wage bargaining under control. Eventually, when unemployment stabilises at a high level, the supply of new short-term unemployed may begin to dry up, in which case wage inflation could start to rise again – despite a now-permanent 'lump' of long-term unemployed workers who have virtually retired from the labour force.

The implication of this approach is that the correct specification of the Phillips Curve relationship should include only the short-term unemployed. However, the number of discouraged workers who are no longer active in the labour market should be added to the NAIRU calculated from such equations. Obviously the larger is this discouraged group, the higher is the overall NAIRU. Layard and Nickell (1985) have attempted to measure this effect, and their results indicate that the total of long-term unemployed indeed has little or no significant effect on the inflation rate.

If true, this result has several implications. First, it suggests that it is very dangerous to conduct a counter-inflation policy solely through demand reductions. While this may be conceived as involving *temporary* unemployment costs for *permanent* inflation gains, the creation of a large and inactive group of discouraged workers means that this result can be partially reversed: some of the unemployment costs become permanent while part of the inflation gains prove only temporary. Second, and more optimistically, there is a very clear implication for future policy. If schemes can be designed specifically to bring down long-term unemployment, there should be no adverse effect on inflation as previously 'retired' workers are rehabilitated into the labour force. This would indeed be the proverbial 'free lunch' for UK policy makers. Third, it is possible that these suggestions account for the fact that the level of unemployment seems in empirical estimation to have a progressively smaller impact on inflation as unemployment rises. (This is because the ratio of long to short-term unemployment has a tendency to rise with the unemployment rate.) Many Phillips Curve estimates suggest that the UK unemployment 'level' effect drops sharply between, say, two million and three million unemployed – which means that cutting unemployment from its present level would initially lead to very little deterioration in inflation. Alternatively, leaving unemployment at over three million will lead to very small further gains in inflation.

We therefore conclude that a long-run NAIRU probably does exist at any given time (since both the level and rate of change of unemployment are important in determining inflation). However, the level of this long-run NAIRU may well depend on the composition of the unemployed, which changes as unemployment rises. The increasing proportion of long-term unemployment in a recession may be one factor accounting for the tendency of the NAIRU to increase in such periods. In addition, the possibility that the NAIRU might change for nebulous political reasons means that it is potentially a very volatile concept, subject to great measurement problems.

Long-Run Policy Ineffectiveness and Inflation – Conclusions

The conclusions of this section are as follows:

1. In most economic models where there is any degree of price flexibility, the long-run solution will involve an eventual return to 'equilibrium' output and employment levels which are not affected by demand management.
2. However demand management can affect the speed at which these 'equilibrium' levels are restored after a shock to the system. This is crucial, since realistic models based on imperfect competition foundations suggest that the economy can get 'stuck' in short-run 'disequilibrium' states for very long periods.
3. The long-run NAIRU in these models is, in itself, subject to influence by economic policies, especially policies that affect the use of monopoly power in goods and labour markets, or change the level of long-term unemployment.
4. Real wages are generated in these models as endogenous variables, depending in part on the relative strength of monopoly elements in goods and labour markets respectively. The observed correlation between real wages and employment does not need to be negative.

5. Inflation emerges as the consequence of the struggle between firms and workers for a higher mark-up/real wage. The long-run NAIRU is produced by that level of demand at which the outcome of this struggle produces constant inflation.
6. The NAIRU can be measured through traditional Phillips Curve-type relationships, which are consistent with the inflation mechanism underlying modern imperfect competition models. Recent empirical work suggests that the NAIRU has been trending upwards in the last three decades, but that the present level of unemployment in the United Kingdom is above the NAIRU.
7. However, the NAIRU itself can be affected by the results of a recession, especially if this increases the ratio of long- to short-term unemployment. Furthermore, since the NAIRU can be affected by such nebulous factors as the political climate, it would be very dangerous to place too much weight on precise estimates of its level at any time.
8. At present levels of unemployment, the short-run Phillips Curve *seems* very flat, so the inflation consequences of cutting unemployment from here would probably be slight. This empirical result may be explained by the fact that the ratio of long- to short-term unemployment goes up as unemployment rises. If so, this reinforces the case for concentrating help on the long-term unemployed.

7 POSTSCRIPT

The main theoretical conclusions of this chapter have been succinctly summarised at the end of Sections 5 and 6. However it may be worth saying a few additional words about the way the UK experience of the last few years has fitted into the theoretical structure which has been developed.

The most important objective of the present administration when it came to office in 1979 was to reduce inflation as rapidly as possible. Although there were some economists who believed that this could be done painlessly (simply by relying on the announcement effects of medium-term monetary targets), the government itself was probably aware all along that some unemployment costs would need to be accepted if inflation was to be curbed. The surprise has been that the unemployment costs have proved semi-permanent, rather than just temporary, and that gains on the inflation side now seem to have stopped prematurely.

This is in fact perfectly explicable in terms of the Keynesian models of the last two sections, which suggest that the processes of price adjustment which are supposed to lead the economy back to full employment after a major contractionary shock (such as the one imposed to reduce inflation in 1979–81) can be painfully slow, or can cease altogether. At the very least, the United Kingdom now seems to be on a flat portion of the short-term Phillips Curve, which would enable the government to reduce unemployment with little or no deterioration in inflation. More worrying is the associated possibility that a prolonged period of recession has actually increased the long-run NAIRU by effectively removing the long-term unemployed from the active labour force, and by reducing the quality of the capital stock.

The government's overall policy mix turned more contractionary in the 1985 Budget after a period in which the fiscal stance (properly measured) had become slightly easier, permitting a recovery in output after 1981, but as yet producing no reduction in unemployment. Maintenance of this more restrictive stance runs the risk of leading to a marked slow-down in economic growth next year, and another upward lurch in unemployment could easily follow. As we have seen only too clearly since 1979, such an eventuality would not be quickly reversible, since it would lead to yet more wastage of the capital stock, both in human and non-human forms. This is how recessions become endemic.

The alternative, as suggested by the Charter for Jobs (1985) and by Dornbusch (Chapter 2) is to break out of this vicious circle by starting a controlled fiscal expansion of a type which is designed to minimise inflation risks. This means concentrating action first on the long-term unemployed and on cost-cutting measures such as reducing employers' national insurance contributions; it means using monetary policy to prevent a major drop in the exchange rate; and it means learning lessons from the 'supply-side friendly' nature of the American expansion. Although there would always be some risk with such a package, it seems unlikely that it would trigger a significant rise in inflation compared to a continuation of the government's present policies. And the risks of doing nothing seem considerably greater.

The government's own justification for turning its back on active demand management has over the years shifted from old monetarism, to a flirtation with new classicism, and now to a more pragmatic concern with the real wage 'problem' and the dangers of re-triggering inflation. Throughout all this, they have kept up a dogmatic refusal to consider fiscal policy (or any form of active demand policy) as a legitimate tool of short- or long-term economic management. The main theme of this chapter has been to argue that such dogmatism is not justified, either in theory or in practice.

Readers with a sense of history will have been struck by the similarity between many of the arguments which have appeared here and those which were raging in the 1930s. Indeed, while the work of Friedman, Lucas and Sargent certainly differs from that of Pigou in its degree of technical sophistication, the theoretical underpinnings of the present monetarists are in most important respects identical to those of their classical antecedents. Furthermore, as Figure 3.3 shows, the experience of the British economy from 1975 onwards bears a remarkable resemblance in many respects to its behaviour from 1925 onwards.[31] Britain's output performance after 1975 has been no better than that in the years after 1925, despite North Sea oil, and despite a much more favourable world trade background. We have fallen into the second Great Depression of the twentieth century.

While it is dangerous to overemphasise similarities with the past, the first Great Depression does have messages for us in Britain today. I would pick out two in particular. First, quite contrary to the vehement statements of classical economists at the time, the level of real wages in 1930/1 did not prevent a rapid recovery from recession when monetary policy was loosened in 1932 (see Worswick, 1984) and when fiscal policy was loosened in 1933/4 (see Middleton, 1981). As two of the panels in Figure 3.3 show, recent changes in UK real wages have been almost identical to those at the same stage of the first Great Depression (though changes in nominal wages have of course been very different). According to the most detailed econometric study on this question by Dimsdale (1984), real wage growth *did* have a restraining impact on employment from 1925 onwards, but this was more than offset by the expansionary impact of world trade and policy changes after 1932. Can the same not happen again?

Second, the present British Chancellor has described stable prices as a 'blessed condition' and the government has always suggested that low inflation is a necessary condition to get unemployment down. Yet stable prices throughout the latter part of the 1920s were certainly not *sufficient* to ensure the maintenance of economic growth, or to stop unemployment from rising to over 15 per cent of the labour force before policy was changed in the early 1930s. Nor, in the subsequent expansionary phase, did a very rapid burst of output growth lead to

***Figure* 3.3 The two great UK depressions of the twentieth century**

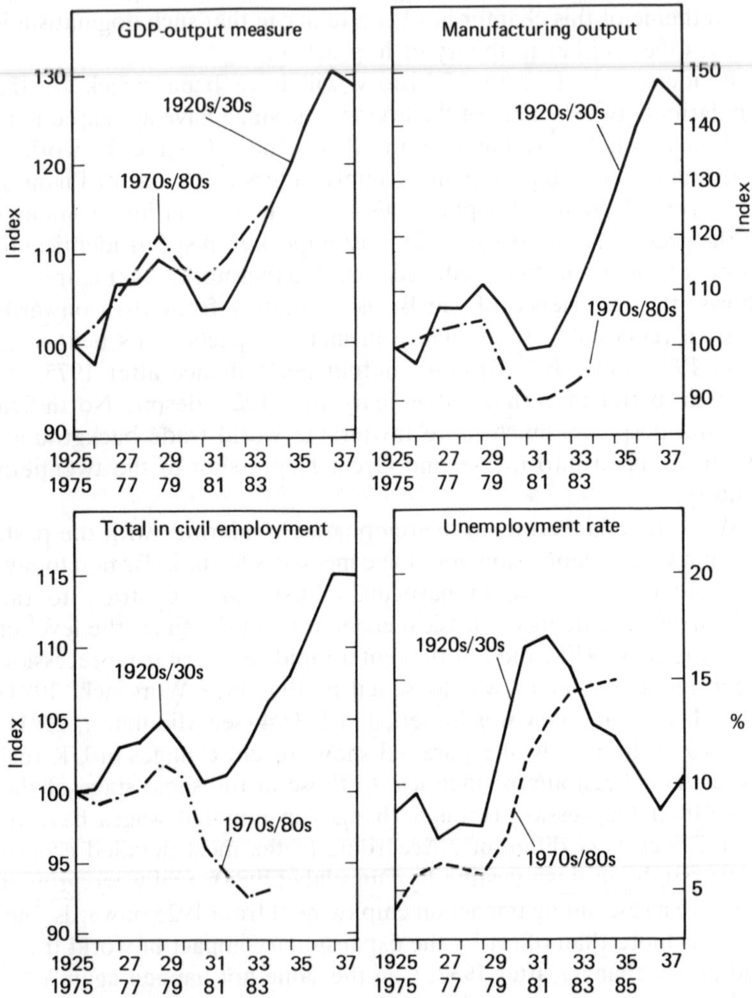

Sources: See Appendix 2

any discernible change in the price trend. The classical dichotomy which lies behind monetarist theory failed, and failed spectacularly.

Unemployment is now approaching the peak levels reached in the inter-war recession. No less than in 1931/2, Britain needs a period of expansionary demand policy to bring unemployment down.

Figure 3.3 cont.

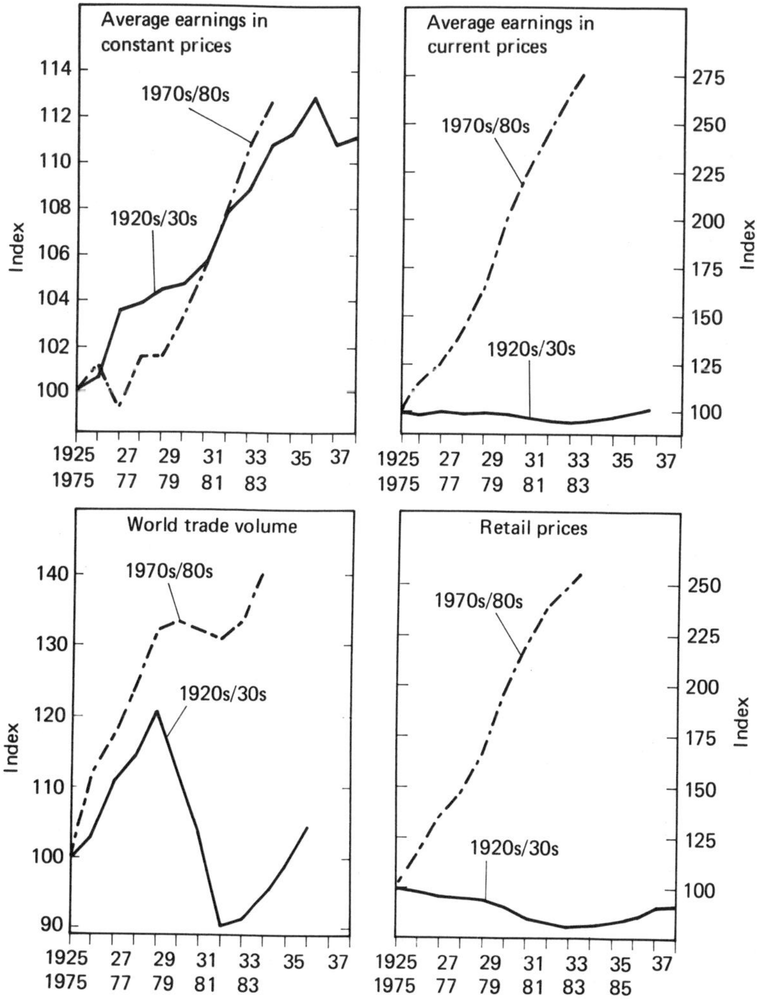

Appendix 1 – The Simple Algebra of the NAIRU

This appendix spells out the simple algebra of the augmented Phillips Curve and the NAIRU. It relates to the discussion in Section 6.6. The four sub-sections demonstrate that:

1. In the usual augmented Phillips Curve relationship, the NAIRU is determined in the long-run by exogenous variables only, and is independent of inflation.
2. There is no long-run NAIRU if inflation is determined by the change in unemployment, with the level having no impact.
3. There are both long- and short-run NAIRUs, if both the level and change in unemployment affect inflation.
4. The long-run NAIRU can be affected by the ratio of long-term/short-term unemployment if these have differing impacts on inflation.

(i) The Augmented Phillips Curve and the Long-Run NAIRU

Using the same notation and equation numbers introduced in Section 6.6, we have:

$$\dot{w} = a_1 + a_2 U + a_3 \dot{p}_e + a_4 X \qquad (3.10)$$
$$\dot{p} = a_5 + a_6 \dot{w} + a_7 Z \qquad (3.11)$$
$$\dot{p}_e = a_8 \dot{p} \qquad (3.12)$$

Assuming a_3 and a_6 both equal unity (3.11) can be substituted into (3.10) to produce:

$$\dot{p} - \dot{p}_e = a_5 + a_7 Z + a_1 + a_2 U + a_4 X \qquad (3.13)$$

In steady-state equilibrium, inflation must be fully anticipated, so that $\dot{p} = \dot{p}_e$. Given this, (3.13) can be arranged to yield:

$$U = (-a_5 - a_7 Z - a_1 - a_4 X) \,/\, a_2 \qquad (3.14)$$

Since $a_2 < 0$ while a_5, a_7, a_1 and a_4 are all greater than zero, this expression is positive. It represents the long-run NAIRU, which is related only to the constants and the exogenous variables X and Z. Changes in any of these move the NAIRU, but it is independent of the inflation rate.

(ii) Hysteresis

Returning to (3.13), for simplicity let $a_5 + a_1 = b_1$ and $a_2 = -b_2$ and $a_4 = a_7 = 0$. We then have the familiar augmented Phillips Curve:

$$\dot{p} = b_1 - b_2 U + \dot{p}_e \qquad (3.15)$$

In this formulation, the long-run NAIRU (when $\dot{p} = \dot{p}_e$) is simply b_1/b_2.

Now let $\dot{p}$ be related only to the change in unemployment instead of the level (that is, let $b_1 = b_2 = 0$ and introduce a new term in the change in U). Using subscripts to denote time periods:

$$\dot{p} = -\, b_3\,(U - U_{-1}) + \dot{p}_e \tag{3.16}$$

When inflation is fully anticipated,

$$0 = b_3\,(U - U_{-1}) \tag{3.17}$$
$$U = U_{-1} \tag{3.18}$$

Inflation will be fully anticipated and steady whenever unemployment is constant at any level. As unemployment rises, the level of unemployment which will keep inflation steady will also rise. In this loose sense, the 'NAIRU' follows the actual rate upwards and downwards. However, if the system is hit by a random shock of any description which changes the actual level of unemployment, there will be no tendency to return to any fixed unemployment rate. In this sense, there is no true NAIRU in this model.

(iii) Short- and Long-Run NAIRU

In (3.16), we eliminated U by assuming $b_1 = b_2 = 0$. Now let us assume that both the level and change in unemployment affect inflation:

$$\dot{p} = b_1 - b_2U - b_3(U - U_{-1}) + \dot{p}_e \tag{3.19}$$

The long-run NAIRU (U_L) exists when inflation is fully anticipated and unemployment is steady. Therefore $\dot{p} = \dot{p}_e$ and $U = U_{-1}$. The long-run NAIRU is therefore still given by b_1/b_2. The change in unemployment does not affect this. Therefore:

$$U_L = b_1/b_2 \tag{3.20}$$

However, there is also a short-run NAIRU (U_s) which exists when inflation is fully anticipated, but unemployment is not constant. In this case:

$$0 = b_1 - b_2\,U_s - b_3\,(U_s - U_{-1}) \tag{3.21}$$

Rearranging, we obtain

$$U_s = \frac{b_1 + b_3U_{-1}}{b_2 + b_3} \tag{3.22}$$

Hence the short-run NAIRU follows a path which is affected by the last period's unemployment level. In fact, U_s will always lie between U_L and U_{-1}.

Since $b_1 = b_2U_L$, we have

$$U_s = \frac{b_2U_L + b_3U_{-1}}{b_2 + b_3} \tag{3.23}$$

Therefore U_s is a weighted average of U_L and U_{-1}. When both the level and change in unemployment affect inflation, the system will still converge eventually on a long-run NAIRU, but the short-run NAIRU will determine whether inflation rises or falls from one period to the next.

(iv) Short- and Long-Term Unemployment

Assume now that short-term unemployment (U_{ST}) has a different impact on inflation from long-term unemployment (U_{LT}). Let us, however, return to the basic system in which only the level of unemployment has any effect on inflation, with the rate of change of unemployment having no effect (that is, $b_3 = 0$).

$$\dot{p} = b_1 - b_4U_{ST} - b_5U_{LT} + \dot{p}_e \tag{3.24}$$
$$U = U_{ST} + U_{LT} \tag{3.25}$$

or

$$U_{ST} = U - U_{LT} \tag{3.26}$$

In the simplest case, let us assume that long-term unemployment has no effect on inflation, so $b_5 = 0$.

Substituting from (3.26) into (3.24), we have with fully anticipated inflation:

$$0 = b_1 - b_4(U - U_{LT}) \tag{3.27}$$

or

$$U = b_1/b_4 + U_{LT} \tag{3.28}$$

The NAIRU therefore moves up with the level of long-term unemployment.

Appendix 2 – Data Sources For 1930s and 1970s/1980s (Figure 3.3)

The following are the data sources for the graphs shown in Figure 3.3. Data have been re-based as necessary.

1. *GDP (output measure) at constant factor cost*. 1925–38: Feinstein (1972) Table 6, T19. 1975–84: ET May 1985, p. 28 and ET 1985 Annual Supplement, p. 84.
2. *Manufacturing Output*. 1925–38: total manufacturing output; manufacturing defined according to the 1948 Standard Industrial Classification. Feinstein (1972) Table 51, T112. 1975–84: total manufacturing output; manufacturing industry defined according to the 1980 Standard Industrial Classification. ET February 1983, p. 26, and May 1985, p. 26.

3. *Unemployment*. 1925–38: total unemployment as a percentage of civil employees in work plus unemployment. Feinstein (1972) Table 58, T128. 1975–85: unemployment (pre-1982 definition) as a percentage of civilian employees in employment plus unemployment. Unemployment Unit (unemployment) and Department of Employment Gazette Historical Supplement No. 1 (employment).
4. *Employment*. 1925–38: total in civil employment (excludes armed forces). Feinstein (1972) Table 57, T126. 1975–84: employees in civil employment (excludes employers, self-employed and armed forces). ET December 1984, p. 36, and May 1985, p. 36.
5. *Average Earnings*. 1925–38: average actual weekly earnings for manual workers in the main industries and services. Feinstein (1972) Table 65, T140. 1975–84: monthly index of average earnings (new series), whole economy, GB, NIER May 1985, Table 8, p. 84.
6. *Average Real Earnings*. 1925–38: average wages deflated by GDP deflator. Dimsdale (1984) Table 2, p. 97. 1975–84: average earnings, NIER May 1985, Table 8, p. 84, deflated by GDP deflator, ET April 1985, p. 6.
7. *Retail Prices*. 1925–38: Retail prices are a measure of the average level of prices of a representative collection of goods and services. Feinstein (1972) Table 65, T140. 1975–84: general index of retail prices (RPI). ET May 1985, p. 42.
8. *World Trade*. 1925–38: quantum of international trade. League of Nations (1935) p. 7 and (1937) p. 7. 1975–84: volume of world trade. NIER May 1985, Table 23.

The data sources are:

Feinstein C. H. (1972) *National Income, Expenditure and Output of the United Kingdom, 1855–1965* (Cambridge University Press).

Economic Trends, HMSO (London) various issues.

National Institute Economic Review (London) various issues.

Dimsdale N. H. (1984): 'Employment and Real Wages in the Inter-War Period', *National Institute Economic Review*, November 1984, pp. 94–103.

Notes

1. Gavyn Davies is Chief UK Economist at Goldman Sachs and a Trustee of the Employment Institute. This text was first published in September 1985.
2. Even the Chancellor seems to believe that his policies are akin to laboratory work. The sub-title of The Mais Lecture is 'The British Experiment'.
3. It makes no difference if the budget deficit is financed by money instead of bonds. This simply leads to expectations of higher inflation, which acts as a tax on money. Individuals save to pay this tax. However it is important to note that the Ricardian proposition applies only to the equivalence of tax or borrowing. Changes in the level of public expenditure which need to be financed by tax or borrowing *can* have real effects. It is *only* the *method* of financing public spending which is held to be neutral.

4. See, for example, Tobin's Yrjo Jahnsson Lectures (1980) which argue against the Ricardian proposition on many different grounds.
5. Equilibrium is used here in the general equilibrium sense. *All* markets must clear before trades are permitted.
6. If there are *n* commodities, there are *n*-1 relative prices. It makes no difference which commodity is used as a numeraire.
7. This is sometimes not fully recognised by economists, at least in textbook accounts. The classical dichotomy tends to get discussed as a prelude to general equilibrium theory, while new classical economics appears as a postscript to the Keynesian model or the Phillips Curve. The extremely close links between general equilibrium theorists and the new classicists are then too easily overlooked.
8. '*Ad hoc*' is a term of considerable abuse among some economic theoreticians. Roughly translated, it usually means that arbitrary assumptions have been added to a body of theory to explain away particular problems which the theory is incapable of handling otherwise. Such assumptions have *deus ex machina* characteristics. Pesaran (1982) however argues that the definition of '*ad hoc*' chosen by the new classicists is in itself wholly *ad hoc*. Tobin (1980) makes a similar point '. . . the capacity of [Lucas'] new macro-economic theory to explain observations, without very questionable *ad hoc* assumptions for which no empirical evidence is offered is exceedingly limited'.
9. The natural level of output, Y_n, can be affected by fiscal policy instruments even in the new classical world. Cuts in the marginal rate of income tax may, for example, induce a permanent increase in the supply of labour and in the natural level of output and employment. But systematic attempts to *stabilise* variations in output around its natural level will not succeed in new classical models.
10. For a demonstration of this result, see for example, Begg (1982a) p. 23.
11. The residue of search unemployment replaces the role of the Walrasian auctioneer as the means of allocating workers to jobs for which their skills are suited. In general, information is assumed to be spread through search unemployment rather than by the auctioneer.
12. A clear and rigorous exposition of this problem is given in Begg (1982a), Chapter 3. If a model contains a saddlepoint (a *unique* convergent path to the steady state), then it is reasonable to suppose that rational, fully informed individuals will proceed along it towards equilibrium, and that this piece of knowledge will be used to form expectations from the start. Hence the solution is unique. Saddlepoints crop up frequently in rational expectations models, but this does not help if the model is either globally stable or globally unstable. Begg suggests that one role for policy might be to ensure that a saddlepoint *does* exist.
13. See the section below on econometric results.
14. Apart from Begg (1982a) see Attfield *et al.* (1985) which is more up-to-date and perhaps somewhat easier for non-economists to assimilate.
15. Financial markets are often claimed to exhibit more flexible prices and more rational expectations than the rest of the economy, and this leads to serious complications, especially in open economy models. We do not discuss these here.

16. One justification for policy activism which is not emphasised in this paper is the belief that the government will usually have superior information sources to those of the private sector. This would indeed be enough to demolish policy ineffectiveness but, apart from publication lags in economic statistics, it is hard to see why it should be true. Even if it is, the appropriate response is surely to open all information sources to the private sector, rather than to attempt complicated intervention through fiscal and monetary policy.
17. Some recent work, for example that of Symons and Layard (1984) covering the manufacturing sector, has reversed these traditional results. But other work, for example by Geary and Kennan (1982) strongly confirm that output changes are the crucial determinants of employment. Increasingly, British macroeconomic models are incorporating both output and real wages as determinants of employment.
18. Shapiro and Stiglitz (1984) show that employment will be below its equilibrium level on average if firms use dismissal as a sanction for workers who 'shirk'.
19. For US evidence see, for example, Eckstein and Wyss (1972). For the United Kingdom see Stromback and Trivedi (1976). Davies (1984) argues that cost-based retail price equations in the United Kingdom have survived the post-1979 recession reasonably intact.
20. See, for example, Hahn (1984) for a series of papers which emphasise the dependence of monetarists on the postulates of perfect competition.
21. Readers who are interested in a full and up-to-date summary of the econometric literature should consult Attfield *et al.* (1985).
22. One problem with this approach is that it assumes that rational agents could have isolated the process determining monetary growth right from the outset of the estimation period. Quite how this is possible when econometricians have to wait until the end of the period before estimating their equations is far from clear.
23. Buiter (1983) raises another problem of observational equivalence. He shows that the usual NC approach, in which a money 'surprise' appears in the output equation is in fact indistinguishable from a completely different approach, in which an output shock appears in the money equation, rather than the other way around.
24. Barro (1977) examined the relationship between unemployment and anticipated/unanticipated money. In subsequent papers, by Barro (1978) and Barro and Rush (1980), the analysis was extended to output and prices.
25. Gordon uses annual US data from 1890 to 1980; Demery employs quarterly UK data from 1963.2 to 1982.2.
26. The explanation for this is that changes in the money supply are cancelled out by opposite changes in the velocity of circulation.
27. Models are non-nested when one cannot be obtained as a special case of the other. The versions of the Barro model which are rejected are those which do not assume that the private sector can forecast government expenditure perfectly.
28. As Michael Prowse pointed out in the *Financial Times*, it is difficult to explain a large change in one variable by reference to another variable which has remained roughly constant. However it might be argued that a

large supply shock in 1979/80 (that is, the oil price rise) necessitated a downward adjustment in real wages to keep employment constant. The failure of this adjustment to occur could have caused unemployment to rise, but this does not explain why the United Kingdom suffered much more on the employment front than either Japan or the United States.

29. This argument has been advanced by the London Business School economists – see Robinson (1985).
30. Strictly, variable *Z* must exclude demand variables for the NAIRU to be independent of inflation.
31. This was pointed out by the National Institute for Economic and Social Research in 1982.

4 Medium-Term Employment Strategies[1]

Jon Shields

INTRODUCTION

The most important economic issue facing governments in Western Europe today is mass unemployment. Just as the fight against inflation dominated political agendas in the late 1970s, so has unemployment now become the central economic concern of voters and political parties.

There are, however, crucial differences in the way these two issues have been tackled. Whilst the British Government gave absolute priority in the early 1980s to bringing down inflation, nowhere is the problem of unemployment being attacked with anything like the same single-minded determination.

The reasons for this failure to deal effectively with high unemployment are manifold. But two stand out:

1. No government is prepared to run the risk of rekindling inflation. Both unemployment *and* inflation must now be conquered together.
2. Faith in conventional remedies for dealing with high unemployment has been lost. No new prescriptions have gained credibility.

There is therefore an urgent need for a new approach. One possibility might be to replace the Medium-Term Financial Strategy by a Medium-Term Employment Strategy. This would maintain the longer perspective towards economic policies, but involve a shift away from tight constraints on public sector finances and a willingness to accept some non-market solutions.

This chapter assesses the way the objectives for such a strategy might be expressed and whether policies are available which would secure achievement of lower unemployment without generating higher inflation.

THE PROBLEM

There can be no escaping the huge additional costs of unemployment over the past six years. Consider the scale of the deterioration since 1979, as shown in Figure 4.1. The increase in the level of claimant unemployment from 1.1 million (on current definitions) in 1979 to over 3.3 million now represents a massive waste of resources. The output of the economy could be 7 per cent higher if unemployment were reduced again to 1979 levels – producing perhaps £25 bn extra goods and services. Looked at solely from the point of view of the public exchequer, the costs in terms of benefits paid to the *additional* unemployed and taxes foregone from those out of work amounts to over £12½ billion,[2] equivalent to the size of the total education budget. The personal and social consequences of unemployment are incalculable – both to those 'on' the claimants register and the hidden unemployed outside it.

No relief from this situation is likely on current policies. Projections of national output in the government's Medium-Term Financial

***Figure* 4.1 UK unemployment (excluding school leavers)**

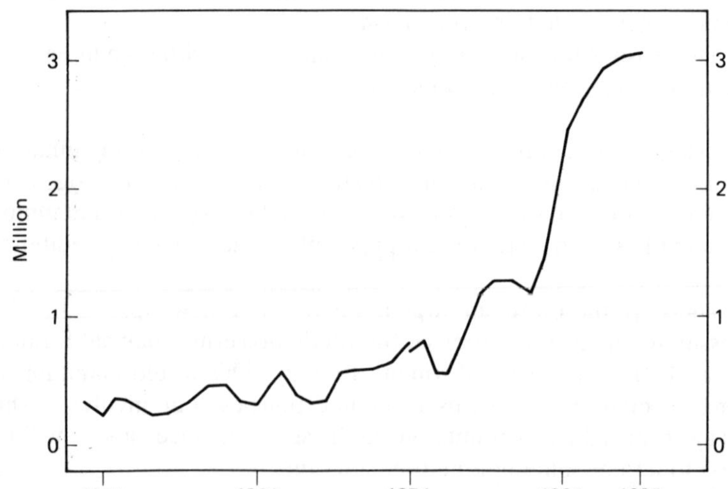

Source: *Economic Trends Annual Supplement 1986* and *Department of Employment Gazette*. The series has been revised since 1971 to take account of changes in the definition of unemployment (see *Employment Gazette*, July 1985)

Figure **4.2 UK retail price inflation, 1950–85**

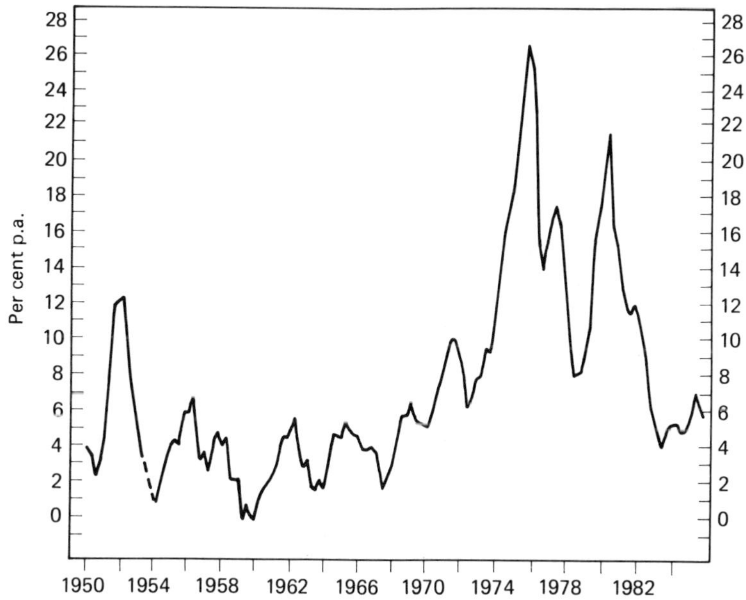

Source: *Economic Trends Annual Supplement 1986.*

Strategy do not imply any substantial reduction in unemployment from current levels. The assumptions about unemployment published in the Public Expenditure White Paper are consistent with this view. Even from the government, therefore, the message is that the prospects for unemployment will remain bleak.

Contrast this with the recent history and outlook for inflation. Retail prices were increasing at over 20 per cent per annum at the beginning of 1980. Inflation now appears to have settled in the region of 5 per cent per annum and government policies are designed to reduce it to perhaps 3 per cent per annum in 1988 and near zero by the early 1990s. See Figure 4.2.

GROUNDS FOR HOPE

If inflation can be reversed so effectively, why not unemployment? Despite the gloomy forecasts, some signs of hope have recently been

Figure **4.3 UK employed labour force**

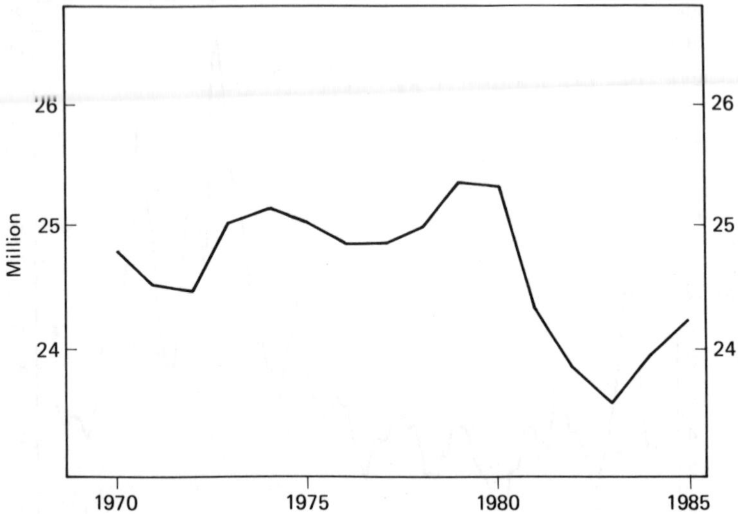

Source: *Economic Trends Annual Supplement 1986.*

identified in the form of the beginnings of a recovery in *employment* levels. The scale of this has been exaggerated by Government emphasis on the very recent past and neglect of the high proportion of part-timers in the total increase (over 500 000 of the 710 000 rise in the employed labour force). But at least the period of job *decline* may now be over. See Figure 4.3.

A more encouraging indication that a genuine improvement in unemployment levels is possible comes from the United States, whose job creation record has been outstanding for a long period. But it is the swift recovery from the 1980–2 recession that is most astonishing. Over eight million jobs have been added in under three years. See Figure 4.4.

The total number of people looking for work in the United States has also been rising very rapidly: an increase of the order of five million since the beginning of 1983. This has not, however, prevented unemployment from coming down appreciably, a lesson for the United Kingdom, where the recent rise in the labour force has been blamed by the government for rising unemployment.[3] Unemployment in the United States has fallen below 7 per cent, not far above the average level of the 1970s. See Figure 4.5.

***Figure* 4.4 United States civilian employment**

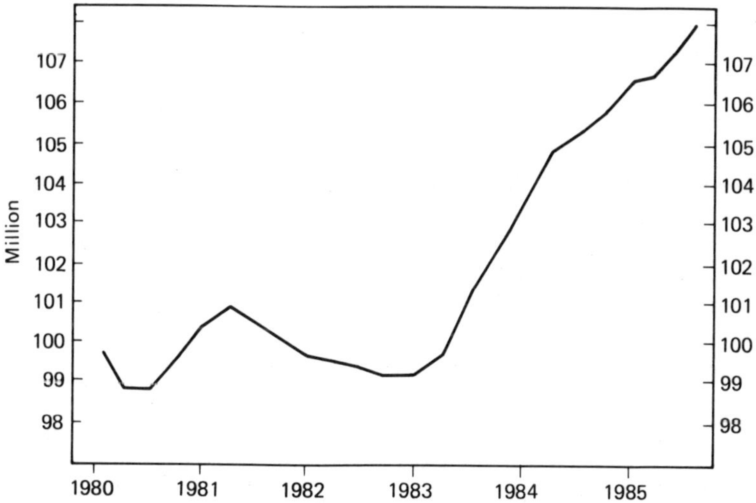

Source: OECD *Quarterly Labour Force Statistics* (No. 4, 1985) and US Bureau of Labor Statistics.

***Figure* 4.5 United States unemployment rate**

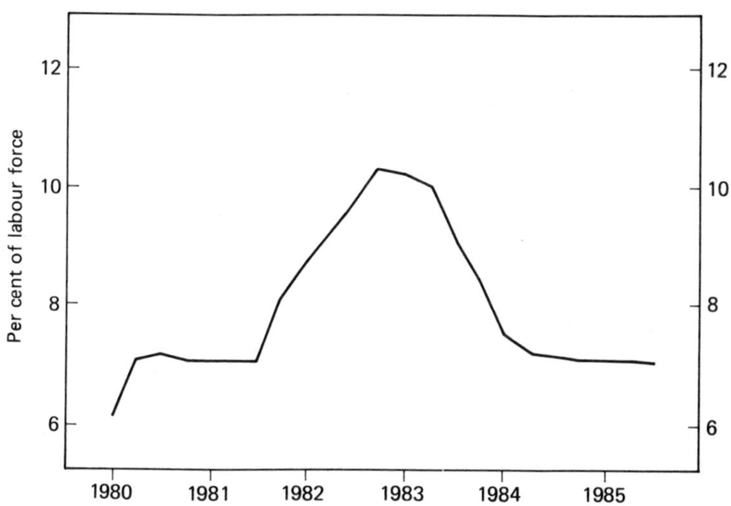

Source: *OECD Quarterly Labour Force Statistics* (No. 4, 1985) and US Bureau of Labor Statistics.

CREDIBILITY

The example of the United States has not so far been taken to heart by European governments or people. Partly this is because the costs of the measures used to achieve the job expansion have been clearly visible. The rise in the US Federal Government deficit has been mirrored by a large balance of payments deficit. An overvalued dollar has hurt parts of American industry and agriculture.

But defeatism in Europe also reflects previous perceptions of failure. Efforts in the 1970s to preserve unemployment at low levels were seen primarily to have accommodated or stoked inflation rather than protect employment. Although the circumstances now are very different, faith in demand management has been lost. Only a radical recasting of such policies has much chance of acceptance.

Can this be achieved? To understand the potential of an apparently fresh approach, it is instructive to look back at the presentation of 'monetarist' policies in the late 1970s. There was, after all, little new in the theoretical underpinnings of these policies. Fiscal stringency, curbs on the growth of the money supply and reductions in public expenditure had all been tried before. But they proved enticing because they were presented as a coherent whole and appeared to be aimed specifically at new problems. Particularly impressive may have been the fact that a long-term commitment to them was being emphasised.

The failure of such policies to restore health to the UK economy should not be allowed to obscure the fact that monetarist prescriptions were packaged and promoted in an extremely effective way. The lesson is that to achieve credibility now a programme to combat unemployment must not only be theoretically valid and feasible (criteria not fulfilled by 'monetarist' policies) but also:

1. Be clearly distinguishable from recent policies associated with specific defects.
2. Be seen to be sustainable – not easy prey to the whims of the foreign exchange markets, oil prices or electoral pressures.

Fundamentally, a programme to combat unemployment must also:

3. Be understood not to be running risks with inflation.

THE ROLE OF OUTPUT

Let us consider the scale and type of problem that now faces us. Since employment levels and the output they produce are closely linked, it is particularly instructive to look at the shortfall of output below what it might have been if unemployment had not risen. We call this 'potential output'.

To determine the current level of potential output we need to know both its level at some point in the past and its growth rate since then. This rate of growth will be determined by two factors: the growth of the labour force and the underlying growth of labour productivity. Estimates of both the level and growth rate of potential output can vary enormously. As an illustration of the issue, however, consider Figure 4.6 which is similar to that produced by Rudi Dornbusch in Chapter 2 of this volume. We look only at non-oil output and take the first quarter of 1977 as a 'normal' level of unemployment. We further assume that potential has grown at an average rate of 2 per cent per annum since then.

In contrast to this assumed steady growth of potential, actual activity levels in the economy have been substantially depressed. Although there has been reasonable growth since 1981, it has simply been insufficient to make up the ground lost in 1979 and 1980. The

***Figure* 4.6 Dornbusch output gap**

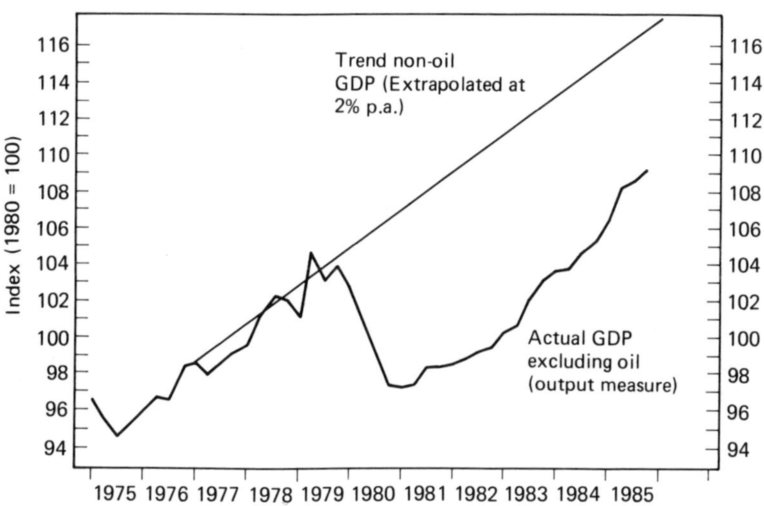

result is the maintenance of a permanent 'output gap' that corresponds directly to involuntary unemployment. How can the output gap be reduced, and with it unemployment? Two ways immediately suggest themselves: increase actual output or reduce potential output. The first suggests a policy to produce a simple expansion of the economy. The second means making the economy less productive by reducing productivity levels or labour supply.

This latter approach, while seemingly defeatist, has been advocated in some form through policies proposed by all the major political parties in the United Kingdom. It is reflected in various programmes put into effect over the last ten years. For instance, schemes to encourage early retirement have led to a smaller workforce. Measures to reduce the real cost of employing lower-paid workers may have produced some lower-productivity job opportunities. Such proposals cannot simply be rejected out of hand, at least in the short term, *if* there are overall constraints on output growth.

A useful synthesis of the higher output and lower productivity approaches is represented by the 'employment-centred growth' policies advocated in the latest EEC Economic Report.[4] The Report suggests that growth in areas where the prospective labour input is highest should be encouraged by creating the right conditions for labour-utilising investment. Such an approach would not only maximise the employment gains of any new prescriptive policy (at the expense of labour productivity). It would also promise to avoid many of the constraints which otherwise threaten to abort new initiatives to expand the economy.

CONSTRAINTS

Ultimately, any policy designed to increase the growth rate of the economy must be judged by its ability to overcome the constraints which have held back economic expansion in the past. This is particularly true of policies addressed at the level of demand.

Two major constraints on growth have beset the British economy over the past forty years: rising inflation and either a deficit on the balance of payments current account (under a fixed exchange rate) or pressure on the exchange rate.

Sources of Inflationary Pressure

Several possible direct sources of inflationary pressure arising out of general expansion can be identified:

(i) Wage Pressure
When demand is growing quickly, increased wage pressure from both employers and employees becomes more likely. Some firms, faced with a greater demand for their output, may find it necessary to increase the wage they offer to attract or keep workers with particular skills who are in short supply. Employees, in turn, may bid for higher wages because they believe that when demand is expanding firms are more able to pay and will suffer greater costs if they resist.
(ii) Margins
Most firms price on the basis of a mark-up on their costs of production. With strong demand, firms may take the opportunity to increase this mark-up. In imperfect markets, profits may be expanded more by raising prices than expanding output, particularly if the additional demand may only be temporary.
(iii) Exchange rates
A general expansion of domestic demand not matched by higher exports would lead to a deterioration in the balance of trade. The exchange rate may fall in response. It might also depreciate if inflationary expectations worsen or if interest rates fall relative to other countries. A lower exchange rate would raise directly the price of imported goods and permit higher margins (and hence prices) of domestic goods.

Balance of Payments Problems

On a number of occasions in the 1960s when the economy faced a chronic current account deficit the government was forced to deflate the economy to a level of activity more consistent with a sustainable current account balance. The current account then represented a serious constraint on growth.

The current account is in surplus at present, largely owing to the contribution of North Sea oil. However oil's contribution to the balance of payments reached its peak in 1985, even before allowing for recent oil price falls. As a result, fears have been expressed that poor performance on the current account in future will limit the scope for expansion.

The situation now is slightly different from that of the sixties. International trade is no longer carried out under a fixed exchange rate regime. Since the early seventies the United Kingdom, nominally at least, has operated a floating exchange rate. In such a situation the current account itself does not represent a constraint. But the real depreciation of the exchange rate necessary to bring the total account into balance (or the interest rates necessary to sustain it) may instead not be acceptable.

Public Expenditure

It has been claimed that both rising inflation and balance of payments pressures are linked to the size of public sector borrowing and the strains this has put on monetary policy. These are not however *direct* influences. A policy must be judged by its ultimate effects on the economy, not on theoretically suspect mechanisms.

This does not mean that the costs of programmes or their implications for monetary growth can be neglected. They *could* have a substantial impact on expectations about inflation or influence the level of interest rates. But the potential impact of borrowing levels on inflation or interest rates can best be assessed in terms of the levels of outstanding debt that will emerge relative to the economy's ability to finance them and not just the immediate effect on public borrowing.

A STRATEGIC APPROACH

A crucial element in the success of any policy must be its effect on expectations. Individuals' and companies' perceptions about the likely future path of events can influence substantially their current behaviour. Views about the likely path of inflation, for instance, will influence the size of wage demands individuals present or companies accept. Appreciation of general prospects for employment will determine whether people take up specific offers of jobs. The likelihood of tax cuts to come may affect expenditure patterns. Companies' levels of investment will be determined by the expected level of demand for their products.

If no guidance is given about the way the government will conduct economic policy it is difficult for the private sector to form any coherent view about these issues. The private sector must know in particular how the government will respond to unexpected or 'undesirable' outcomes for the economy. What is the government trying to achieve and what will it do if it is blown off course?

One way of making clear the government's *intentions* might be for it to publish a comprehensive plan for the whole economy consistent with a higher rate of growth. But the problems experienced in the past – the UK National Plan in 1966 being no exception – show the risk of excessive claims involving the government's power to deliver. Indicative plans – such as those operated in France for much of the postwar period – offer a happier model. Neither, however, is necessarily *essential* if the main purpose is simply to allow the private sector to understand the principal strands of policy and to come to a view about the way the economy in general is likely to develop.

There are three major areas of concern for the individual in respect of the domestic economy as a whole: the outlook for inflation; the outlook for the level of demand and for domestic production; and the outlook for employment and unemployment. When it comes to likely changes in policy instruments under government control, the three variables that there will be particular uncertainties about will be: interest rates; the exchange rates; and tax rates.

A strategy which sets out clearly what the government *expects* to happen in these areas, what they *would like* to happen and how they would seek to bring the two nearer together should greatly help private individuals make their own plans for the future. What does this require of the government in the way of policy making and presentation?

Fundamentally, it demands a medium- or long-term perspective. Horizons for making decisions about employment or investment are (or ought to be) much longer than the single year for which Budget plans are produced. More specifically, it implies that the government should be prepared to publish:

1. a projection of what is likely to happen to the economy over the medium term if policies are not changed;
2. a feasible objective for reducing unemployment over a number of years;
3. a path for national ouput consistent with 2;
4. the use which is expected to be made of the various instruments of economic policy (tax changes, increases in expenditure, improvements in training, etc) to achieve the unemployment objective;
5. the expected implications for inflation, the balance of payments and public borrowing;

6. how policy would respond to deviations from the main objectives or the threatened breaking of the constraints specified in (5) and the relative importance assigned to each.

An absolute minimum in terms of public statements by the government would, on this reasoning, be a clear indication of the direction in which both the economy and policy are expected to move. Unless there are firm undertakings that the government is prepared to encourage growth (while not underwriting inflation) the private sector cannot be expected greatly to increase capacity or improve the quality of its labour force.

We now have the basic elements, if not the detail, of an approach towards economic policy which would constitute a realistic 'Medium-Term Employment Strategy'.

LEARNING FROM THE MTFS

The formalisation of such a strategic approach towards economic management would not need to start from scratch. Some of the groundwork – and many of the pitfalls – have been revealed by the Medium-Term Financial Strategy (MTFS).

The Medium-Term Financial Strategy

First introduced in the 1980 Budget and updated in every Budget since then, the Medium-Term Financial Strategy (MTFS) outlines the government's intentions in the financial policy area for four (sometimes three) years ahead. The main objective of the strategy has always been to control the rate of inflation by reducing future rates of growth in the money supply. The strategy has been expressed in terms of targets for monetary growth rates. Projections for public borrowing (PSBR) are also provided in the expectation that a lower PSBR will permit the main monetary objectives to be achieved at minimum cost in terms of interest rates.

The MTFS marked an important break with previous economic policy. It shifted the focus of the government's attention away from regulating output and employment, towards the sole objective of controlling inflation. It also sought to provide the business and financial communities with a clear guide to the future development of financial policies.

The fundamental premises behind the MTFS were disarmingly simple. It was assumed that the relationship between changes in the rate of monetary growth and national income would be stable enough to allow national income to be controlled via monetary growth; that monetary growth was itself controllable by the government; that the recession would not be worsened by overriding the 'automatic stabilisers' of public borrowing and that the publication of the strategy and experience of the government's resolve would in themselves be sufficient to reduce inflationary expectations and hence affect wage and price decisions.

All of these premises have so far proved very wide of the mark. Changes in the financial markets have increasingly distorted the already unstable relationship between monetary growth and national income. The government has neither been able in theory nor prepared in practice to stick to its announced targets for monetary growth. And few in the City – let alone the wider business community or households – have understood the potential implications for inflation or output of the government's targets.

The result of these failures has been that the MTFS has actually contributed to instability and output loss. Neither in the monetary field (where the exchange rate and interest rates bore the brunt of shocks elsewhere in the economy) nor in the rest of the economy (where industry and employment were hit by declining real demand, an uncompetitive exchange rate and high real interest rates) were decisions or behaviour assisted by the rigours or vagaries of the MTFS. At the end of the day, the policy delivered something like the growth of nominal GDP that had been expected. But the costs incurred on the way were enormous and the economy was producing far less than we now know it could have been. Meanwhile the deceleration in inflation was no more dramatic than had been achieved (if only temporarily) by the much-abused counter-inflation policies of the 1970s.

The MTFS has established some useful precedents. It has shown that a government can plan financial and economic decisions within a framework of several years rather than a single year. It has made the government reveal a little more about its expectations for its own finances and the economy. And it has established the principle that monetary and budgetary decisions are interlinked and that judgements about expenditure and revenue should be made together.

At the same time it has failed several crucial tests:

1. It has not provided a clear guide either to future economic (rather than financial) developments or the government's policy response. In particular, it has not produced stability or predictability in the tax regime.

2. It has been vague about its ultimate objectives – inflation rates – but too specific about unattainable and perhaps irrelevant intermediate targets – money growth rates.
3. It has offered no formal trade-offs: the reduction of monetary growth and hence inflation has been given, in theory, absolute priority over output, employment, profitability, productivity or income distribution.
4. It has failed to allow the 'automatic stabilisers' of the economy to operate.
5. It has abandoned or fudged its own targets.
6. It has failed to deliver low interest rates or a climate for employment creation.

The lessons for an employment-centred medium-term strategy are clear:

1. The ultimate targets must be attainable.
2. All appropriate instruments of economic policy should be utilised.
3. While maintaining a stable framework, including the overall tax regime, flexibility in targets and instruments must be preserved.

SETTING OBJECTIVES

What would constitute a reasonable objective for reducing unemployment within an employment strategy? Ultimately the limit will be set by the impact of a higher rate of growth in the economy at large on the specified constraints: growth more than a couple of percentage points above the growth rate of potential is likely to increase substantially the risks of inflation or balance of payments problems. But experience in the United Kingdom in the past and the United States recently suggests that it is possible even in peace time to achieve rapid reductions from high levels of unemployment. Between 1932 and 1937, for example, the UK unemployment level (on postwar definitions) fell from 17 per cent to 8.5 per cent, as shown in Figure 4.7.

Such a swift fall may be more difficult to achieve in the 1980s. Unemployment is now even more deeply entrenched than in the 1930s,[5] and there is concern about rising rather than falling prices. Even allowing for this and the destruction of much industrial capacity, however, it would be wrong to rule out completely the possibility of a

Figure **4.7 Unemployment rates – 1930s**

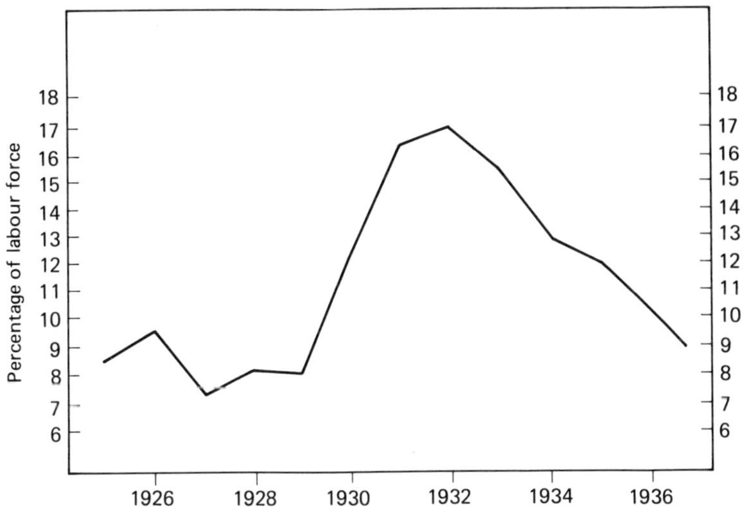

Source: *National Income, Expenditure and Output of the UK 1855–1965*, G.H. Feinstein.

reduction which matched the 1.9 million *rise* in unemployment between 1979 and 1983 in terms of size and speed.

This suggests the possibility of setting a fairly *ambitious objective*: a return within, say, four years to a level of claimant unemployment *below one and a half million*. It would imply a very high rate of job creation. Well over half a million jobs would have to be added every year to absorb, as well as the fall in claimant unemployment, a take-up of jobs by people not on the register and the expected increase in the supply of labour. There is no reason to suppose, however, that this performance, equivalent to an increase in jobs of 2 per cent per year, would be impossible. Employment in the United States has been rising at 3 per cent per year since early 1983.

There may none the less be problems in basing a strategy on such an optimistic objective. An objective needs to be clearly credible; and it needs to be robust in the face of shocks to the economy. What may be possible in a perfect environment is far more likely, in the real world, to fall foul of adverse developments. While an important attribute of a successful strategy should be to permit the best feasible outcome to occur, it is more likely to be effective if its aims are perceived to be attainable even in a relatively hostile environment.

Figure **4.8 Unemployment: medium-term objectives**

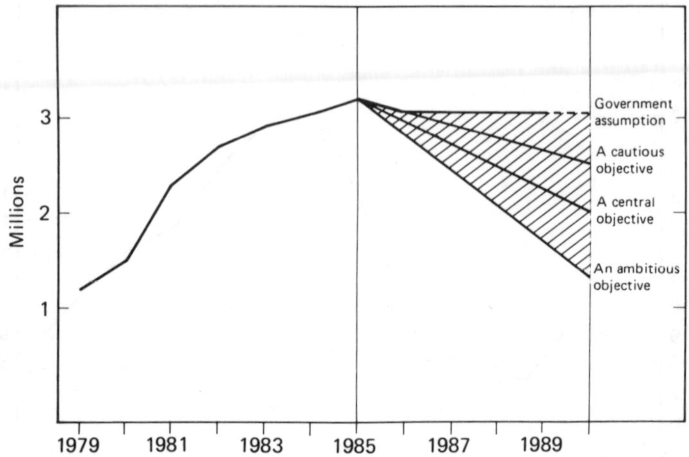

Source: Historical data from *Department of Employment Gazette*. Government assumptions from Autumn Statement 1985.

An alternative approach would therefore be to go for a fairly '*cautious*' *objective*. Aiming to reduce unemployment to, say, two and a half million by mid-1990 would demand a fall in unemployment of about 200 000 a year. With the supply of labour expected to grow at a slower pace over the next few years, recent rates of job creation (averaging perhaps 250 000 per year) might alone be enough to achieve this – *if* the pace were sustained and *if* the new jobs were full-time rather than part-time.

Would it be necessary to make a choice between two such contrasting objectives? A more attractive option might be to preserve enough flexibility in the strategy *either* to achieve the ambitious objective if it proved possible *or* to settle for the easy objective if the external environment or constraints proved too adverse. This would imply setting a *range* for the unemployment objectives of the strategy. In some ways, this might dilute the message, however reasonable in practice it is to accept that other factors may rule out the specification of a unique aim. So there may also be a role for a '*central*' objective within the range. If such a central objective were set at two million, the aims of the strategy could be illustrated in terms of the 'target cone' in Figure 4.8.

PRIORITIES

Setting such a 'central' target of reducing unemployment to two million within four years would demand large-scale action by the government and a considerable increase in the growth of output. But one substantial and needy group in the population might not benefit immediately. Those who have already been out of work for a year or more – the long-term unemployed – have in many cases suffered a considerable loss of morale. Employers are wary of their abilities to return quickly to full-time work. So they may be the last to get taken on.

Special help and special programmes may be the answer in the short term. The Charter for Jobs has consistently argued for a guaranteed offer of a job for at least a year to be made by the government to the long-term unemployed. The House of Commons Select Commitee on Employment has recently endorsed this call, recommending a practical scheme to realise a job guarantee within three years.[6] The places would either be in the current Community Programme or in one of three new schemes: a building improvement programme carried out by the private sector but subject to tenders submitted to the MSC; additional employment in the health and personal social services; or job subsidies to employers to take on the long-term unemployed.

These proposals seem practical and well targeted. By providing direct assistance, training and re-motivation they will improve the quality of our labour force. And it is unlikely that any significant change in wage pressure will result since these people are in many senses so detached from the rest of the work force that they cannot currently exert any downward influence on inflation.

The Select Committee's measures are designed to reduce the number of long-term unemployed by 750 000. The impact on the *total* number of people claiming benefit may be rather less because some displacement might occur. But it is reasonable to assume that the size of the register will be reduced by at least 600 000 by 1989 if the guarantee is put into effect.

NEW JOBS

If the number of unemployed can be reduced by 600 000 (if only temporarily) in this way, how many further jobs would have to be created elsewhere in the economy to satisfy the aims of a Medium-Term Employment Strategy? The calculations below suggest that to achieve the 'central' objective of two million claimant unemployed would require a further 700 000 people being removed from the count:

	Millions
Current level of claimant unemployment	3.3
less effect of job guarantee	0.6
less 'Central' objective for unemployment	2.0
Extra required reduction in claimant unemployment	0.7

However this is not the whole story. Official figures for unemployment measure only how many people are actually claiming benefit. There are substantial numbers outside the claimant count who suffer just as badly from unemployment and whom it is as essential to get back into regular employment.

Many of these 'non-claimant unemployment' would in fact manage to take up employment opportunities before those on the claimants register. Research by the National Institute of Economic and Social Research (NIESR) for instance, suggests that recently, out of every four extra people employed in the non-manufacturing sector, a reduction of only one has occurred in the official unemployment count. It is unlikely that such a pattern will be maintained in a broadly-based general upturn which involves a revival in manufacturing employment and more full-time jobs, but it would be wise to assume that no more than three-quarters of the new jobs (say 70 per cent) go to people 'on' rather than 'off' the register.

Allowance also has to be made for new entrants to the labour force. Although there are always people retiring from work, their numbers are generally exceeded by school-leavers and those wishing to start returning to work. The Department of Employment estimates that, over the next four years, the labour force will expand by nearly 400 000 people. This means that about 1.4 million jobs will have to be found if unemployment is to be brought down to two million:

	Millions
Extra reduction needed in claimant unemployment	0.7
Associated reduction of non-claimant unemployment	0.3
Expansion of the labour force	0.4
Total new jobs required	1.4

THE TASK OF NEW POLICIES

Tight as government policy currently is, the partial relaxation since 1983[7] has permitted the creation of a limited number of new jobs. Most forecasters expect this process to continue. Some see the likely increase as being sufficient to bring about a small fall in unemployment. Others see it as barely keeping pace with the expansion of the labour force (a rise of 0.4 million), even now oil prices have fallen. *A reasonable assumption is that about 0.4 million jobs would be created over the next four years on current policies.*

To achieve the 'central' objective, therefore, once the 'job guarantee' is in place, other new policies need to create *one million more jobs* than will present policies:

	Millions
Total new jobs required	1.4
less expected job creation under current policies	0.4
Jobs requirements of 'new policies'	1.0

A million jobs is equivalent to nearly 4 per cent of the employed labour force. Although many of these jobs will be taken by people with skill levels below the average, we generally observe better-than-normal productivity gains being achieved in an upturn. Output may therefore need to rise by an extra 5 or 6 per cent over four years. Another way of expressing the policy requirement is therefore that it needs to ***increase output growth on average by 1 to 1½ per cent per year over four years. This (and the implementation of the job guarantee) would mean that growth rates for the whole economy of up to 4 per cent per year (before allowing for the expected decline in North Sea oil extraction) would need to be averaged.***

POLICY ALTERNATIVES

The central argument expounded by Charter for Jobs has been that restrictive government policies on the demand side have been the main reason for the steep rise in unemployment since 1979; and that only a reversal of such policies will create the right conditions for a sharp fall in the immediate future. In particular, a relaxation of fiscal policies is needed. The scope for such measures can easily be illustrated by a couple of examples:

1. There is a wide consensus of the need for a substantial build-up of expenditure on the public sector infrastructure: roads, railways, sewers, land, housing, education and health services. Memoranda prepared for the National Economic Development Council (NEDC) have identified a large number of projects ready for implementation. There is a gap of at least £2 billion between what the TUC and CBI[8] consider necessary just on investment in roads and what the government is currently prepared to fund. A recent Department of the Environment report has also revealed that nearly £19 billion of work is needed on the nation's housing stock. Although the net cost of employing additional labour on construction may in general be larger than the £5000 per job expected in the proposed Building Improvement Programme, costs can be held down by careful targeting of projects and techniques. Nearly half a million fewer people are employed in the construction industry than in 1974.
2. Reductions in employers' national insurance contributions represent a very cost-effective way of increasing employment. They not only act as a general stimulus to the economy by reducing costs and therefore prices, but also reduce the relative price of labour. Simulations published by Andrew Britton in the February 1986 issue of the *National Institute of Economic and Social Research Review* suggest that a near-abolition of employers' National In-

surance contributions might increase employment levels by one and a half million over five years compared with present policies.

Monetary policy may also have a role to play, perhaps in concert with other countries. Real interest rates are currently at exceptionally high levels. Part of this reflects international factors. With the world inflation outlook now exceptionally favourable (not only oil prices, but those of most international commodities have been falling over the past year) the potential for concerted action to reduce world interest rates seems high. It may be necessary for Germany, rather than the United States, to take the lead but a reduction of about two percentage points appears perfectly feasible. This would mirror the rise between 1980 and 1982 which OECD estimates suggest contracted the world economy by about 1¼ per cent.

On the supply side, several potentially powerful (if slower-acting) policy instruments are available:

1. The productivity of labour can be increased by improving educational standards and skills of school-leavers and by expanding facilities for retraining; employers can be involved more purposefully in this process through subsidy or taxation.
2. Matching workers to jobs by improving information or encouraging mobility can overcome bottlenecks – increasing potential non-inflationary output – and improve competitiveness.
3. Attempts to overcome regional imbalances by subsidising labour, improving the local public and private sector capital stock, or compensating industries directly for moves to areas of high unemployment can improve their domestic and international competitiveness.
4. Costs of employing labour can be held down by reducing taxes on employers or encouraging a deceleration in wages.
5. Incentives can be provided for capital investment in industries with a large labour input. As part of a general strategy for re-industrialisation, research and development activities can be fostered and the resources of local authorities, enterprise agencies and financial institutions can be mobilised.

Empirical estimates of the effects of such supply-side measures are much harder to find than those of a demand-side stimulus. The costs of not undertaking them can, however, be considerable, as bottlenecks prevent the expansion of the domestic economy and production moves abroad.

If joint action were taken on supply and demand many of the constraints which have previously held back output growth may be overcome. Balance of payments pressures could be alleviated by the maintenance of healthy levels of competitiveness and the elimination of bottlenecks. Inflation could be held down by concentration on cost-cutting modes of production and targeting expenditure on areas of high unemployment or the long-term unemployed.

However a strategy for the medium term would demand a more formalised specification of the constraints, so that a reasonable balance could be struck between progress towards the main objective (employment creation) and the avoidance of unacceptable side-effects. The absence of such formal trade-offs for unemployment and the real exchange rate made the concentration of the MTFS on inflation objectives so destructive for the rest of the economy.

SPECIFYING THE CONSTRAINTS

How might a Medium-Term Employment Strategy formally recognise the need to accept certain constraints? The first principle to be accepted would be that *forecasts* of what was likely to happen in these critical areas would be allowed to affect decisions rather than waiting until the economy has already strayed beyond some 'acceptable' point.

The second principle would be the acceptance of *uncertainty*. No forecast can be completely accurate; no policy will work exactly as intended. To attempt to massage the economy in too fine a manner (or achieve a precise set of multiple objectives) is doomed to failure.

These considerations suggest that, as with the unemployment objective, it would be sensible to specify the constraints in the form of 'acceptable ranges' of expected outcomes. If deviations are likely to occur, policies need either to be reined back or made more ambitious.

The prime worry about any expansionary policy must be its effect on the rate of inflation. Other areas of concern might be the balance of payments on current account (because the prospect of a large deficit may cause further difficulties for the exchange rate), labour productivity (to prevent losses in efficiency or income) and resource allocation (particularly if investment is to be subject to administrative fiat or incentive).

How would 'acceptable ranges' for such constraints be set in practice? A simple example may be instructive. The first step would be to consider a 'no policy change' forecast of the economy. This might show that only a small fall in inflation was expected. If policy makers felt that *any* sustained rise in the inflation rate from the current rate of nearly 6 per cent should be avoided, they might then set an 'acceptable' band of, say, 3 to 6 per cent a year. Similar considerations would arise with the balance of payments, where a small deficit rather than the forecast small temporary surplus might be thought acceptable.

The process of setting constraints alongside targets involves a recognition both that objectives must be feasible and that most economic policies involve costs. Crucial to the issue of expansionary policies (particularly on the demand side) is whether it is domestic output which responds to the new stimulus or whether the impulse leaks through instead to domestic prices or imports. If subsidiary policies can be identified which mitigate these effects, constraints will prove to be less of an obstacle to expansion.

OTHER POLICIES TO ATTACK THE CONSTRAINTS

The failure of the MTFS over the last few years to bring about a deceleration in the growth rate of earnings[9] has shown the difficulty of relying on market forces or 'expectations' to achieve lower sustainable rates of inflation. Alternative approaches are now needed.

Better presentation of the aims, power and trade-offs of a comprehensive economic strategy may be one answer. But policies to influence incomes and prices directly should not be ruled out. Three approaches in particular tend to be on offer: a 'legal' norm limiting the size of any wage increase that employers can offer or prices they can charge; a 'voluntary' or consensus approach involving organised labour and major employers; or tax-based policies under which employers are penalised but not prevented from giving 'excessive' wage increases.

The history of the first two is clearly chequered but by no means as bad as current rhetoric would have us suppose (see Figure 4.9 for a comparison of inflation in the late 1970s and in the early 1980s). Tax-based policies are untried, but there is a growing volume of literature on both theoretical and practical aspects.

There are of course costs associated with these policies. They stop

Figure **4.9 Inflation comparisons**

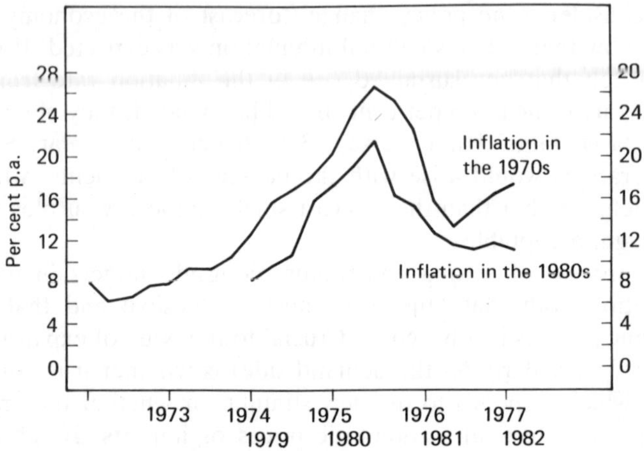

Source: *Economic Trends Annual Supplement 1986*.

employers and employees making fully independent decisions. Sometimes the strains are obvious: staff shortages in profitable companies hoping for expansion; tension in the public sector because policies may seem to be being policed more rigorously than elsewhere; or a widening gap between management able to exploit loop-holes and a workforce tied to fixed wage rates. But if the choice is between some such inefficiencies and 'living with' either high unemployment or high inflation the priority now should be to develop effective variants of such policies; not to reject them on grounds of dogma.

In the absence of such policies, much of the burden of holding down inflation may continue to be borne by monetary policy. This would involve primarily the use of domestic interest rates to influence the exchange rate (and hence the direct transmission of inflationary pressures) rather than precise targeting of the money supply.

Interventionist policies in the industrial area may be able to limit the potential damage to the balance of payments of expansionary policies. Some forms of protection are allowable even within EEC rules. An alternative approach would be to concentrate on policies designed to strengthen the supply side of the economy, particularly on the industrial side, so that the competitiveness of UK industry and its ability to withstand foreign pressure would be improved.

The impact on the balance of payments could also be minimised by 'targeting' an expansion towards areas where it is known that domestic industry is competitive or there are few foreign substitutes available. Thus if public services are expanded or labour-intensive renovation work is undertaken, the direct effect on the balance of payments would be small.

The most effective way to minimise the external constraints on expansion is of course to encourage other countries to adopt similar policies. The extra demand this would produce for our exports and the additional freedom it would permit for monetary policy (less need for the use of interest rates to limit the impact on the exchange rate) would provide invaluable assistance.

FINANCING

Most of the policy measures considered above would involve additional government expenditure or loss of tax revenue. In the short term, public sector borrowing would rise. This would subsequently be reduced by flowbacks to the Exchequer in the form of lower payments to and higher tax receipts from the newly employed. Faster growth would also increase the taxable capacity of the whole economy.

The MTFS has laid great stress on the need for lower public sector borrowing so that interest rates can be brought down for a given rate of monetary growth. There is however little evidence that such a relationship exists. Certainly the experience of the last few years provides little support for the proposition. A much clearer influence has been the level of real international interest rates.

Even if a relationship between the PSBR and interest rates were well established, there is no reason to suppose that this would imply an absolute constraint on the rate at which the economy could be expanded by fiscal means. The impact of high interest rates on spending patterns is generally thought to be much smaller than the direct effects of most forms of public expenditure or taxation. High interest rates might reduce the effectiveness of expansionary policies (and act as a disincentive to investment) but, if spare resources are available, they would not nullify the impact. Financial 'crowding out' of this sort should be seen as a feature of certain theoretical models rather than of the real world.

Perhaps of more concern is the possibility of a crisis of confidence in domestic and overseas financial markets if a programme of fiscal expansion were announced. This might reflect fears that a large part of the increase in the public sector deficit would be monetised (implying a subsequent rise in inflation) or simply doubts about the long-term sustainability of the public sector's level of indebtedness.

Such considerations might lead to the choice of measures being dictated solely by their 'cost-effectiveness' in terms of the size of reduction in unemployment they achieve for a given increase in the PSBR. This is one appealing feature of special employment measures (as exemplified in the proposals for a 'job guarantee'). Direct employment in the public services will also quickly generate revenue flow-backs, so that the initial effect on public borrowing may be limited. Similarly public expenditure can be redirected away from 'employment-weak' areas towards 'employment-rich' ones.

Efforts to bring about a co-ordinated reduction in world interest rates offer a mechanism for reducing unemployment without reliance on higher public borrowing. Indeed public borrowing might be substantially reduced as a result since interest payments in the United Kingdom are one of the largest items in government expenditure.

A further way in which employment growth might be stimulated with little adverse effect on public sector borrowing would be if the exchange rate fell in real terms. Output and employment in the traded sector would expand, generating useful revenue flowbacks.

These measures would of course involve other costs. Productivity growth might be slower if much of the extra employment were concentrated in the public sector. A depreciation of the exchange rate could exacerbate inflationary pressures. Lower interest rates world wide might disturb international confidence. Thus, while the implementation of such measures might involve only modest increases in public sector borrowing, the other costs involved might divert policy makers to opt instead for a package involving large increases in the PSBR.

A crucial question is how much extra borrowing the markets could bear in the context of a consistent and coherent strategic approach. There seems little shortage of available finance at the moment. The markets have withstood well the initial impact of expected tax revenue losses from the North Sea. A rise involving initially, say, two to three billion pounds per year in the PSBR should not present major problems.

Much larger packages have been suggested, however, by some commentators. In chapter 2 of this volume Professor Rudiger Dornbusch advocates, writing in 1985, an immediate fiscal stimulus worth 1½ per cent of GDP in the first year and 3 per cent in the second year. Given this large initial shock, the momentum to the economy would be sufficient to allow a rundown of the stimulus thereafter. Conscious of the possible impact of the package on foreign exchange markets, Professor Dornbusch suggests that domestic interest rates should be raised sufficiently to ensure stability in the exchange rate.

This judicious use of monetary policy could also support a slower-acting fiscal stimulus with higher initial costs. Reductions in employers' national insurance contributions, for instance, should ultimately have only a small impact on the PSBR because of substantial revenue flow-backs. Lower contributions would also have a beneficial effect on inflation. In shaky financial markets, however, some reassurance may be needed. An alternative approach would be to phase in such measures only slowly, over a number of years.

One of the important contributions which a Medium-Term Employment Strategy might be able to make would be to demonstrate the complex interaction between the PSBR and the rest of the economy. Two critical concerns should be the permanence of any change and the ability of the economy to finance the additional borrowing. This suggests that the Employment Strategy might specify what *levels* of debt (or ranges of levels) would be appropriate given the expected increases in output and inflation.

Figure 4.10 below shows how the (gross) level of public sector debt

***Figure* 4.10 Ratio of public debt to national income**

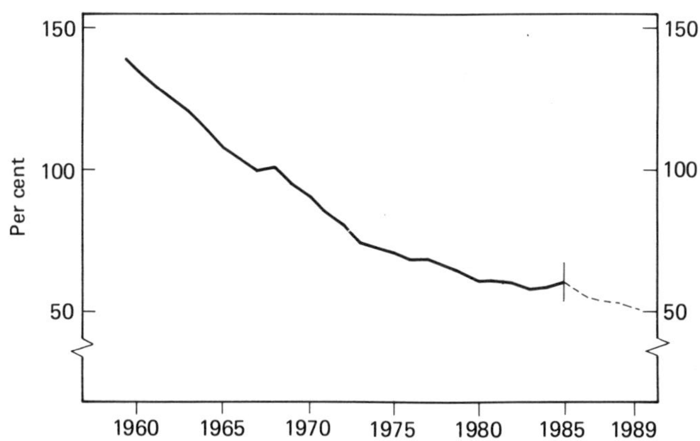

Source: CSO, Financial Statistics Table S1 and *Economic Trends Annual Supplement 1986.*

has been performing relative to national income (GDP). The trend for the last thirty years has been progressively downwards (the recent rise reflects in part the way that the government has been intervening in the financial markets rather than a rise in net indebtedness). Yet government plans are to push it down further over the next three years.

With expansionary policies in place, national income would grow faster than the government is currently assuming (the forecast figures in Figure 4.10 are taken from the 1985 MTFS and the Autumn Statement). But even if they took the growth rate no higher than 8 per cent per annum in money terms, there would be no threat of a rising ratio of debt to income even with a doubling of the PSBR compared to present plans over that period. Given the current depressed state of the economy, it might be thought appropriate for this ratio in fact to rise.

CONCLUSIONS

We have shown that a Medium-Term Employment Strategy could contribute towards a framework for an expansion of the economy and the creation of a substantial number of extra jobs. It could avoid the mistakes of the Medium-Term Financial Strategy – a narrow focus of action and emphasis on a single priority – and be designed to accommodate the complexities of modern economies and the need to use a number of policy instruments in consistent fashion.

A Medium-Term Employment Strategy could involve a quantified set of objectives. These would specify feasible goals for higher employment and output; and limits for the inflation rate and other potentially adverse factors. They would be in the form of ranges of possible outcomes to be achieved over a period of years.

Identification of a set of objectives would clarify the government's priorities. They could indicate that, whilst the reduction of unemployment had become the prime aim of policy, unacceptable risks would not be taken with inflation. They would provide a clearer guide for the private sector about the likely course of the economy and policy than the narrower intermediate objectives specified in the Medium-Term Financial Strategy.

The credibility of a Medium-Term Employment Strategy would depend on the provision by the government of detailed forecasts of the economy and evidence of the effectiveness of available policy measures. Measures could include well-targeted increases in public expenditure and reductions in taxes on jobs to stimulate the demand for labour; improved facilities for training, mobility and investment to ease the supply of labour and capital; and consideration of the roles of both monetary policy and forms of prices or incomes policies to influence the price level. Efforts could also be made on the international level to promote more growth-oriented policies.

The choice of domestic policies in any particular period would be determined both by the aim of steering close to the chosen paths for the main objectives and the need to preserve reasonable stability in the instruments of policy: tax rates, interest rates, expenditure plans and so on. This would reduce the uncertainty which the emphasis in the MTFS on precise targets for monetary growth rates and the PSBR has generated for short-term interest rates and tax rates.

There is no reason to suppose that an approach such as this would be an *essential* component of a successful drive against high unemployment. There are, for instance, powerful arguments for preserving greater flexibility for governments in dealing with potentially hostile financial or labour markets. But it would show the government's commitment to firm action and provide an incentive for the private sector to plan for growth.

In the drive to overcome defeatism and despair about mass unemployment, the case for embedding economic policy within a Medium-Term Employment Strategy seems to deserve detailed consideration.

Notes

1. This text was first published in a Charter for Jobs Economic Report in March 1986.
2. 'The Real Cost of Unemployment', by Professor Adrian Sinfield and Neil Fraser, BBC North-East, 1985.
3. See Charter for Jobs 'Economic Report' No. 4.
4. 'A co-operative growth strategy for employment', EEC Economic Report 1985–86.
5. See Charter for Jobs 'Economic Report' No. 1.
6. See Charter for Jobs 'Economic Report' No. 5.
7. See Charter for Jobs 'Economic Report' No. 3.
8. 'Infrastructure Investment', TUC Memorandum to NEDC July, 1985.
9. Earnings have grown at a fairly steady rate of 7½ per cent per annum since the middle of 1982 despite rising unemployment and prospects of declining inflation.

5 The State of Britain To Come[1]

Edward Heath

THE ORGANISATION OF SOCIETY

I have no doubt that the talents of our people are as prolific as in the past. The fundamental question that we face is about the structure and organisation of our society. We must so order it as to provide the incentives, opportunities, support and assistance to permit talent to achieve its full potential. Sadly, in recent years, the debate about the organisation of our society has descended into a sterile trench warfare between rival ideologies. Discussion has been dominated by the supporters of *laissez-faire* on the right and the exponents of social central planning on the left. They have happily traded insults and each assailed the facile philosophy of the other, with scant concern for the real world. This is remote from the British tradition of empiricism.

When we speak of the organisation of society, we imply a whole range of things including the spiritual and philosophical values summed up in great concepts like freedom and justice. On this occasion I shall confine myself to the organisation of society for the creation and distribution of wealth. For some people wealth creation begins with a production process. But it is impossible in a complex modern society to consider production by itself. It rests on so many diverse bases.

The days of unskilled labour are substantially over. Production now depends on education and training designed to turn out men and women capable of high standard production work. It rests increasingly on high-quality research to generate new ideas and to test and refine them until they can be applied profitably. Production without profit is doomed. But the overheads carried by our productive industries are integral with their operations. They are indissoluble from their success. That is why our national infrastructure is so important. Traffic jams, customs clearance delays, inadequate roads, decaying bridges or crumbling sewers all help to tip the competitive balance away from Britain to younger rivals abroad. That is why it is meaningless for even the most dedicated champion of *laissez-faire* capitalism to ignore the need for nation-wide co-ordination in both planning and provision.

At the highest level, responsibility for co-ordination rests with the Cabinet itself. It is its job to assess and set priorities, to allocate funds and to inspire initiatives. It is a sad fact that in the complex modern world, no Cabinet can have the command of detail to perform this co-ordinating role except in the broadest terms. And below the level of the Cabinet this function has not been carried out entirely satisfactorily in the last few years.

There are some in government who will not lament this. They have never really accepted the need for a Department of Trade and Industry with a wide brief to co-ordinate industrial development. They believe that the invisible hand of the free market will produce the optimum distribution of all the factors involved in production. Universities will conduct the research that industry requires; further education colleges will train people in the necessary skills; the right roads and railways will appear on time and in the right places to support the needs of the commercial sector. I have no such faith. I believe that there is an essential role for government in planning and co-ordinating our industrial efforts on a regional basis.

There is one part of the United Kingdom that has practised the style of industrial co-operation that I recommend. That is Scotland. The excellent work of the Scottish Development Agency supported by the Scottish Office should not go unremarked and unpraised. Nor should the stewardship of George Younger, who has a worthy successor in Malcolm Rifkind. The SDA pursues a market oriented strategy. It attempts to ensure as far as possible that Scotland's industry capitalises upon its strengths and seizes its commercial opportunities. It does not attempt to fly in the face of market forces. It helps business to make the most of these, even to anticipate them. With proper guidance from the Department of Trade and Industry, this approach can be emulated in other parts of the United Kingdom.

The decline of our manufacturing industry has been graphically charted by the recent report of the Lords Select Committee on Overseas Trade.[2] It correctly points out that, just as there was no automatic process by which the existence of a large surplus in our oil trade led to a high exchange rate and a destruction of jobs and whole industries, so there will be no automatic process by which the value of sterling will fall as oil production declines and those jobs and industries will be recreated. It was the lack of a realistic exchange rate policy which made it impossible for our businesses to maintain their share of our home market or to compete in international markets. When oil production declines, a reduction in the value of sterling will no doubt follow, but that will not of itself recreate businesses that have perished. Nor will it foster new ones.

AN INDUSTRIAL STRATEGY

The key element of British industrial policy in the period over the next seven years, until the oil revenues begin to decline sharply, must be a deliberate and purposeful strategy to recreate a modern British industry capable of outdoing the modern industries of our competitors. There are pessimists who believe that we are already too late, and that Britain's only hope lies in service industries and investment overseas. Nobody doubts the importance of services but there is a critical – even symbiotic – relationship between manufacturing and services. It is simply stated: service industries need something to service.

The fashionable doctrines of the 1970s have done us great damage. Schumacher's thesis that small is beautiful paints only half the picture. Small is very often weak, vulnerable and in need of protection. Small firms may grow into large ones – and we certainly need many to do just that – but in most cases the process is long and hard and attended by grievous pitfalls. I admire the enterprise and courage of many small firms; I shall support the government in giving them all the assistance that I can.

But my message to the government is that in assisting the small businesses it should not underestimate the importance for the economy of our largest firms. When a large factory closes it takes many, many small businesses to replace the jobs that have been lost. And it may well be easier to rehabilitate old firms: to find for them the advice and assistance required to allow them to restructure their operations and compete once more in the market place.

At Consett, for example, the run-down and closure of the steelworks led to the loss of seven thousand jobs. Six years later, after a great deal of effort including government assistance, the most optimistic of estimates put the number of new jobs created no higher than 2000 (despite the excellent work of the Derwentside Development Agency). And few of the jobs created have been suitable for former steelworkers because so many of them are part-time and for women.

Yet the truth remains that few British businesses are 'too big'. Even the mighty GEC, one of our largest industrial concerns, is only medium-sized by international standards. General Electric of the United States is far bigger. And do politicians in the United States criticise it for expanding too much? Is IBM damned for its size? Of course not. They are applauded as outstanding examples of industrial success.

We must learn to manage great enterprises on this scale for ourselves and make a success of them, not to run and hide and resign ourselves to our inability to match the Americans and Japanese. Such fatalism about our abilities and capabilities must be abandoned. It is undermining our very will to survive as an industrial force in this modern world. There is a lack of ambition in Britain today that alarms me. A lack of will and a lack of drive. An assumption of automatic failure. This mood must be replaced by one of new resolution.

PROMOTING EUROPEAN INDUSTRY

In the reconstruction of our industries, we must have in the front of our mind the nature of the market in which we need most to compete. This is the international market increasingly dominated by enormous American and Japanese corporations, enjoying the economies of scale of huge home markets far greater than our own, or for that matter than the immediate home market of any of the middle-sized European nation states.

We too now have a home market of great size. It is the market of the European Community. It now stands at over 320 million, half the size again of that in the United States. We must learn to exploit it. In reconstructing our industries we must create the firms that are capable of exploiting it: truly European firms, feeding off the domestic market and capable of taking on the biggest and the best that Japan and America can offer in the market-place of the world.

Let me illustrate part of what I mean with reference to the recent controversy over the proposed sale of British Leyland. Of course the government was right to worry about the long-term future of the employees in British Leyland. But the government was undoubtedly wrong to translate that concern into secret unilateral negotiations with a single American company. I admire and like the Americans, but I, like the vast majority of my fellow countrymen, could not support the sale of this central British industry to the Americans without fully exploring the alternatives. To offer ownership and control to foreign firms, without allowing the same facilities to us British to buy government-owned firms of high industrial reputation, is indefensible.

I am glad that in the end public opinion persuaded the government to re-examine the options and to abandon their proposals for the sale of British Leyland overseas. I know full well that if the shoe had been on the other foot, and British Leyland had sought to buy General Motors, the people of Detroit and of the whole United States would have rejected the sale of such a potent national symbol to a foreign company. Would this make them anti-British? Not for one moment. It would mean just that they wanted to keep control in their own hands of a firm of which they are proud and upon which so many of them depend for their jobs and livelihoods.

We all recognise the vital importance of the partnership between North America and Europe through the Atlantic Alliance for the defence of the free world. It must remain our priority to consolidate and strengthen the Alliance. It was President Kennedy who spoke to me of the twin pillars of the Atlantic Alliance and fully backed Britain's membership of the European Community. He did so because he recognised the need for Europe to draw together and strengthen itself so that the Alliance would rest on tall strong pillars on each shore of the Atlantic. He did so because he knew that Alliance and partnership can only be maintained in the long run on the basis of equality. The relationship can then be conducted without raising sentiments of domination, inferiority and wounded pride.

Yet individually the nations of Europe can never speak as equals to the United States. This is not a sound basis for an enduring relationship. And this is one more reason why Europe must fulfill the potential that our population of over 320 million gives us, in order to become better and more effective allies of the United States within the North Atlantic Treaty Organisation.

It is to Europe as a whole that we must look for Britain's destiny. Through Europe, we can co-operate with the United States on equal terms. The same should be true of British companies in their associations with the vast American multinationals. If General Motors had been permitted to acquire British Leyland, it would not have been a merger, but a take-over. Control would have passed outside the United Kingdom; it would have passed outside Europe and away from the influence of the institutions of the European Community in which we have such a powerful voice. It would have passed to a United States corporation influenced by a United States government before whom we British are only supplicants. We would have had no more rights or claims for consideration than many others.

The plain fact is that, at a time when there is almost limitless cash ripe for investment opportunities, all that a *laissez-faire* industrial policy will achieve is the sale of many of our industries to the larger and more powerful American and Japanese multinationals. Of course a rump of our largest companies will remain, but many of our wealth-creating enterprises will end up as subsidiaries of foreign companies, with all the consequences for control over our own lives.

There is an alternative. But it will require resolution and a reorientation of our industrial policy. It is to seek answers for our industrial problems within the European Community. This will require a new determination from our own government and agreement with our partners. It will require a more assertive stance by the European Commission, combined with a willingness to grasp the initiative.

Just as our firms are mostly too small, so are the vast majority of firms in Europe. They are geared to individual national markets that are generally too small for optimum efficiency and too small to foster the cost savings that permit competition in world markets. The ideal would be to bring together compatible firms of roughly equivalent size and merge them into European-wide organisations: fully committed to the whole vast European market.

It would have been in the long-term interest of all concerned if such a solution could have been found for Westland. It is imperative that the possibilities are explored for Leyland before any final decisions are taken about its disposal.

We must not hand over our technology or the fruits of our research and development efforts. They are the guarantee of our future prosperity and employment. And with joint British and European ownership we can ensure that our technology is exploited in our own interests and that manufacturing jobs do not ebb away.

TRADE POLICY

A strategically planned industrial policy must be supported by an equally vigorous policy for trade. As a nation we have been slow to emulate the aggressive national marketing efforts mounted by other countries in pursuit of contracts and orders. As a result, we have seen our market share eroded and the loss of many jobs. We have failed to make available either sufficiently early or in sufficient quantity the sort of favourable trade finance that our competitors have so often used to undercut our industries.

I welcome the government's concession in making available special credit terms for trade with China and Indonesia. This is undoubtedly a step in the right direction. Unfortunately the sums involved are relatively trivial when set against the size of the world market, the efforts of our competitors, and the scale of the challenges.

The other complaint I hear so often from those abroad who otherwise seem so keen to trade with Britain, is that our export promotion effort is ill-co-ordinated. This is not to denigrate the British Overseas Trade Board or the commercial staff of the Foreign Office and our embassies abroad. They do the best job they can with the scant resources they have at their disposal. It is simply to point out that our competitors devote far greater resources and effort to ensure that their firms are properly supported in overseas markets, that as far as possible they do not cut each other's throats and that they co-operate as closely as possible to present a cohesive package.

We must emulate our competitors. I cannot accept the argument that financial constraints will not permit the extra staff and facilities required to do so. The cost is small in comparison with the potential return which could be achieved.

The government can impose its own form of market economy on this country. What it cannot do is to impose it on the rest of the world. When our competitors provide better financial packages, lower interest rates and longer term loans than we do they inevitably oust our manufacturers and building contractors from world markets. We do not want to be bellyaching about their success. We will only succeed by offering the world better terms than they do.

CO-ORDINATED EXPANSION

Industrial reform and the restructuring of industry and trade is best carried out during a period of economic expansion. I have described in the past the type of 'supply-side friendly' fiscal and monetary regime which I believe is required to ease this process. There are a number of measures I would like to see acting as the suitable backdrop to a concerted drive to strengthen our industrial base.

Our own budget judgement can only be made in the context of the prevailing international situation. Elsewhere I have devoted myself to a detailed explanation of the current state of the world economy. In a nutshell, the position is this: the United States budget deficit of over $200 billion and trade deficit of $150 billion is unsustainable in the long run. The US economy has been expanding as a result of the fiscal stimulus represented by the deficit. This has pulled the world economy up from the trough in which it found itself between 1981 and 1983, but it has not been sufficient to produce a recovery in any meaningful sense.

In the developed economies belonging to the Organisation for Economic Co-operation and Development about 30 million people are without work. For other areas no record exists.

The US economy is running out of steam. Unless the other major trading nations of Western Europe and Japan move to expand their economies to take over from the American locomotive as it slows, there is a strong risk of the onset of a new depression. This is why I have urged a co-ordinated reflation of the international economy. At this time of falling oil and commodity prices, such a move need not be inflationary. But it must be *co-ordinated*, particularly within the European Community. The French experience of 1981–2 shows why. It was misguided to reflate at a time when France's major trading partners were contracting their economies – and, incidentally, to achieve reflation by measures which directly increased costs for domestic industry.

LOOSENING THE STRAIT-JACKET

Some say that more government borrowing will lead to higher interest rates. It is undoubtedly true that in some circumstances high borrowing causes interest rates to rise. But, with careful management of all the mechanisms at the government's disposal, this need not be so, especially at a time of vast unused reserves of plant and manpower. My critics argue that the financial markets would not view it that way. My answer would be that the financial markets must be educated. They were broadly Keynesian in their sympathy once. They are now following the monetarist fashion. The rigid monetarist philosophy of 1980–1 bred markets in its image. But there is a great deal that the government can now do by itself.

First of all, the Chancellor must loosen the financial strait-jacket that is stifling the real economy. It makes no sense to deny funds for capital investment on the infrastructure upon which our industry depends, when by the Treasury's own calculations there are literally hundreds of projects that would bring a strong positive real rate of return. They would bring us clear economic benefits. They would help our industries to be more competitive. It costs us dear not to spend or indeed to borrow the necessary funds to allow these projects to go ahead.

There is an important parallel between the finances of an individual firm and those of the nation. If firms ignore opportunities to invest, whether they fund their investment from profits or by borrowing, they quickly fall behind their competitors. The same remains true for Britain. In the crucial manufacturing sector, output is still lower than in 1973 and, perhaps even more worrying, so is investment. And yet we have had the excessive capital write-offs of the past four years, unprecedented levels of bankruptcies, and billions of pounds of plant and equipment scrapped.

The financial markets should never be allowed to enjoy a veto over policies any more than other powerful groups like the CBI or the Trade Unions. They too must be persuaded and encouraged to rediscover a sense of responsibility that seems to be slipping away fast in the world of 'get rich quick'. I suspect that those who will benefit most from the free-for-all will be the Japanese, with their highly-developed system of consensus, social responsibility and national loyalty.

The key to the strategy must be investment. Investment – rather than the stimulation of current consumption through tax cuts. Investment – rather than sucking in imports from abroad via tax cuts. Investment that – according to the overwhelming weight of economic analysis – will produce far more jobs more quickly and cheaply than tax cuts. Investment that provides the basis for a modern competitive economy with quick and efficient communications and cheap and reliable services.

A NATIONAL TRAINING SYSTEM

Modern capital is more than just physical objects: *people* are our most important resource. And we must invest in people; we must create human capital, as we create docks and railways. This means we must develop first-rate programmes for education and training.

I fear the consequences of long-term unemployment. I know from my experience in the North-East that long-term unemployment, quite apart from the human misery it brings, leaves men and women demoralised and quite incapable of holding down a job. I agree with the Charter for Jobs and with the House of Commons Select Committee on Employment,[3] that the Government must now guarantee jobs for the long-term unemployed. Charter for Jobs has calculated that this would result in a net annual cost of less than £3½ billion to provide 750 000 extra soundly useful jobs over the next three years.[4]

But the creation of jobs both for the young and the long-term unemployed cannot be seen merely as an exercise in managing the unemployment figures. These must be real jobs and the advantage should not be missed to impart both to our young people and to the long-term unemployed the skills and knowledge that will enable them to make a valuable contribution to the production process in this era of rapidly evolving technology.

In short, we need a national training scheme. I strongly favour the creation of a Ministry of Employment and Training, to take on both the present functions of the Department of Employment and the responsibility for non-advanced further education and certain parts of the advanced further education sector which presently lie within the Department of Education and Science. These could then be welded together to form the basis of a National Training System to be co-ordinated with existing provisions by employers and their organisations. Training is one of our chief national failures. Comparative surveys suggest that we fall far short of France, Germany, Switzerland, Japan and the United States both in the quality and quantity of the training that we undertake.

A PROGRAMME OF NATIONAL CONSENT

There are also pressing social reasons why we must reduce the numbers of unemployed and devote more resources to education and training. It is no coincidence that the regions of Britain which are most depressed are those with high rates of crime: the West Midlands, the North-East, Merseyside, South Wales and Central Scotland. The sense of hopelessness felt by many people living in these areas, particularly when they have no prospect of finding a job, must be a contributing factor. Decay in our inner cities has now run beyond anything to be found elsewhere in the European Community.

Comparative studies between Liverpool and Turin in the aftermath of the terrible events in Brussels last year showed that the standards of living of many in Liverpool were far worse than their Italian counterparts.

In these inner city areas, there has grown up a sense of alienation as deep as any to be found across the Atlantic. If our society cannot offer the opportunity or hope of a stable job, decent housing, and a reasonable standard of living, how can we expect allegiance to society, loyalty to its institutions and obedience to its rules? Our laws and institutions will only command assent for as long as all our people feel that they have an equal chance through their own endeavours to enjoy the rewards that society brings.

If a significant number of our fellow citizens come to feel that they no longer have a realistic prospect of sharing in prosperity, then alienation is inevitable. This is particularly so if people find themselves isolated because of their racial background or religious beliefs. And alienation brings with it the prospect of crime and social breakdown. Why obey the rules if obedience offers one nothing?

In my view, it is now clear that we need, and the time is now ripe for, a fresh emphasis and a change of direction in policy to meet the challenges that face our country. New ailments demand new prescriptions. And the time now grows shorter. We must have an open debate about what level of resources and manpower we need to devote to different aspects of our common purpose. It should be a debate involving all those who have an open mind, who are prepared to abandon dogma and construct a programme that will command national consent.

If our people believe that their voice has been heard and listened to; if, as a result of open discussion, they do not feel that their interests have been sacrificed for those of privileged groups in society, they will respond. They will regain the motivation that is tragically lacking today. Then the future for Britain can be brighter than many dare to hope.

Notes

1. This is an extended version of an Employment Institute Lecture delivered on 4 March 1986 at the Josiah Mason Lecture Theatre, Birmingham. The Rt. Hon. Edward Heath, MBE, MP, a patron of the Employment Institute, is the Conservative Member of Parliament for Old Bexley and

Sidcup. He was Leader of the Conservative Party from 1965 to 1975 and Prime Minister of the United Kingdom from June 1970 to February 1974.

2. Report from the House of Lords Select Committee on Overseas Trade, 1984–85, HMSO.
3. 'Special Measures and the Long-Term Unemployed', First Report from the House of Commons Employment Committee, 1985–86, HMSO (199).
4. Charter for Jobs 'Economic Report' No. 5.

6 Full Employment and the Balance of Payments

Andrew Britton[1]

INTRODUCTION

The movement of the balance of payments into substantial deficit on current account is fresh reason for anxiety about the condition of the British economy. How can anything like full employment be restored in this country if we are running a deficit on the balance of payments even when output is so depressed that two or three million people are unemployed?

It must seem very strange to the non-economist that full employment and a balance on external account should be difficult to reconcile. Surely the answer is simple: put the unemployed to work making goods for export (or to replace imports). Just so. It is indeed a sad reflection on the working of the economy that such an obviously desirable outcome is so difficult to achieve. The argument of this chapter is that its achievement is not impossible, that full employment could be restored and that the constraint placed on economic activity by the balance of payments is not absolute. The policy choice is nevertheless a difficult one, which may be helped by a wider discussion of the alternatives.

In the next section we outline briefly the balance of payments situation of this country. After that we look at the consequences for imports of increasing demand in a conventional Keynesian way so as to stimulate activity and employment. We consider at a little length the superficially attractive proposition that the balance of payments does not matter any more. As there seems little cause for complacency on that account we go on to look at depreciation and industrial policy as measures to improve the balance of payments prospects, before drawing some conclusions.

HISTORY AND PROSPECTS FOR THE BALANCE OF PAYMENTS

The balance of payments was an almost continuous preoccupation of British policy makers throughout the 1950s and 1960s. At that time

Table 6.1 Indicators of the trade and payments performance of the UK economy

	Balance of payments on current account (Billions of pounds)	*Balance on visible trade in oil (Billions of pounds)*	*Competitiveness of manufacturing industry (Index, 1980=100)*	*Sterling effective exchange rate (Index, 1975=100*
1975	−1.6	−3.1	77.9	100
1976	−0.9	−3.9	75.5	85.7
1977	−0.1	−2.8	79.7	81.2
1978	1.0	−2.0	84.5	81.5
1979	−0.7	−0.7	90.4	87.3
1980	2.9	0.3	100	96.1
1981	6.1	3.1	98.1	95.3
1982	3.9	4.6	92.2	90.7
1983	3.1	7.0	89.2	83.3
1984	1.2	6.9	87.6	78.8
1985	3.5	8.2	89.7	78.3
1986[1]	−0.1	2.7	85.5	72.9
1987[2]	−2.6	2.6	84.8	68.2

Note:
[1]Partly out-turn, partly estimates made by the National Institute of Economic and Social Research in February 1987.
[2]NIESR forecasts (February 1987).

the exchange rate was fixed and a current account deficit almost inevitably led to a drain on the official reserves of foreign currency. When sterling was eventually devalued in 1967 it was hoped that external balance would no longer be a concern of economic policy. In the event that hope was not fully justified.

In the 1970s the 'external constraint' on the British economy took a new form. The danger signal now was not a loss of reserves but a fall in the value of sterling. Such a fall would result directly in higher import prices and hence threaten higher inflation. Moreover as capital movements came more and more to dominate trade-related transactions in exchange markets the rumour of an incipient current account deficit might be enough to send the pound into a downward spiral. That was the situation up to 1976 when the last major sterling crisis occurred.

Thanks partly to North Sea oil and gas production, and to the high prices dictated by OPEC, the British current account was in surplus in every year from 1980 to 1985 (See Table 6.1). This gift of nature (and of OPEC) removed for a period any suspicion of an external constraint. In fact, however, the opportunity for faster growth was not taken; on the contrary the low level of economic activity following the 1979–80 recession cut back imports sharply and further increased the size of the balance of payments surplus. The consequence was a sharp appreciation of the pound, despite continuing inflation, so that the relative price competitiveness of British industry suffered a very severe blow.

This appreciation, although it took place nearly a decade ago, is very important to an understanding of the predicament of the British economy today. It contributed to the reduction in inflation that followed, but in every other way it was highly damaging. Although the exchange rate has subsequently fallen (see Table 6.1) and competitiveness has to some degree improved again, the damage, once done, cannot easily be undone. British industry is still the weaker as a result of what is now widely recognised to have been a mistaken monetary policy in the period 1977 to 1981.

The legacy of this period is the obstinately high level of unemployment (relative to other countries and to our own past experience). Had employment been maintained the balance of payments would never have moved into sustained surplus, the exchange rate would not have been so excessively strong and competitiveness would have been better maintained. This is the origin of what we now perceive as a 'balance of payments constraint' on output and employment growth.

A continuing underlying deterioration in the balance of payments position has since then been masked by the surplus on trade in oil. The balance of trade in manufactures particularly has moved from large surplus into deficit. Our exports of manufactures continue to lose their share of world markets. (When world trade in manufactures rises by 10 per cent our exports typically rise by just 6 per cent.) Imports continue to grow faster than domestic production. Sooner or later such trends must lead to large deficits again on the balance of payments, unless the growth of output and incomes in this country is held back so as to restrict the demand for imports.

The world price of oil was halved during 1986, from about \$30 a barrel to about \$15 (although it has since recovered to about \$18). This brings forward the decline in the UK oil surplus which was expected even before oil prices fell. The level of oil production in the North Sea is now beginning to fall. Oil consumption in this country, on the other hand, is likely to rise now that oil is cheaper relative to other fuels. The period when we could rely on oil to solve our balance of payments problem is drawing to an end.

Opinions differ as to the scale of current account deficit to be expected this year and forecasts of the balance are notoriously uncertain. But the need to address the balance of payments problem does not arise just from one particular forecast of a particular year. It arises from the underlying deterioration we have already seen over a number of years and the almost unavoidable assumption that this will continue. Moreover the present position and prospects for the balance of payments must be seen in the context of unemployment continuing at an unacceptably high level.

Concern over the balance of payments now may be exaggerated or premature if nothing is done to restore full employment. My purpose is not to express immediate anxiety about the balance of payments in these circumstances. It is rather to stimulate discussion of expansionary policies that will bring about a major reduction in unemployment over the next few years. We consider next therefore the rise in imports which is likely to follow from a higher level of economic activity in this country.

IMPORTS AND DOMESTIC DEMAND

No-one would question that (other things being equal) a higher level of domestic demand in this country would entail a higher level of imports. Imports of goods and services now account for 23 per cent of total final expenditure. (This includes imports of finished goods, semi-processed goods and raw materials.) The import content of different kinds of spending varies quite considerably, being very high for example in the case of consumer spending on durable goods and company investment in plant and machinery, much lower for some kinds of public spending and consumer spending on services. Generally the marginal import content of spending is higher than the average; in other words an increase in spending results in a more than proportionate rise in imports.

It follows that any policy measures taken to increase domestic demand so as to raise output and employment will also raise imports. Some very crude arithmetic might indicate the orders of magnitude involved. To create a million jobs would require an increase of about 4½ per cent in employment; if output rose in proportion to employment and imports rose twice as fast as output, then (with prices unchanged) the value of imports of goods and services would increase by about £9 bn a year. If nothing else changed that would simply be added to the current account deficit in perpetuity. By using a macroeconomic model of the economy we can be rather more precise than that, and can distinguish between the effects of different kinds of economic expansion.

Table 6.2 shows the effects, as estimated by the National Institute's macroeconomic model, of two different kinds of demand expansion: current spending by the public sector on goods and services and consumer spending by the private sector (including both durable and non-durable goods). These model estimates, or simulations, take account of a large number of estimated relationships linking different parts of the economy and are therefore very much more sophisticated than the simple arithmetic described above. In both cases it is

Table 6.2 Estimated economic effects of increased spending

(a) An addition of £1 billion a year (at 1980 prices) to public spending on goods and services

		Output (GDP)		*Imports of goods and services*	
		£ Billion at 1980 prices (annual rate)	*percent*	*£ billion at 1980 prices (annual rate)*	*percent*
1987	1	1.1	0.5	0.3	0.3
	2	1.2	0.5	0.4	0.4
	3	1.1	0.5	0.4	0.5
	4	1.0	0.4	0.4	0.5
1988	1	0.9	0.4	0.4	0.5
	2	0.9	0.4	0.4	0.5
	3	0.9	0.4	0.4	0.5
	4	0.9	0.4	0.4	0.5

		Employment (thousands)	*Unemployment (thousands)*	*Current account of the balance of payments in billions of pounds (annual rate)*
1987	1	104	−49	−0.4
	2	108	−47	−0.5
	3	113	−46	−0.6
	4	116	−46	−0.6
1988	1	119	−45	−0.6
	2	122	−45	−0.6
	3	124	−45	−0.7
	4	126	−45	−0.7

(b) An addition of £1 billion a year (at 1980 prices) to private consumption at given income

		Output (GDP)		Imports of goods and services	
		£ Billion at 1980 prices (annual rate)	percent	£ billion at 1980 prices (annual rate)	percent
1987	1	0.8	0.3	0.4	0.5
	2	0.9	0.4	0.4	0.5
	3	0.9	0.4	0.5	0.7
	4	0.9	0.4	0.6	0.7
1988	1	0.9	0.4	0.6	0.7
	2	0.9	0.4	0.6	0.7
	3	0.9	0.4	0.6	0.7
	4	0.9	0.4	0.6	0.7

		Employment (thousands)	Unemployment (thousands)	Current account of the balance of payments in billions of pounds (annual rate)
1987	1	11	−6	−0.6
	2	23	−11	−0.6
	3	34	−16	−0.8
	4	45	−20	−0.8
1988	1	56	−24	−0.8
	2	67	−28	−0.8
	3	77	−31	−0.8
	4	87	−34	−0.8

assumed that the exchange rate is virtually unchanged. This means that the effect on inflation is also very small.

The direct import content of public spending is relatively low and mainly for that reason the percentage addition to imports in Table 6.2(a) is little more than the percentage increase in output. However the reduction in unemployment in thousands is much less than the addition to employment. This is because many of the extra jobs would go to workers (for example part-timers) who would not otherwise have been counted in the unemployment figures. Suppose a million jobs were created in this way over a period of two years. The effect on the unemployment total would be only 360 000 (that is, less than the employment effect in the ratio 45 to 126 – see Table 6.2(a), final line).

The effects of an increase in private consumption shown in Table 6.2(b) are different in kind because it takes more time for a stimulus to output to affect employment decisions in the private sector. Suppose a million jobs were created by additional consumer spending. After two years, the effect on unemployment, as measured, would be 391 000 and the balance of payments would be worse by £9 bn at an annual rate. This is, as it happens, broadly in line with the crude arithmetic set out above.

In the National Institute *Review* for November 1986 the results of a much more complicated simulation were published. The changes incorporated in the simulation were intended to correspond broadly with the announced policy intentions of the Labour party. They included an increase in consumer spending resulting from higher social security payments as well as an increase in direct public spending on goods and services. The simulation also included a cut in employers' national insurance contributions, which helped employment without adding much to output, and some special measures to assist the long-term unemployed. (No account was taken of the proposed industrial policy, as not enough detail was available to the authors for its effects to be quantified.) After a few years the estimated effect of the package of measures on unemployment reached a million. The balance of payments cost (if the exchange rate moved in line with domestic inflation) reached about £7½ billion a year by the fifth year. This is rather less than the crude arithmetic quoted above would suggest. The special measures and the cut in NI contributions which were included in the package both raise employment without a commensurate rise in output and therefore with relatively little effect on the balance of payments.

Taking these calculations together with our assessment of the underlying balance of payments situation leads inescapably to a qualitative conclusion. Reflation on a sufficient scale to restore full employment would open up a current account deficit of substantial size. How might we deal with that situation? First we consider whether any special policy response is called for at all.

DOES THE BALANCE OF PAYMENTS MATTER?

The current account of the balance of payments is the difference between receipts and payments by UK residents in respect of sales and income transfers. It can also be defined as net borrowing or lending by residents from or to the rest of the world. It is sometimes described as a measure of the extent to which the country is 'living within its means'. As such it is a very misleading measure since it takes no account of investment in fixed assets within the domestic economy. An emotive attitude to the balance of payments can only lead to mistaken policies. It would not be imprudent for the country as a whole to borrow from abroad in order to finance investment at home, especially if the return on that investment was relatively high.

Since the abolition of exchange control there has been a continuing outflow on capital account representing the net lending by financial institutions to the rest of the world. This is one counterpart of the surpluses we have been running on current account. In the absence of policy intervention (such as that advocated by the Labour party) that outflow is likely to continue. This does not mean, however, that the country has to remain in current account surplus. The outflow from the pension funds is just one element in the complex and volatile pattern of capital account transactions. It might for example be possible to attract a larger inflow of foreign portfolio or direct capital into the United Kingdom. Failing that we might be able to borrow from the world banking system. The way the institutions allocate their funds should be considered on its merits, not as an adjunct to macroeconomic policy making.

The balance of payments is difficult to define precisely or to measure accurately and is therefore not a good index of the success or failure of economic policy. Perhaps the most important problem of definition concerns the treatment of net property income. The return on overseas assets as measured in the balance of payments figures includes interest, profits and dividends but not capital gains. Partly for tax reasons much of the gain to holders of foreign assets may be in the form of capital appreciation rather than income as defined in the statistics. The full return on overseas assets may be far in excess of the payments recorded in the balance of payments figures. A better account of external borrowing and lending can be derived from estimates of the external balance sheet published regularly by the Bank of England. This suggests a very strong external position indeed in recent years, substantially stronger than indicated by the current account as officially defined.

Problems of measurement are also very serious for the 'invisible' items in the balance of payments account. The unremitted profits earned by UK companies abroad are especially difficult to measure. Some of the better statistical sources were lost when exchange control was abolished. It is also worth emphasising that an error of measurement in visible trade flows either into or out of the country of only 5 per cent would make a difference of some £4 billion a year to the balance of payments. Moreover the presence of a large 'balancing item' in the accounts demonstrates that either the current or the capital account is not measured at all accurately. Since 1984 that 'balancing item' has averaged £5½ bn a year, implying either a substantial over-recording of the net capital outflow or else a substantial under-recording of the current account surplus. A further reason for questioning the accuracy of the figures is provided by international comparisons. By definition the current account balances of all countries should sum to zero. In fact they sum to a very large deficit. If the figures themselves are so uncertain, and so imprecise, does it really matter if the country appears to run a sizeable deficit from now on?

Public concern with the trade figures and the balance of payments still reflects the experience of the three decades following the war, rather than the circumstances of the last ten years. We still retain the habits of mind appropriate to a fixed exchange rate system, when most transactions in currency markets were related to trade and when 'speculation' was officially frowned on and limited by controls. Nowadays a balance of payments deficit only matters if foreign exchange market operators interpret it as an indicator of imminent weakness in the currency. If the market decides that a substantial deficit on current account is sustainable, then the volume of business on capital account is such that there will be no difficulty in financing it.

From the point of view of national economic policy or priorities there seems little reason to adopt any specific objective for the current account. A surplus can be regarded as one form of investment, a deficit as one form of borrowing. There is no presumption that the return on overseas assets is higher or lower than the return on domestic investment, nor indeed is there any presumption that in all circumstances investment is to be preferred to consumption at the margin. If a determined effort were made to raise output and put the labour now unemployed to productive use then a period of borrowing from overseas might be deemed not just acceptable, but indeed appropriate.

That is one side of the story; the other is not so encouraging. We may wish to qualify the current account figures in a variety of ways, throwing doubt on their definition or the way they are measured. We may say that a current account deficit is nothing to worry about in its own right, and a surplus no cause for complacency. Nevertheless there is evidence[2] that the current account (or perhaps the visible balance) is a statistic to which the foreign exchange market reacts.

The nature of foreign exchange markets has changed profoundly in recent years. It is no longer necessarily true that a deficit on current account implies an excess supply of sterling. Trading on capital account dominates trading associated with the current balance. (Speculation in futures markets has recently been added to speculation in spot and forward markets.) Exchange controls on UK residents have been abolished. We have yet to see what effect that has on the behaviour of sterling if confidence were to be really undermined. So a current account deficit presents a problem if, and only if, the market interprets it as a sign of imminent sterling weakness. Such expectations are likely to be self-fulfilling.

An exchange rate fall does not of itself necessarily constitute a crisis or a defeat for a policy of demand expansion. It may indeed be the necessary means of correcting the balance of payments deficit that provoked it. While it is happening it can no doubt be a source of some anxiety to policy makers, lest it get out of hand and precipitate a political rather than an economic crisis. It may also go too far for the good of the economy and risk setting off an inflationary spiral. We turn next therefore to the consequences of exchange depreciation, for good as well as for ill. After that we shall consider whether the scale and timing of exchange-rate changes can in practice be handled effectively by the monetary authorities, without having to put into reverse the expansionary policies which are necessary to reduce unemployment.

THE CONSEQUENCES OF EXCHANGE RATE DEPRECIATION

An exchange rate is the relative price of two currencies. It is often convenient to use an index of the value of sterling relative to the currencies of the major competitors of the United Kingdom. This is called an 'effective' exchange rate index. But changes in this index must be interpreted in the light of relative inflation rates, since what matters to traders is the relative price of goods produced at home and abroad measured in terms of the same currency. Several different measures of competitiveness or of the 'real' exchange rate are available. If a depreciation of sterling is to have any effect on trade flows it must change these competitiveness indices; in other words it must not be offset by a proportionate rise in domestic prices. Provided competitiveness does improve the volume of exports should rise and the volume of imports should fall at any given level of economic activity and employment in the domestic economy.

The immediate direct effect of depreciation is to *worsen* the current account, because it makes imports more expensive in sterling terms. Provided, however, that the volumes of imports and exports respond sufficiently to the improvement of competitiveness the net effect on the current balance will become favourable in due course. This pattern of response (first adverse, then favourable) is commonly called the J-curve (from the shape of that letter).

Table 6.3 shows some further estimates or simulations using the National Institute's macroeconomic model. The story is quite a complicated one, but it is important to understand the value and limitations of depreciation as a means of correcting an external payments imbalance. The first part of the table shows the effects over a five-year period of a 10 per cent depreciation. The effect on the price level builds up over this period to 7 per cent, so by the end of five years only one third of the initial gain in relative price competitiveness remains. If therefore the estimates were to be continued for another period of, say, five years the benefits to output and to the balance of payments would be very gradually reversed.

As it is, the effects on output are quite large, and the effects on unemployment, which come rather later, become substantial after about three years. The higher level of activity results in a higher level of imports, so the benefit to the balance of payments is delayed. It only *begins* after three years in this simulation. No doubt these calculations of economic effects that take several years to manifest themselves are highly uncertain. Nevertheless the qualitative results of these calculations seem reasonably robust. If depreciation is to have a *quick* effect on the current balance it must be accompanied by *deflationary* action to save imports, not by any stimulus to domestic demand.

This conclusion can only be reinforced by examination of Table 6.3(b). Here the exchange rate is assumed to be devalued by 10 per cent *in real terms*. In other words it continues to fall (after the initial 10 per cent drop) sufficiently to maintain relative price competitiveness. This means that inflation tends to spiral upwards and after five years the estimates show the price level up by about 17 per cent. (In other words inflation on average over that period is more than 3 per cent a year higher than it otherwise would have been.)

The addition to exports and hence to output is now much larger and the effect on unemployment is very large by the fourth or fifth

Table 6.3 Estimated economic effects of depreciation

	Output (GDP) per cent	Level of consumer prices per cent	Unemployment (thousands)	Balance of payments on current account* in billions of pounds (annual rate)
(a) A 10 per cent reduction in the exchange rate from the first quarter of 1987 with no change thereafter.				
First quarter of: 1987	0.5	0.0	−15	−£2.7
1988	1.3	3.1	−101	−£0.4
1989	1.1	5.3	−179	−£0.1
1990	1.1	6.3	−237	−£0.1
1991	0.9	6.7	−276	+£1.2
1992	0.7	7.0	−301	+£2.5
(b) A 10 per cent reduction in the exchange rate from the first quarter of 1987 with sufficient further depreciation to offset the effect of inflation on competitiveness.				
First quarter of: 1987	0.6	0.0	−20	−£2.8
1988	1.9	3.5	−147	−£2.3
1989	2.3	7.6	−300	−£1.3
1990	2.6	11.2	−459	−£2.5
1991	2.8	14.2	−617	+£0.1
1992	2.9	16.9	−770	+£3.0

*includes an 'off-model' adjustment to the balance on interest, profit and dividends.

year. The changes shown here *on their own* would be enough to restore full employment according to some definitions of that concept. For that very reason the initial additions to the balance of payments deficit are large and the turn-round on external account is even longer in coming than it was in Table 6.3(a).

These estimates are based on the Institute's macroeconomic model, which represents, we believe, the present state of knowledge in so far as it can be incorporated in estimated statistical relationships. Before leaving the question of the effects of exchange rates on the economy it is nevertheless worth mentioning some considerations which the model may not fully take into account.

It has been said that the appreciation of the exchange rate around 1979 resulted in damage to UK industry that was irreversible. The Institute model, like all others of its kind, assumes a kind of symmetry of response so that the effects of an appreciation are just like those of a depreciation with the signs reversed. In all such models after an exchange rate has gone up and down again the initial state of the economy will eventually be restored. The real world may be less resilient. It is easy to believe that a sharp appreciation of the exchange rate could lead (as indeed it did in 1979) to a sharp fall in output and large-scale job losses. It is rather less easy to believe that a sharp depreciation could put the whole process into reverse. The model simulations are undoubtedly the right starting-point for considering the response of the economy to a depreciation, but some caution in interpreting them seems essential. This is one reason for guessing that the size of the additions to output and employment may be rather smaller than the model suggests and that the benefits to the balance of payments may be even slower to arrive.

There is another question worth raising about the effects of depreciation. To what extent does the size and speed of the response to changes in competitiveness depend on expectations as to the durability of the change? In recent years applied macroeconomists have been much concerned with the way in which expectations influence the behaviour of firms (and, to a lesser extent, households), but this refinement is not often introduced into the discussion of trade flows. Further work is needed to investigate the practical importance of the issue, but the point is valid at least in theory. The response of both purchasers and producers to an improvement in the competitiveness of British industry will be greater and swifter if there is a reasonable assurance that the improvement will not be undermined either by a renewed appreciation of sterling or by domestic cost inflation.

If the estimates in Table 6.3 are even broadly correct the depreciation route is not an easy one to take. In particular the estimates suggest that something ought to be done to secure the initial gain in competitiveness without setting off a wage–price inflationary spiral. In the next section we consider what measures might be taken in combination with exchange depreciation to offset its adverse effects and to neutralise the effect on inflation.

THE THREAT OF INFLATION

Some economists would say that the idea of a balance-of-payments constraint on growth is misconceived. The real constraint, they would say, is fear of the inflationary consequences of exchange rate depreciation. Put this way the issue is largely semantic. Nevertheless it is worth being precise about the nature of the threat of inflation that is being considered here. It is *not* being argued that the process of demand expansion is necessarily inflationary in its own right, for example because it involves raising the growth rate of the money supply. It is *not* being accepted that the current level of unemployment is the 'natural' rate somehow defined, or that a lower level of unemployment would inevitably result in accelerating inflation. It *is* accepted that a fall in the exchange rate would have an immediate and direct effect on import prices and hence the price of many consumer goods. That in turn would lead to higher wage settlements, and the inflationary spiral would be under way.

One response to this difficulty is to recommend that the required improvement in competitiveness come about not through depreciation of the exchange rate but through a reduction in wages. A more 'realistic' proposal would be that wage increases should be lower than those of our competitors. In principle this may be an attractive idea, but one must question its speed of operation. Suppose wage settlements in this country were to be brought down every year to 1 per cent below that of our competitors (Japan, Germany and so on). That would be no mean achievement. Even so it would take ten years to achieve the competitiveness gain that would come literally overnight from a 10 per cent depreciation of sterling.

Moreover the 'wage cutting' solution does not escape the need for an exchange rate policy. If wages were held down in the way described it is more than likely that the exchange rate would appreciate, thus negating the whole of the immediate purpose of the sacrifice by wage earners.

Another response open to the government would be to offset the effects of depreciation on the price level by cuts in some form of taxation or explicit subsidies on expenditure. That would mean that wages need never rise above the level they would have been at had the depreciation not occurred. In other words the inflationary spiral could be stopped before it ever got under way.

The *direct* effect of a 10 per cent depreciation on the price level (that is, with wages unchanged) is probably about 3 per cent.[3] The response would take some time to come through, for example because increases in the price of raw materials would take some time to affect the cost of goods in the shops. The current price value of consumer spending is now about £250 billion a year, so that the tax or subsidy cost of reducing its price by 3 per cent would be about £7½ billion a year.

It is doubtful whether one would ever want to superimpose such a large injection of public funds on top of a 10 per cent depreciation. As Table 6.3 shows, depreciation itself is a powerful expansionary force. It is very likely therefore that any revenue lost by cutting expenditure taxes would have to be made good by raising other taxes or by cutting public spending. Taxes on spending[4] are being cut *not* to stimulate demand but to prevent wages rising in response to the rise in import prices. If that means that domestic demand rises too much, then the purely 'demand management' component of the package might be contractionary. This would be a matter for judgement at the time the package was introduced.

No mention has been made so far of incomes policy. This is deliberate since the success of an expansionary policy does not depend crucially on the political feasibility of 'wage restraint'. Nevertheless it is easy to see that incomes policy would be a very valuable addition to the range of policies available in the circumstances described.

If wages could be prevented from responding to the rise in import prices by some kind of administrative action or 'deal', then there would be no need to cut taxes on expenditure. That in turn would mean there was no need for the other tax increases or public spending cuts which would otherwise have to be enacted to finance the element of 'price subsidy' in the package. So wage restraint might be said in these circumstances to 'buy' a higher level of public spending as well as a higher level of employment.

It may be said that the strategy described, especially in the absence of incomes policy, is a complex and tortuous one. But that in itself is not a criticism. If there were neat and simple solutions to such public policy problems there would be no need for economics. If there were obvious and painless solutions they would have been adopted already. The task of policy makers is to unravel the complexities as well as they can and to distribute the costs of restoring full employment as equitably as possible amongst the rest of the community.

We turn next to a different threat and a different source of complications. So far the exchange rate has been treated as if it were an instrument of policy under the control of government. But the truth is far otherwise. An attempt to secure a modest real depreciation may result in no depreciation at all or an exchange crisis that gets quite out of hand. This is the subject of the next section.

THE EXCHANGE RATE AS A POLICY INSTRUMENT

Can the exchange rate realistically be treated as an instrument of policy? Is it not rather the product of market forces on which the authorities have only limited effect? Failure to control the exchange rate has been the downfall of many, perhaps most, attempts (in this country and others) to secure employment growth by expanding domestic demand. The control problems are of two kinds: first, the fall in the rate has to be brought about without creating market conditions, or political reaction, that forces a reversal of the policy; second, the rate has to be sustained for a period, possibly stretching over many years when the balance of payments actually gets worse (as a result of the J-curve described above). Neither will be possible unless the markets regard the whole strategy as 'credible' and 'responsible'.

The sterling crisis of 1976 demonstrated the consequences of a general loss of confidence by the market. Although interest rates were raised progressively from under 9 per cent to over 15 per cent, sterling remained persistently weak. Although some fall in the exchange rate was required at that time, the authorities were unable to keep control of the markets and did not give a clear signal as to their intentions for the exchange rate. As a result the persistent weakness of sterling, coupled with political pressure, forced a change of domestic economic policy and recourse to the IMF for a loan. On this occasion therefore the consequence of a loss of market confidence was *both* a fall in the exchange rate *and* a 'stabilisation' package. The alternative of allowing the currency to find its own level while persisting with expansionary policies was not pursued. The memory of this episode has had a profound influence on discussion of policy options in this country ever since.

A more recent episode in France in 1981 seems to confirm the difficulties of economic expansion in a relatively small open economy.[5] When the Mitterrand government was first elected its top priority was the reduction of unemployment. The expansionary policies introduced were in fact quite modest in scale, their overall impact on output being estimated at between 1 and 2 per cent of GDP. Nevertheless the current account deteriorated and the franc came under strong pressure. The response was a fiscal contraction and a shift to a quite different economic strategy.

The case of the United States is clearly quite different. There the current balance moved into deficit in 1982 thanks partly to a strong expansion of domestic demand, reinforced by tax cuts. Nevertheless the dollar was extraordinarily strong. Initially this strength was the result of tight monetary policy and high interest rates, but most observers saw some additional element of self-fulfilling speculation which drove the rate well above any level that could be justified by the 'fundamentals'. In 1986 the reaction set in and the dollar fell very sharply. This in turn will ultimately tend to correct the current account deficit but the process will be very long-drawn-out.

The recent history of America demonstrates the power of the capital account to swamp current account transactions. Nevertheless it would be unwise to draw a close parallel between market reaction to the policies of President Reagan and its likely reaction to fiscal expansion in this country. The US monetary authorities are better able than our own to dictate the movement of capital by adjusting relative interest rates. Moreover essential ingredients of the US situation were low inflation, monetarist rhetoric and a booming stock market. The sheer size of the US economy, the wide and deep market for dollar assets and the absence of alternative currencies to hold may all have been important as well. It is not an example we can follow at all closely in this country.

Market participants are not in general professional economists. Although they may have professional economists as advisers they may not attach great weight to the advice they are given. To convince the market that a strategy is 'credible' and 'responsible' it is not enough to win the support of economists, it is also necessary to win the support of a rather tightly-knit community of bankers, businessmen, officials and financial journalists – but especially bankers. Within this community it cannot be said that British governments (of any political party) enjoy a high reputation for consistency, responsibility or even credibility in matters of financial policy. A policy of expansion and controlled depreciation would have a much better chance of success if it were in some way endorsed or even 'underwritten' by some weighty international body as well as by the British government.

Two options of this kind might be worth exploring. One would be to work with the IMF. A strategy of the kind described would not necessarily be anathema to the officials of that organisation, but they would undoubtedly have some hesitation in giving it support. The time to secure their support would be before any expansionary measures at all were taken. They would then be involved in the design of the policy and would undoubtedly be very cautious about the speed with which a return to full

employment by this route was attempted. The second, and perhaps more natural, approach would be to join the exchange rate mechanism of the European Monetary System. Here, too, the extent of depreciation, and the measures that accompany it, would be a matter for bargaining. The UK position in such a bargain would be somewhat strengthened by the manifest wish of some European states that Britain should participate in the system and that progress be made towards the elusive goal of closer monetary co-operation. The choice between an EMS or an IMF solution to the difficulty of market management involves wider political questions besides those of economic policy. There would certainly be an interaction with issues of trade and industry policy discussed below.

From what has been said it is clear that the exchange rate should ***not*** be thought of as a policy instrument under the control of government. It would be wrong therefore to characterise the approach advocated in this chapter as a depreciation strategy. Depreciation is not in the gift of government. What is proposed is rather a strategy of expansion and economic development. If, as seems likely, its consequences include the opening up of a deficit on the balance of payments, the exchange rate may well come under pressure in the markets. Should that happen it would be wrong to reverse the strategy, as has so often happened in the past. The exchange rate should be allowed to fall, by at least as much as the market expects, but it should then be defended vigorously, and in co-operation with other monetary authorities, at the new rate.

DEVELOPMENT POLICIES

Undoubtedly the most satisfactory way of eliminating anxiety about the balance of payments and of restoring full employment would be to raise the productivity and improve the international competitiveness of British industry. Indeed these would be very worthy objectives whether the balance of payments is proving troublesome or not. It may be helpful therefore to distinguish between two groups of policy measures which might be recommended in the current situation. The first group consists of measures which are justified 'on their own merits', that is to say they are worthwhile irrespective of the balance-of-payments situation. The measures in the second group are by contrast definitely 'second best'. They would not be worth taking if the balance of payments were in healthy surplus, but they could not be dismissed if the balance of payments were in serious deficit.

This is not the place to elaborate all possible measures that fall into the first category. My own list would include the following:

1. encouraging capital inflow, especially when this involves foreign management, to demonstrate how productivity can be raised to international standards;
2. getting government to support industrial training and establishing differentials that reflect the relative scarcity of skilled and unskilled labour;
3. cutting labour costs by means of a reduction in the national insurance contributions of employers, recouping the lost revenue by increasing either employees' contributions or corporation tax.

Any of these proposals might improve the outlook for the balance of payments in the long term, but the extent of the improvement is difficult (or even impossible) to quantify. While it is possible that these measures will be adopted, it would be unreasonable to assume that an incipient balance-of-payments problem will necessarily be solved in this way. We must also consider other proposals that fall into the second category, that is proposals which have less intrinsic merit but which might act more directly and reliably to release a constraint on growth posed by the balance of payments.

Traditionally the policy instruments considered in these circumstances are tariffs or quantitative import controls. Such measures, however, have not in fact been used in this country in response to any of the recurrent balance of payments troubles since the Second World War. On the contrary, the level of protection against imports has been progressively reduced as a result of international negotiation through GATT or in the context of joining the EEC. This country, with others, has benefited from this multilateral trade liberalisation and the consequent expansion of our exports. In the late 1980s tariffs and general import controls can be rejected as impractical on political, as much as on economic grounds. This follows from our membership of the EEC. An expansionary policy would be sustainable only if it enjoyed some international support. An explicit use of protection would seem certain to alienate just that body of opinion on which we would be most dependent.

This does not mean that we cannot have a policy for development in which the balance of payments is given priority over domestic real income or consumption growth. The establishment and maintenance of a competitive real exchange rate would be the most important element in such a strategy. There may, however, be a need for other policy intervention as well, which would be designed to assist the beneficial effects of exchange rate depreciation – not as a substitute for it. In effect we would be intervening to speed up the response of producers and consumers to the better competitive position of British goods and services. That would be helpful since one of the main problems which we have identified with depreciation is the delay in trade response, and the resulting 'J-curve'.

Some of the measures one might recommend in this context would be specifically linked to meeting the costs of adjustment. For example, help might be given to firms undertaking the investment necessary to profit from the competitive advantage, whether it was in new equipment, marketing networks or vocational training. Such assistance would be temporary of its very nature. It would not include a continuing subsidy to production.

Official assistance with the adjustment process might not be limited to the provision of finance, whether grants or loans. One reason for delay in adjusting to a new competitive advantage is simply the slow dissemination of information. The framework could be provided by the existing National Economic Development Office and its Economic Development Committees. One cannot say what quantitative effect a better co-ordination of plans by different firms and industries might have. It is nevertheless widely believed that similar exercises in France and in Japan do improve the overall performance of those economies. If the strategy adopted by the government was one of more rapid industrial development and employment creation, then each firm would need to reassess its own strategy in response. Some exchange of information could benefit all, provided that the exchange of information between firms was really mutual.

So far as public purchasing is concerned the arguments are very similar. A permanent preference for domestic production is just a special case of protection, and no more attractive than any other. But, in the course of adjustment to a better competitive performance by British industry, it might be helpful if the public sector were to take immediate action to switch to domestic suppliers wherever the long-term advantage pointed to a move of this kind. Again it is a matter of acting more quickly than one otherwise would, rather than doing something totally different.

CONCLUSIONS

Policies that would restore full employment in Britain have to surmount the hurdle of external balance. Some would argue that, in a strict sense, the constraint is not the balance of payments as such, but the difficulty of achieving balance-of-payments adjustment in an economy prone to inflation or to excessive growth of real wages. The issue seems to be largely semantic and need not detain us. However defined, the risk of running into a constraint associated with balance-of-payments adjustment seems a real one. The substantive issue behind the semantic one is the appropriate policy mix to secure full employment.

Fiscal policy is under the immediate control of government. It should be made expansionary so as to set the economy on a path back towards full employment.[6] If, as seems likely, the balance of payments moves into deficit, that should not be accepted as a constraint. The answer should be a controlled depreciation.

It is argued here that the exchange rate, left to itself, may either fail to fall enough, or fall too far. Market confidence in the strategy as a whole must be secured at the outset, and maintained. Britain on its own would find this difficult to achieve. International support might be obtained from the IMF, or from fellow-members of the EMS.

Having secured a controlled depreciation, the difficulties are not over. Wages and prices must not rise so as to nullify the real value of that exchange rate fall. Whilst incomes policies are certainly an attractive route to achieving wage moderation, it has been argued that they are not the only one open. The alternatives could involve cutting those taxes that affect wage costs or inflation. Thus the loss of real incomes which depreciation entails would be borne, not by wage earners or employers, but by the exchequer. If the loss of revenue could not be financed by borrowing, other taxes would have to be raised or spending cut instead.

Provided a strategy of this kind can be followed, there is no reason why the balance of payments should constrain output or employment. There is no need to have recourse to trade restrictions or any other special policies which are protectionist in intention. Industrial policies and other structural interventions can be considered on their merits, not ranked according to their 'side-effects' on the current account. In practice explicitly protectionist measures would mean forfeiting the international support for expansion which has been argued to be essential for its success.

It has been argued that an explicitly development-orientated strategy should be adopted with full employment and balance of payments equilibrium as its objectives. It is in this context that a limited and controlled depreciation is most likely to be accepted by international political opinion as well as the markets. There would be a role for industrial policy in bringing forward the response of the economy to a better competitive position.

In real-world economics, as opposed to the theoretical world of the textbooks, policy analysis is never simple. Policy recommendations have sometimes to be quite complicated, and their effects on the economy cannot be predicted with certainty. Nevertheless it is clear that a strategy of development and expansion offers more hope of a return to full employment than does the very cautious approach followed in the last few years.

Notes

1. Andrew Britton is Director of the National Institute of Economic and Social Research and was a Trustee of the Employment Institute from 1985 to 1987. This text was first published in April 1987.
2. See for example Wren-Lewis, S., 'Introducing Exchange-Rate Equations into a World Econometric Model', *National Institute Economic Review*, February 1987, and Currie D. and S. Hall, 'The Exchange Rate and the Balance of Payments', *National Institute Economic Review*, February, 1986.
3. The reform of the retail prices index in 1987 raised its import content and the effect on it of the exchange rate because of the inclusion of the cost of foreign holidays.
4. An attractive alternative would be to cut employers' national insurance contributions. For a fuller account of the advantages of this option see 'Can Fiscal Policy Cut Unemployment?' *National Institute Economic Review*, February 1986.
5. See Barker, K., A. Britton and R. Major, 'Macroeconomic Policy in France and Britain, *National Institute Economic Review*, November 1984.
6. It is *not* being argued that fiscal expansion on its own will achieve full employment. There is a very important role also for supply-side measures and special employment measures, but these are outside the scope of this chapter.

7 The Plain Man's Guide to Fiscal and Financial Policy

Charles R. Bean and Willem H. Buiter[1]

1 THE PUBLIC SECTOR: SHIBBOLETHS AND STATISTICS

One of the most remarkable features of economic policy making in the United Kingdom over the last seven years has been the extent to which the size of the public sector and of the government's borrowing requirement has taken centre stage. In so far as targets for public sector borrowing over the next few years have forced the ministers responsible for public spending to acknowledge the revenue implications of their decisions this is a development to be welcomed. Under the British system public expenditure decisions have tended to be taken independently of taxation decisions made at Budget time.

Now there is a much greater awareness amongst politicians that expenditure and taxation are two sides of the same coin. Nevertheless the pursuit of sensible, yet sound fiscal policies has been hindered by the focussing of political and media attention on just one or two indicators and the attribution to them of almost mystical significance.

Before discussing possible rules for fiscal policy, we have to ask some basic questions. First, just how big is the public sector? This is not an easy issue. The central problem is to decide how to treat bodies like the nationalised industries. The answer is bound to depend on the focus of interest. Much of the current debate, for example, centres on the extent to which the public sector absorbs resources from the private sector and/or inhibits investment. If nationalised industries act just like private companies (hiring and firing, undertaking new investment, and raising funds from the capital markets on the basis of profitability) there need be no serious worries about misallocation. This provides a good case for excluding them from the public sector.

After all, if the issue is whether current spending will 'crowd out' investment, it is of little concern whether the investment is private or public if investment projects in both sectors have to be equally profitable at the margin. By contrast, if nationalised industries do not behave in the same way as private companies and are instead run in the interests of particular groups (perhaps the workforce), there are good reasons for keeping them in our consideration of the public sector. Ultimately the appropriate definition must depend on the final use made of the statistics.

The second major question, having decided on the appropriate borders to the public sector, is to select a specific definition of expenditure. There are three conceptually different forms of public spending:

1. expenditure on goods and services from which society benefits now, such as refuse collection (current expenditure);
2. expenditure on goods which yield benefits in the future, such as building dams or motorways (capital expenditure);
3. monetary payments to private individuals, such as pensions and unemployment benefit (transfers).

Unfortunately the dividing line between these categories is not always clear. For instance, expenditure on education (other than actually building schools) is usually classed as current expenditure within the national accounts. Yet it has a very significant investment element. Indeed a major objective of education is to raise the productivity of the future workforce. Equally, as expenditure on health care improves the quality of the workforce and raises productivity by reducing working days lost through illness, it also contains a significant investment element.

We can now begin to look at magnitudes. Table 7.1 displays the share in total domestic output of each of these components of general government spending (that is, *excluding* nationalised industries) over the last fifteen years. Some sub-categories, like current spending on health and education, are also shown. The great and growing importance of transfer payments is immediately apparent, having risen more than seven percentage points since the beginning of the 1970s This is owing to improved pension provision, increased unemployment and increased interest payments on government debt. These last two items are only partly under the control of the government in the short run. Also apparent is the decline in capital spending. By

Table 7.1 UK general government expenditure (as percentage GDP)

	1970	*1975*	*1980*	*1985*
Spending on current goods and	19.9	24.1	24.6	24.0
services of which: Health	4.1	5.1	5.6	5.5
Education	3.9	5.5	4.9	4.4
Spending on capital goods[1]	5.5	5.2	3.3	3.0
Grants and transfers[2]	18.2	20.5	23.1	25.4
of which: Debt interest	4.5	4.3	5.5	5.7
Total spending	43.5	49.9	51.0	52.4

[1]Gross domestic fixed capital formation *plus* increase in stocks. The figures exclude sales of government assets.
[2]Excludes lending activities and sales of government assets.

Source: Central Statistical Office, *National Income and Expenditure Blue Book*.

contrast the share of current spending has remained roughly constant in the last decade. The disparate movements in current and capital spending are even more marked if spending on education is treated as investment.

Discussion about the size of the public sector often focusses on something like the figure for 'total spending' that appears in the bottom line, but it is not clear that this is necessarily the most meaningful measure. One of the most important issues to be addressed is the extent to which the public sector directly determines what is spent and hence itself absorbs *real* resources. Only the first two categories, of spending on current goods and services and spending on capital goods – together termed *exhaustive spending* – contribute to this. By contrast, transfer payments merely redistribute purchasing power *between* different members of society. It could of course be argued that the 'bottom line' total spending figure accurately reflects the government's need to raise revenue through taxation or borrowing, and therefore does capture some notion of the scale of the public sector. Even this is misleading, however, because there are further problems of classification. Should those transfer payments which are subsidies for specific types of expenditure or production be treated as expenditure or should they really be a negative tax? At the moment the public sector accounts are inconsistent. Some subsidies are treated as expenditure whilst others, such as mortgage interest relief, are hidden as an offset to revenue.

Table 7.2 UK general government revenue (as percentage of GDP)

	1970	*1975*	*1980*	*1985*
Income taxes[1]	22.2	24.6	22.5	24.7
Expenditure taxes	18.6	14.6	18.3	18.5
Other	5.4	4.7	4.7	4.6
Total taxes	46.2	43.9	45.5	47.8
of which: North Sea Oil taxes	0	0	1.9	3.7

[1]Includes social security contributions.

Source: Central Statistical Office, *National Income and Expenditure Blue Book*.

This brings us naturally to the revenue side of the public sector accounts. Table 7.2 shows how the share of tax revenues in total output is broken down into its major components. It is notable how little the share of income taxes has changed over the last decade, despite the Conservative Government's objective of lowering the income tax burden (even the 1p and 2p reductions in the 1986 and 1987 Budgets take the ratio only back to 1970s levels). A simple, aggregate figure does, of course, conceal quite disparate movements of the average and marginal tax rates on individuals in different tax brackets. The growing importance to the exchequer of North Sea oil revenues is also apparent, although the total yield from this source is still small compared to that from income and expenditure taxes.

The inherent difficulty of defining exactly what in the way of taxes and transfers constitutes expenditure and what constitutes revenue suggests that it is most fruitful not to focus on either 'total spending' or 'total taxes', but rather on the government's spending on currently produced goods and services, that is, exhaustive spending, and total taxes less grants and transfers, that is, *net* taxes. This is not to deny that the detailed structure of the tax and transfer programme will have important allocative and distributional effects. But it does concentrate attention on the major preoccupation of this study, namely the effects of government spending and their mode of finance on demand. For, once the government's exhaustive spending programme has been agreed upon, important policy choices still remain. Exhaustive spending can be financed by borrowing and by 'printing money' as well as by taxation.

Table 7.3 Financing and the deficit

	1970	*1975*	*1980*	*1981*	*1982*	*1983*	*1984*	*1985*
Public Sector Financial Deficit (as % of GDP)	−1.5	8.0	5.4	3.8	3.2	4.3	4.7	3.2
Public Sector Borrowing Requirement (as % of GDP)	0.0	10.7	5.9	4.9	2.1	4.5	3.7	2.5
Net borrowing[1] (as % of PSFD)	115.4	90.0	102.1	68.0	73.9	82.4	68.7	90.5
Money creation (as % of PSFD)	−33.9	8.9	3.4	8.2	6.3	7.3	4.7	4.4
Exchange reserves (as % of PSFD)	18.4	8.6	−2.7	29.6	19.3	5.4	6.9	−18.1
Sales of assets (as % of PSFD)	0.1	−7.5	−2.8	−5.8	0.5	4.9	19.7	23.2

[1]Includes accruals adjustments and balancing items.

Source: Central Statistical Office, *National Income and Expenditure Blue Book*.

Table 7.3 provides a breakdown of how the Public Sector Financial Deficit (PSFD) has recently been financed. Because these figures relate to the total public sector and not just general government (that is, they include the nationalised industries and other public corporations) the PSFD is not quite the difference between the series for total spending and total taxes in the two previous tables.

The public sector's deficit can be financed in essentially four ways: (i) borrowing from the public; (ii) printing money; (iii) running down the exchange reserves; and (iv) selling off public sector assets. The last item might cause some surprise. Proceeds from the privatisation of British Telecom, British Gas and the like and the sale of council houses are viewed as a way of *financing* a given deficit, not as a negative expenditure. Such sales merely represent a transfer of ownership of the assets involved, and do not represent any change in the government's command over currently produced goods and services. The fact that the conventional Public Sector Borrowing Requirement (PSBR) figures place them 'above the line' is just one of its more obvious deficiencies as a fiscal indicator.

Table 7.3 reveals that even in 1975 when the inflation rate exceeded 25 per cent the contribution of monetary growth was really

Figure 7.1 **UK national debt–GDP ratio 1801–1983**

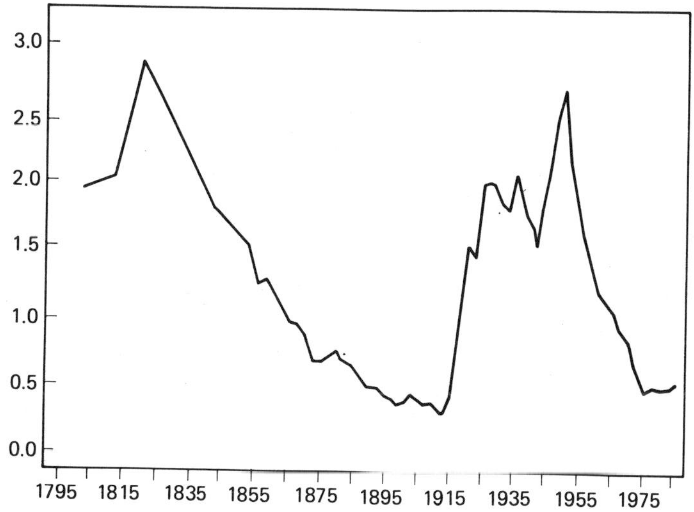

Sources: National debt: Mitchell B.R. and P. Deane, 1962 *Abstract of British Historical Statistics*, Cambridge University Press; Mitchell B.R. and H.G. Jones (1971) *Second Abstract of British Historical Statistics*, Cambridge University Press; *Annual Abstract of Statistics and Financial Statistics*, various issues. GDP: 1801–51: Mitchell and Deane (1962) p. 366. 1855–83: Mitchell and Dean (1962) p. 367 and *Economic Trends*, various issues.

very small (the revenue from this source amounted to less than ¾ per cent of output). This is tiny compared to the 44 per cent share of conventional taxes.

A central tenet of conservative economic thinking is that public sector deficits are intrinsically harmful and inevitably lead to trouble – however they are financed. If they are financed by money creation, they are thought to lead to more inflation now. If they are financed by borrowing, they are supposed to raise interest rates and crowd out private investment. Prolonged deficits will lead to a vicious circle of increased interest payments and a growing debt burden. Ultimately this has to be met by increased monetary growth and hence inflation again – or there has to be a severe fiscal contraction.

How much truth there is in these views will form the substance of Section 6, but by way of background Figure 7.1 plots the ratio of the UK national debt to output since the Napoleonic war. Not surprisingly this rises most dramatically during wars, falling back during

***Figure* 7.2 Historical public debt–GDP ratios for five major OECD countries (%)**

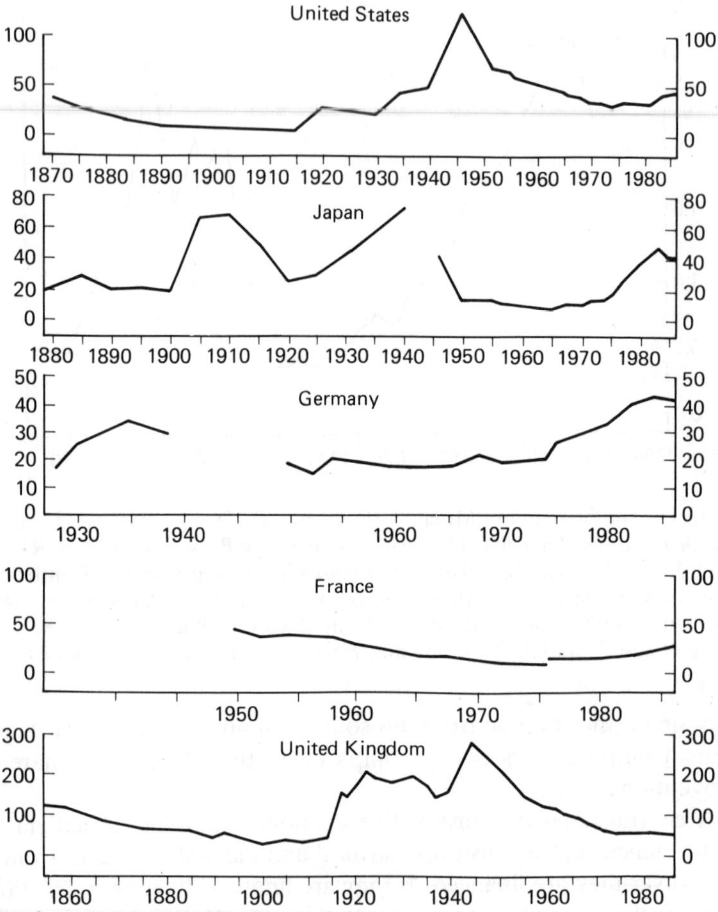

Source: OECD *Economic Outlook*, 37, June 1985, p. 7

peace time. However it is currently at almost its lowest level ever, suggesting that concern about an excessive debt burden is somewhat misplaced. Figure 7.2 presents some comparable figures for other countries (with debt expressed as a percentage rather than a ratio of GDP). It shows that the UK's debt–output ratio is also not excessive by international standards.

With these figures as background, let us turn to a detailed examination of the role of government spending and the design of financial policy. The next section looks at the effects of balanced budget changes in government exhaustive spending, that is, changes in spending that are paid for by changes in current taxes, while Section 3 examines the implications of money or debt-financing of a change in spending. Section 4 presents some numerical calculations that illustrate the arguments in the two previous sections. Section 5 briefly discusses measures of fiscal stance. Section 6 considers the connection between government deficits and inflation that has occupied such a central role in recent debates and elaborates the requirements for government solvency. Section 7 draws the preceding strands together by discussing when governments should (and should not) run deficits. Finally, Section 8 restates a few of the main conclusions.

2 INCREASING TAXES TO PAY FOR GOVERNMENT SPENDING

It is impossible to divorce a discussion of the effects of government spending *per se* from a consideration of how it is to be financed. A change in spending matched by an offsetting change in revenue will generally have different effects on the economy from an equivalent change in spending financed by borrowing.

First of all we shall look at changes in spending that are tax-financed, postponing for the time being the intertemporal issues raised by debt-finance. It is most important to realise that changes in spending that are accompanied by changes in taxes which leave the budget deficit unchanged will nevertheless affect the level and composition of output, independently of any effects they may have on the supply side of the economy through incentives.

The classic example of this is the so-called 'balanced budget multiplier'. Suppose that government spending on domestically produced goods is increased by £100m. Then the incomes of workers and the profits of the firms who produce those goods will also rise by £100m. If the government were now to increase taxes on those same workers and firms by £100m, the government budget would be unchanged. But aggregate demand would, at the existing level of interest rates and prices, be exactly £100m higher. Of course, the government would probably raise taxes in general rather than just on the firms and workers who supply the goods to the government. Nevertheless the general principle still stands: an increase in government spending that is matched by an increase in taxes will usually have an effect on aggregate demand even though the budget deficit is unchanged.

Effects on Demand

Clearly, in the first instance, a tax-financed increase in government spending will generally increase aggregate demand in the economy. However it is also likely to affect private spending decisions. These effects can either be direct or can work indirectly through changes in interest rates, the exchange rates or prices induced by the extra spending or its financing.

The direct effects on private spending are fairly straightforward to describe although varied in impact. Most goods provided by the government are, to a greater or lesser extent, substitutes for private expenditure. Thus public spending on health and education will, more or less directly, displace private spending on the same. Other publicly provided goods and services, however, have what is referred to as a 'public good' aspect. Such goods and services serve many members of society simultaneously. Examples are the police and the armed forces. It is quite possible that a reduction in expenditure on the police could lead to a considerably greater increase in private expenditure on security firms and the like. Still other forms of public expenditure, for instance on maintaining the national parks, may increase private expenditure, for example on hiking boots.

Thus public spending interacts with private spending decisions in a complicated manner. The most pronounced effect of this direct link between public and private spending, however, is likely to be on the *composition* of demand rather than its overall total, although this is not invariably the case, and public spending may have a *direct crowding out* (or crowding in) effect on private spending.

As a general rule the *net* effect of a public spending increase will be to boost aggregate demand if we assume that there are no induced changes in interest rates, the exchange rates or prices. Whether demand will *in fact* be increased once induced changes in interest rates and the exchange rate (the effect on prices is discussed later) are allowed for will depend on several factors:

1. the monetary policy pursued by the authorities;

2. how the public's holdings of money responds to changes in interest rates;
3. how easily financial capital can flow between countries;
4. the exchange rate regime in force.

As Britain has – pending any entry into the European Monetary System – a more-or-less cleanly floating exchange rate and financial capital is free to move into and out of the country we assume that these remain in force during the following analysis. But on monetary policy we need to consider two polar cases. First let us assume that the original path of the money stock is maintained when spending is increased (so that interest rates are allowed to vary). In the second case we assume that short-term nominal interest rates are kept constant (and the Bank of England meets the resulting demand for cash and reserves by the banks and private individuals).

How do we assess the impact of these different policy reactions on behaviour? What we are after is the degree of *financial crowding out* that characterises the economy and so offsets the impact effect on demand of the increase in spending. This in turn depends on how sensitive the demand for money balances is to changes in interest rates. If the demand for money is totally insensitive to interest rates (the assumption of 'constant velocity' implicit in classical monetarism) there will be complete financial crowding out. Interest rates will simply be bid up as the higher *ex ante* demand for goods and services chases a constant money stock. Eventually they will have to rise by enough to choke off completely the incipient boost to demand. If, instead, money demand is slightly sensitive to interest rates there will be some crowding out, but it will be less than 100 per cent. However, if the public's holding of money is very responsive to interest rates, interest rates need hardly rise at all and there is no crowding out of interest-sensitive private spending.

Note however that all this financial crowding out of demand is a *policy choice*. The authorities could choose to peg the interest rate and supply the additional demand for cash and reserves at the higher level of activity. This would prevent any financial crowding out occurring.

If the Bank of England does accept some crowding out, which component(s) of demand are affected? The increase in taxes paying for the higher spending will reduce private incomes and hence also the amount of planned private saving. What will be crowded out are the interest-sensitive components of demand, such as housing, other fixed investment and inventory accumulation. Nevertheless, to the extent that the increase in government spending falls on capital rather than consumption goods, *total* investment in the economy can still be increased.

There is, however, considerable evidence that excess capacity strongly discourages private investment. An increase in current spending may therefore end up *stimulating* private investment rather than crowding it out. Necessary conditions for this are, first, an initial situation with considerable slack and, second, interest-sensitive money demand and/or (partially) accommodating monetary policy. Under these conditions the investment-depressing effects of higher interest rates may be dominated by the investment-stimulating effect of higher rates of capacity utilisation. In such circumstances a long-lived fiscal expansion may be *more* effective than a transitory one, because firms are only likely to increase investment if the increase in demand is durable. Thus increases in government spending certainly need not reduce capital formation and growth.

Even without supply-side bottlenecks, another cause of 'crowding out' of a fiscal stimulus can be an appreciation of the exchange rate, resulting in a loss of international competitiveness. A tax-financed increase in spending will, if there is sufficient international capital mobility, cause an appreciation of the currency provided it is not accompanied by monetary expansion (and provided the public believe this). The upward pressure on domestic interest rates caused by the fiscal stimulus attracts financial inflows of capital which more than offsets a worsening current account and puts *upward* pressure on the currency. Against this, however, it should be pointed out that, with fixed money wages, the appreciation will also boost the real incomes and wealth of consumers and may increase consumer demand. If this effect is sufficiently strong, the exchange rate appreciation could actually produce *crowding in*.

In either case, monetary accommodation (or interest pegging) can prevent this crowding out (in) of demand through the exchange rate from occurring. Financial crowding out (in) of aggregate demand remains a policy choice, *not* an act of God or nature.

Supply Effects

Just as public spending decisions can directly affect private spending, they can also directly affect the supply side of the economy. The beneficial effects of education and health care have already been cited. However the most discussed supply-side effects of the policy in question relate to the way the accompanying changes in taxes and transfers might affect incentives to work and hence the supply of labour.

There is no general agreement on even the *direction* of the effect of a change in the marginal rate of income tax on the supply of labour and effort and its magnitude is subject to even greater dispute. This ambiguity arises because an increase in the rate of income tax, although it reduces the return to working additional hours (at given wages), also reduces the net income from the hours that are already worked. Some people may decide to offset some of the resulting decline in post-tax income by working longer hours. Labour supply may thus rise rather than fall. What empirical evidence is available suggests that the net effect of a rise in the standard rate of income tax is negligible on the labour supply of adult males and unmarried women, but there is a small negative effect on the labour supply of married women. However changes in tax rates may have very significant effects on particular individuals, for instance those in the 'poverty trap'.

Increases in income (or expenditure) taxes may nevertheless have harmful effects on employment because they may raise *ex ante* wage pressure. Work by Richard Layard and Steve Nickell, and others[2] has suggested that this is indeed the case, in at least the short run, with a rise in taxes leading to high (nominal) wage settlements for given levels of prices, inflation and unemployment.

Expenditure by the public sector on transfer payments may also have incentive effects on output and employment. Higher unemployment benefits, relative to income from employment, are likely to make the unemployed more choosy about accepting jobs. They may also encourage unions and employers to take a more sanguine view of the possibility of unemployment, leading them to agree to higher wages and hence lower employment. Patrick Minford has claimed an important role for unemployment benefits in influencing labour supply and employment. However his results have been disputed by Nickell and others.[3] Studies of the behaviour of individual unemployed workers suggest that small variations in unemployment benefits around their present level in fact have a minimal effect on labour supply.

When the economy is at or near full employment – or, more correctly, at the 'natural' or 'non-accelerating inflation rate of unemployment' (NAIRU) – expansionary fiscal policy must be crowded out. This will not be through financial effects but because of bottlenecks in domestic supply (perhaps mitigated if the fiscal stimulus also increases the level of full employment output) and/or spill-over into a deficit on the current account of the balance of payments. The interest sensitivity of money demand and the degree of accommodation of monetary policy become quite irrelevant for the aggregate degree of *real resource crowding out* or the spill-over into current account deficits, which will now be complete.

A final effect to note is that, in the long run, an increase in government spending on consumption (rather than capital) goods will tend to lower the nation's capital stock and its capital–labour ratio, unless the country does not have any influence on the long-run real interest rate it faces. This might be because it is a small participant in a very large internationally integrated set of capital markets. Even if Britain were in that position, the reduction in saving would result in an increased external indebtedness or a reduction in net external asset holdings. Larger trade balance surpluses (or smaller deficits) would have to be generated to service the increased foreign debt.

3 OTHER WAYS OF FINANCING GOVERNMENT SPENDING

As we noted in the introduction, an increase in government spending can be financed not only by increased current taxation (including any tariff revenue from public sector services), but also by printing money, running down foreign exchange reserves, borrowing at home or abroad, or by sales of public sector assets, or any combination of these. The choice of financing mix matters because the behaviour of the inflation rate, interest rates, the exchange rate and the level and composition of real economic activity in the short run and in the long run depend on it. This view, that the financing mix matters, is shared by most, but not all, macroeconomists. A brief summary of the view that financing does not matter may be helpful, precisely because it helps to clarify why in reality financing *does* matter.

'Debt Neutrality' or the 'Irrelevance of Government Financing'

The 'debt neutrality' or 'irrelevance of government financing' view goes as follows. The full impact (and cost) of the government's spending and revenue raising activities is measured by its spending on currently produced goods and services, that is, by its exhaustive spending programme. Whether this spending is financed by current taxes, by printing money or by borrowing is a matter of indifference.

Printing money is simply another form of taxation (hence its occasional description as an 'inflation tax'). A rising price level imposes a tax on the holders of money balances because it reduces the purchasing power over real goods and services of their money holdings. The command over real resources exercised by the government through the operation of the printing presses is sometimes called 'seigniorage', recalling the traditional rights of the sovereign through his monopoly over the minting of legal tender.

Borrowing is merely deferred taxation. Government interest-bearing debt must be serviced. The resources required to pay the interest bill and repay the principal will ultimately have to be raised through taxes – either conventional taxes or the inflation tax. Servicing the debt through further borrowing is not an option that can be exercised indefinitely. Such a 'chain letter' policy (technically known as a Ponzi Game) must break down because the repeated compounding of interest on the debt causes the debt service burden to grow faster than the government's ability to raise taxes. Ultimately the government's solvency will be threatened, and the risk of default or repudiation will drive the authorities out of the credit markets. An asset in the private sector's portfolio – government debt – is thus exactly matched by, and cancelled out by, a liability – the present discounted value of the future taxes required to service this debt.

According to this 'debt neutrality' view, the true cost of government exhaustive spending is therefore incurred as and when the spending takes place. It is then that real resources are preempted and absorbed by the public sector. Whether this spending is formally financed by current conventional taxes, by future conventional taxes, by the current inflation tax or by the future inflation tax is of secondary (or even of no) importance.

Stating the 'irrelevance of government financing' proposition like this is to refute it. Consider, for instance, the proposition that, since borrowing is merely deferred taxation, it will have the same effects as current taxation. There are umpteen different reasons why private agents will not be indifferent between having to pay taxes today and having to pay them in the future, even when the present discounted value of these future taxes (using the interest rate on the government's debt to discount the future taxes) is the same as the value of the current taxes.

First, the incidence of the future taxes is uncertain. Current tax payers may also realise that they will not be around forever, and that part of the future tax bill will be paid, not by them, but by future tax payers as yet unborn or in diapers. To these rational grounds can be added irrational but very human myopia, resulting in future tax burdens being discounted excessively or even ignored altogether. There are further grounds for private sector discount rates to exceed the interest rate at which the government borrows. Governments, at any rate in tolerably well managed economic households such as the United Kingdom, have easier and superior access to financial markets. Not only can they borrow at lower rates than virtually all private agents and institutions, they are also much less likely to encounter credit rationing, the inability to get credit at any price. This reflects the government's unique command over two sources of revenue: the power to tax and the ability to declare some of its liabilities (currency) to be legal tender. The stream of future national income, the ultimate tax base, is collateral for borrowing superior to the future earning power of any individual or the future profit stream of any corporation.

These and other arguments lead to the inescapable conclusion that effective private sector discount rates exceed the government's borrowing rate, and that the government debt is *not* cancelled out by the present discounted value of the future taxes required to service the debt. Government debt is, to some extent, private sector wealth.

The argument that printing money means imposing an inflation tax and that this is equivalent to explicit current taxation is also unsound. It is clearly incorrect if there is sufficient excess supply or spare capacity in the economy. In that case the extra money injected into the system to finance the government's spending does not raise the general price level, but instead leads to an expansion of real economic activity, output and employment. The inflation tax argument thus relies on a fairly strict (and empirically invalid) version of the neutrality of money: an x per cent increase in the stock of money leads immediately to an x per cent increase in the general price level. Even if this were to hold for the UK economy, it must be noted that the inflation tax is a special kind of tax which penalises holders of non-interest-bearing money balances in strict proportion to their holdings. It will induce private agents to reduce their money balances and switch into assets that provide better hedges against inflation. The consequences of such a tax are certain to be quite different from those of a tax on labour income, a corporate profits tax or a value added tax that raises the same amount of revenue. Different taxes have different effects on private incentives. To say that money financing imposes a tax, even when it is correct, is not very informative. This is merely one application of the general proposition that the structure of taxation can be as important as the total amount of revenue raised. While *average* tax rates determine revenue, *marginal* tax rates govern incentive effects. The same amount of revenue can be raised with very different degrees of efficiency loss. The 'financing does not matter' view glosses over the different incentive effects of alternative taxes, and for that reason alone can be dangerously misleading.

Effects of a Debt-Financed Increase in Government Spending

Having established that the form of finance *does* matter, we can now address the question of the impact of an increase in government spending (or a tax cut for that matter) financed by increased borrowing. This raises all the same issues discussed above in connection with a tax-financed increase in spending and more besides. In particular any or all of direct, financial and real crowding out can occur, and once again financial crowding out can be avoided by pursuing a suitably accommodating monetary policy whilst real crowding out can only be offset by measures to increase supply.

An additional complication, in the case of a debt-financed increase in spending, results from the accumulation of public debt that occurs as long as the deficit persists. This continued growth in the stock of government debt will tend to make interest rates higher than they would otherwise have been, and crowding out pressure grows as the debt builds up. Anticipation *now* of these future debt build-ups may cause *current* long-term interest rates to rise and the prices of government stock to fall. However, if the government has access to the international capital market and is a reasonably small borrower in world terms (the UK case) then the importance of this channel is likely to be much diminished. In any case, with sufficient idle resources, such crowding out can always be avoided by increasing the share of money financing in the total deficit financing mix. If resource constraints are binding, however, the consequences of sustained deficits will be less easily avoided.

It follows that a temporary debt-financed fiscal expansion could have a *stronger* effect on demand than a long-lived one, because it does not run into the effects of adverse expectations through high long-term rates of interest and depressed stock markets. This is even more the case if the fiscal expansion takes the form of a tax cut which encourages the reallocation of expenditure over time, for example a temporary investment subsidy which encourages the bringing forward of future investment plans to take advantage of the subsidy. The *credibility* of a government when it announces a temporary fiscal expansion is therefore crucial to its effectiveness. Governments with a sound reputation for long-term fiscal rectitude will be able to use fiscal policy for cyclical stabilisation. Governments plagued by a lack of private sector confidence in their underlying commitment to fiscal rectitude will be the prisoners of the financial markets and their attempts at stabilisation policy will be frustrated.

4 SIMULATING THE EFFECTS ON THE ECONOMY

Our discussion so far has established that a question such as 'What is the effect on output and employment of an increase in government spending of £1 billion?' is virtually meaningless because it is incompletely specified. It will first of all depend on the nature of the increase in spending itself – for instance whether it is current or capital expenditure (another issue is whether the goods in question are import-intensive or not). The effect on activity will also be different according to whether it is financed by raising taxes, printing money or borrowing from the capital markets. It will depend on whether monetary policy is accommodating or not, and whether the exchange rate is fixed or floating, since this will affect how much financial crowding out occurs. It will depend crucially on the extent of spare capacity in the economy and the degree to which the resulting increase in nominal spending is converted into wage and price rises as opposed to increases in activity, that is, how much real crowding out takes place. Finally, but by no means least, the impact on expectations matters; permanent increases in spending will have different effects from temporary ones (and from anticipated increases in future spending).

To give some idea of the orders of magnitude involved we have performed some simulation experiments on a small model of the UK economy estimated at the Centre for Labour Economics, London School of Economics.[4] We looked at the effects of a 5 per cent (approximately £3½ bn) increase in current government expenditure on goods and services for a variety of assumptions about how it is financed, and the stance of monetary and exchange rate policy. The model assumes that operators in financial and exchange markets form their expectations in the most efficient fashion possible, given the information available to them, that is, their expectations are 'rational', in the economist's jargon. The expectations of those making investment decisions are also assumed to be rational. This forward-looking behaviour on the part of financial operators and investors means that everything in the perceived *future* profile of public spending, taxes and so on will affect the economy *today*. By contrast, the expectations of households respond only sluggishly to past events. Consequently it takes some time for consumer spending to adjust to changes in income, and for wage settlements to respond to changes in inflation or the tightness of the labour market. This means that the economy will not continually be at the 'natural rate' of output and employment, and changes in government spending and taxes *can* affect demand and employment. Variables under government control – in particular tax rates – also affect the underlying 'natural rate' through their impact on wage bargaining and investment decisions.

Of course, one should not take exercises of this kind too seriously. All macroeconomic models are very imperfect reflections of reality – as those who build them would be the first to admit – but nevertheless they are useful in giving an idea of the relative importance of the various channels through which policy affects the economy, and of the broad orders of magnitude involved. Policy makers who ignore the lessons of history that are embodied in such models do so at their peril.

We have carried out six simulations in all. The first three look at the effect of a permanent increase in government spending, while the last three assume that the increase lasts for a single year. We make two alternative assumptions about financing – firstly, that the spending is financed by increased borrowing and, secondly, that it is covered by an increase in current income taxation. In both cases it is assumed that there is no change in the rate of monetary growth and that the exchange rate floats freely. Finally, we also look at the case of a debt-financed increase in spending when the authorities use monetary policy to maintain a path for the (nominal) exchange rate rather than the stock of money. This means that (nominal) interest rates do not change because the model in question assumes that international capital mobility is very high. This loosely corresponds to the case where monetary policy is accommodating and there is no financial crowding out. It is, of course, of some interest because it shows how the scope for activist fiscal policy might be altered were Britain to join the European Monetary System.

The astute reader will immediately wonder how a 'permanent' debt-financed increase in government spending could be feasible. The model assumes that Britain is a small borrower on the international capital markets, and that its borrowing and lending decisions have a minimal effect on the level of world interest rates. This is probably not a bad assumption for relatively small variations in the government's financing programme. However a truly permanent increase in the deficit would (assuming that real interest rates exceed the rate of growth of international capital markets) eventually lead to the United Kingdom absorbing a larger and larger share of the rest of the world's savings. Clearly the assumption that the terms on which the United Kingdom can borrow are independent of its actions would no longer be justified, and real interest rates would rise. For technical reasons this channel is omitted from the model and therefore the negative effects on investment from permanent debt-financed deficits alluded to in the last section are necessarily absent. Thus this 'permanent' increase in public spending is probably best thought of as a reasonably *long-lived* increase during the transition to a new higher debt–income ratio, with no adverse effects on long-term real interest rates.

Tables 7.4, 7.5 and 7.6 present the effect of this fiscal stimulus on output, inflation and employment in each of the six cases. To see the impact of the choice of financing mode, compare rows 1 and 4 with rows 2 and 5 in Table 7.4. For instance a permanent 5 per cent increase in government spending financed by borrowing raises output by nearly 1¾ per cent in the first year but by only about ½ per cent if it is

Table 7.4 Percentage increase in output due to a 5 per cent increase in government spending

Year	*1*	*2*	*3*	*4*
Permanent increase, debt-financed	1.7	1.5	1.5	1.5
Permanent increase, tax-financed	0.6	−0.1	−0.2	−0.3
Permanent increase, debt-financed, fixed exchange rate	1.1	1.4	1.4	1.4
Temporary increase, debt-financed	0.9	0.0	−0.1	−0.1
Temporary increase, tax-financed	0.3	−0.2	0.0	−0.1
Temporary increase, debt-financed, fixed exchange rate	1.0	0.1	0.0	0.0

Table 7.5 Percentage point increase in consumer price inflation due to a 5 per cent increase in government spending

Year	*1*	*2*	*3*	*4*
Permanent increase, debt-financed	−1.5	0.3	0.0	−0.1
Permanent increase, tax-financed	0.0	0.0	−0.3	−0.2
Permanent increase, debt-financed, fixed exchange rate	2.1	1.7	0.5	−0.4
Temporary increase, debt-financed	0.7	−0.3	−0.3	−0.2
Temporary increase, tax-financed	0.5	−1.2	0.3	−0.1
Temporary increase, debt-financed, fixed exchange rate	1.8	−0.7	−0.9	−0.6

Table 7.6 Percentage increase in employment due to a 5 per cent increase in government spending

Year	*1*	*2*	*3*	*4*
Permanent increase, debt-financed	0.9	0.6	0.5	0.5
Permanent increase, tax-financed	−0.2	−0.8	−0.7	−0.6
Permanent increase, debt-financed, fixed exchange rate	1.0	0.7	0.3	0.2
Temporary increase, debt-financed	0.6	−0.3	−0.1	0.0
Temporary increase, tax-financed	−0.3	−0.3	0.0	0.0
Temporary increase, debt-financed, fixed exchange rate	0.8	−0.4	−0.3	0.0

financed by current taxation. This demonstrates both that the actual budget deficit cannot be a good measure of fiscal impact (since it does not change under tax financing) and that the 'debt neutrality' view discussed in Section 3 is equally invalid. It is probably worth pointing out that, even though output rises with a tax-financed increase in spending, *employment* actually falls somewhat (see Table 7.6). This is because the higher income tax rates lead to increased wage demands and a switch to less labour-intensive forms of production by producers, outweighing any beneficial effect from increased demand.

Next compare the first-year impact on output and employment of a permanent increase in public spending with a temporary increase of the same magnitude under the same mode of financing. To be specific look at the debt-finance case, rows 1 and 4. The impact of a permanent increase is generally considerably greater – 1¾ per cent as against a little under 1 per cent for a temporary increase. There are two reasons for this. First, expectations of higher *future* demand and profits lead to increased investment today. Second, under a non-accommodating monetary policy (fixed money supply) a fiscal expansion tends to produce an *appreciation* of the exchange rate because of the upward pressure on domestic interest rates and resulting inflows of capital. The forward-looking nature of operators in the exchange market means this appreciation is much larger for a permanent increase in spending (5½ per cent) than a temporary one (1 per cent). Domestic inflation is moderated (see Table 7.5) and this in turn leads to some moderation of domestic wage pressure, and an increase in employment and output. Of course, under a fixed exchange rate this second channel is absent and that is why the difference in the first-year impact in rows 3 and 6 is much less pronounced. This comparison clearly demonstrates, then, the importance of identifying the whole future profile of expected levels of government taxes and spending.

Finally let us see how the stance of monetary policy affects the degree of financial crowding out, by comparing rows 1 and 4 with rows 3 and 6. In the case of a temporary increase in spending, we find exactly what we would expect. With a non-accommodating monetary policy (row 4), interest rates rise (about 6 percentage points) choking off demand somewhat. With an accommodating monetary policy – here necessitated by the fixed exchange rate regime – there is no rise in domestic interest rates and output rises about one-tenth per cent more. However, in the case of a permanent increase in spending the ranking is reversed. The reason for this is the beneficial effects of the exchange rate appreciation under flexible exchange rates on wage pressure and employment already referred to. In this case, therefore, there is actually financial crowding *in* via the exchange rate rather than crowding out. The moral is clear: when expectations of future policy are allowed to enter the calculations matters are considerably more complicated than they seem at first sight.

5 MEASURING FISCAL STANCE

By now the reader will have grasped that the interaction of the public sector and private sector is exceedingly complex. Government spending decisions can affect private spending decisions directly, or else indirectly through the financial markets, or through the exacerbation of supply constraints. The time profile of government spending can also be important when people in financial (and other) markets are forward-looking (this is especially true when the increase in spending is financed by borrowing). It should be clear that actual budget deficit measures such as the PSBR tell us very little about the impact of the public sector on the rest of the economy, and that prescriptions to maintain continuously a balanced budget from year to year and the like are in no sense desirable. Some commentators have suggested that governments should instead try to maintain a constant (possibly zero) budget deficit corrected for the state of the business cycle. This allows for the fact that tax revenues rise in booms and fall in slumps (spending on unemployment benefit accentuates these effects). However there is no reason to believe that the built-in variation of taxes and spending – the 'automatic stabilisers' – is in any way optimal. Other commentators have recommended that a new measure of the budget deficit should be calculated which corrects for the capital gain received on nominally denominated debt when prices rise. This 'corrected' measure would then be targeted. Such a procedure is similar to the 'permanent deficit' and 'net worth' calculations discussed below. However there the focus is on the adjustment necessary to ensure long-run solvency rather than the short-run demand impact and, as pointed out below, there is no reason why the government should aim to stabilise any of these measures either.

Thus, however appealing simple measures of fiscal impact may be, there is ultimately no short cut in assessing the effects of the government's taxing and spending decisions that obviates the need for a complete specification of the profile of spending, how it is to be financed, and an explicit assessment of how the economy works. Model-free policy prescriptions may be appealing to policy makers, but in the end are no more than a mirage. Worse, by concentrating on a misleading or irrelevant indicator, they are likely to exacerbate rather than promote economic stability and growth.

6 DEBT AND DEFICITS: THE CHANCELLOR'S NIGHTMARE(S)

The first part of this chapter has, among other things, dealt with one of every Chancellor of the Exchequer's big concerns in trying to decide whether further government borrowing is desirable – namely that it will crowd out private borrowing and reduce investment. We saw that this may be a well-founded fear when the economy is operating at full employment, but is symptomatic of a misguided monetary policy if it happens when there is spare capacity in the economy. We shall now turn to his (or her) other big fear – that increased deficits will lead to inflation or bankruptcy.

Debt, Deficits and Inflation

Increased deficits can lead to increased inflation through a variety of channels. First, increased aggregate demand is likely to put upward pressure on prices. However this will not lead to sustained inflation unless the government seeks permanently to run the economy at an excessively low level of unemployment, that is, below the 'natural rate'. If the government did try permanently to run the economy at an excessively high level of activity by a mix of expansionary fiscal and accommodating monetary policies, ever-accelerating inflation would be the result. The only way to achieve higher activity is somehow to increase supply.

This might be termed the 'cock-up' theory of inflation since it results from an overly optimistic assessment of the amount of spare capacity in the economy. Governments would presumably not knowingly pursue such a course. However there are more subtle mechanisms which may encourage, or even necessitate, increased monetary growth and inflation. First, a government with a large outstanding stock of nominally denominated, that is, non-index-linked, debt may be tempted to use *unanticipated inflation* to reduce the real value of that debt. Second, by adding to the real debt burden the government may eventually be *forced* to resort to higher monetisation and inflation to finance this deficit. Unlike the previous case this inflation could be completely *anticipated*.

Amortising the Public Debt through Inflation

The price of long-dated, nominally denominated debt can be seen as the present discounted value of future after-tax 'coupon' payments plus the present discounted value of the redemption value of the debt at maturity. With nominal debt, the future nominal coupon payments are discounted using expected future nominal interest rates. An upward revision of future inflationary expectations is likely to be associated with an upward revision of future expected nominal interest rates. The counterpart of this is a fall in the current price of the debt. For a given increase in inflationary expectations, the fall in the price of a bond will be larger, the greater the time remaining till maturity. A government wishing to reduce the real value of its debt (say because it prefers penalising current bond holders to taxing future wages and profits to service the debt) might be tempted to engineer an unanticipated increase in the rate of inflation. The mere possibility of this is likely to lead holders of nominally denominated debt to ask for a higher return than on other assets, and this 'risk premium' will be larger the higher the stock of public nominally denominated debt and the longer its maturity.

In Britain, the attractiveness of using unexpected inflation to 'pay off' part of the public debt in real terms has, however, been diminished since the Second World War for two reasons. First, the average maturity of the national debt has declined. In 1970 more than 40 per cent of government debt had a maturity of more than 15 years. By 1985 that had declined to less than 30 per cent. Since the reduction in the real value of a nominal bond associated with a given percentage jump in the rate of inflation is smaller the shorter the maturity of the bond, the incentive to indulge in a bout of surprise inflation has fallen. Second, marketable index-linked debt has been issued since 1981, and index-linked debt removes the incentive to inflation provided by nominal debt. Currently, more than a third of the public debt is index-linked. Indexation of its debt, far from making inflation more likely, might well enhance the credibility of a government commitment to price stability, by removing the option of reducing the real value of nominal debt through surprise inflation.

The Eventual Monetisation of Deficits

The argument that deficits *must*, sooner or later, be monetised and lead to inflation goes as follows. Ignoring, for simplicity, the running down of foreign exchange reserves and the sale of public sector assets, any excess of spending or taxes must be financed either through borrowing or by printing money. Assume the government chooses to borrow. There is some upper limit on the debt burden which the country, or international capital market, can tolerate. Once that upper limit is reached, all further deficits must be financed by printing money, that is, by the inflation tax.

While this argument has a kernel of truth in it, it must be treated very carefully, lest misleading conclusions be drawn. First, the upper limit does not relate to the value of the debt or even to its real value but to the value of the debt relative to the ultimate tax base, national income. Formally:

$$s = d + (r - n)\bar{b}, \tag{7.1}$$

where s is the amount of money (seigniorage) the government must print as a percentage of national income, d is the *primary* deficit as a percentage of national income, that is, excluding interest payments on the debt, r is the *real* interest rate, n is the rate of growth of the economy, and $\bar{b}$ is the upper limit on the debt–national income ratio. The debt–income ratio is therefore multiplied *not* by the nominal interest rate, but by the *real, growth-corrected* interest rate in order to allow for the fact that nominal national income, which is the denominator of $\bar{b}$, increases at the rate of inflation plus the rate of growth of real output. Thus use of the *actual* deficit which includes nominal interest payments could give a very misleading picture of the prospects for future inflation. For instance, while the nominal interest rate is today around 10 or 11 per cent, the real rate of interest, though much higher than in the 1960s and 1970s, is only about 6 per cent, while the growth-corrected real rate is only about 3 per cent.

To derive the eventual implications for the rate of inflation, π, we first need to note that if the ratio of nominal national income to the stock of money (known as the velocity of circulation and denoted v) remains constant over time, then

$$vs = \pi + n$$

or

$$\pi = vs - n$$

and equation (7.1) can be transformed to give

$$\pi = v[d + (r - n)\bar{b}] - n. \tag{7.2}$$

We can use this equation to calculate not only the eventual implications for inflation once the debt burden reaches its upper limit, but also to evaluate the inflationary consequences of stabilising the debt–income ratio at *any* given value. Now the current national debt–national income ratio is a little under 50 per cent, and the velocity of circulation of the monetary base (which is relevant here) is about 20. With a growth-corrected real interest rate, $r - n$, of 3 per cent and a real growth rate also of 3 per cent, there would actually have to be a primary surplus of about 1⅓ per cent of national income if inflation were to be maintained at zero indefinitely. There was a primary surplus in 1986, but its level was rather greater than this, at around 2 per cent of national income. This would imply an eventual *deflation* rate of about 13 per cent per annum! This hardly suggests that the current debt–income ratio is alarmingly high in terms of any long-run inflationary implications, and matters would look even better than this if the growth-corrected real interest rate were to fall from the current historically very high level as real interest rates decline and growth accelerates.

However, equation (7.2) may seem to provide some justification for concerns about any expansion of the deficit, because it implies that each 1 percentage point increase in the primary deficit requires a 20 percentage point increase in the inflation rate for a given debt–income ratio and given real interest and growth rates! However, this assumes that the new primary deficit levels are sustained *indefinitely*. In fact, as Table 7.3 amply demonstrated, seigniorage from money creation has been a negligible source of revenue in the United Kingdom, amounting to less than a quarter of 1 per cent of national income in recent years. Yet, between 1980 and 1985, a Conservative government dedicated to a reduction of the tax burden actually raised taxes by more than 2 per cent of national income. Financing the deficit purely by monetary growth is, in terms of the political calculus, extremely costly compared to the alternative of raising taxes or reducing spending precisely *because* it would have such a big effect on inflation. But fear of inflation need not stop even a minimally astute government from using variations in the taxation-borrowing mix for macroeconomic stabilisation purposes. Neither need it lead the financial markets to greet any fiscal relaxation with prognostications of a return to the days of double-digit inflation or worse.

Debt, Deficits and Default, or the Chancellor's Ruin

It will come as no surprise that the public debt cannot grow indefinitely at a rate faster than the government's ability to service that debt, without raising the spectre of government insolvency and debt default. The power of compound interest is such that, in the long run, a real interest rate in excess of the growth rate of real national income means that the government either has to run a *surplus* on the primary (non-interest) account or resort to seigniorage. Rewriting (7.1) we get

$$s - d = (r - n)\bar{b}. \tag{7.3}$$

A debt-burden of $\bar{b}$ is sustainable, that is, consistent with continued government solvency, if and only if, given the real interest rate and the real growth rate, the government is willing and able to extract seigniorage (s) or run primary surpluses ($-d$) that satisfy (7.3).

Much is disguised within the symbols of (7.3), and it is informative to spell out exactly what 'solvency of the government' really means. A government is solvent if its spending programme, its tax-transfer programme and its planned future use of seigniorage are consistent with its outstanding, initial financial and real assets and liabilities (in the sense that the present value of its spending programme is equal to its comprehensive net worth). Equation (7.4) below spells out the comprehensive government balance sheet in somewhat greater detail.

$$\left\{\begin{array}{l}\text{Present value of exhaustive} \\ \text{consumption spending} \\ +\,\text{present value of transfers, grants} \\ \text{and subsidies}\end{array}\right. = \left\{\begin{array}{l}\quad\text{public sector financial assets} \\ =\text{public sector financial debt} \\ +\,\text{public sector real assets} \\ +\,\text{present value of taxes} \\ +\,\text{present value of seigniorage} \\ +\,\text{present value of public sector} \\ \quad\text{capital formation}\end{array}\right. \tag{7.4}$$

The left-hand side of this equation contains the present discounted values of the government's exhaustive consumption spending and of its transfer payments. The right-hand side, referred to as *public sector net worth*, indicates how these spending streams are financed, now and in the future. Note that the relevant spending total on the left-hand side *excludes* public sector capital formation. If public sector investment earns a cash rate of return for the government equal to the government's (marginal) cost of borrowing, then the government's elbow room for consumption spending and transfer payments will, in present value terms, be *completely unaffected*. If the cash return to the government of its capital formation programme exceeds the opportunity cost of borrowing then the item 'present value of public sector capital formation' on the right-hand side will be positive, and the government's intertemporal budget, or solvency, constraint is relaxed. If the cash return falls short of the cost of borrowing, then the present value of public sector capital formation will be negative and the solvency constraint becomes more binding. In this respect, spending on education and health may generate cash returns to the government if productivity is thereby enhanced and thus output and the tax base are raised.

Note that this relationship between the cost of borrowing and the cash returns on public sector investment says nothing about the *desirability* of the investment. The desirability of the investment will depend on whether the *social* rate of return exceeds the opportunity cost of the funds invested. This social rate of return may well exceed the cash returns to the government if, as is often the case with infrastructure or social overhead capital, it is too costly or politically undesirable to impose user charges that cover costs. It is also possible for the cash returns to exceed the social rate of return, for instance when the investment is undertaken by a public sector monopoly which cannot be restrained from using its monopoly power. All that equation (7.4) has to say about public sector capital formation is that if the government intends to invest in programmes whose cash returns to the government are low (regardless of how high or low the social returns are) then it must cover the difference between the cost of borrowing and the cash returns out of other sources of revenue, or cut other parts of its spending programme.

Four remarks are in order about the remaining items in the comprehensive balance sheet on the right-hand side of (7.4). First, public sector financial assets include such things as the stock of gold and foreign exchange reserves, public sector loans to the domestic private sector or overseas, and minority government shareholdings in private enterprises.

Second, public sector real assets include the value of the stock of social overhead capital (road, bridges, sewers, hospitals, schools, power lines and so on), of the capital stock in the nationalised industries and of the government's ownership of natural resources such as North Sea oil. Again, these values do not measure the contribution to social welfare that these resources are likely to make, *but only their ability to generate cash income for the government.* A typical British motorway therefore registers a zero on this scale, while a toll road would show a positive value. Industries like British

Coal or British Rail which have tended to be secular loss makers will, if this performance is extrapolated into the future, show up as negative items in the balance sheet.

Third, the value of the government's ownership rights in natural resources, such as North Sea oil, is influenced powerfully by the current and prospective future market price of these resources. In 1986, for instance, the collapse in the price of oil put quite a dent in the government's balance sheet. It is estimated that a $1 fall in the oil price reduces tax revenues by around £½ billion per annum.

Fourth, this comprehensive balance sheet provides us with a good opportunity for fulminating against one of the accounting abominations in the PSBR, that of classifying asset sales as negative public expenditure rather than, correctly, as financing. To a first approximation, it is a matter of indifference whether the government finances an excess of spending over revenue by borrowing (increasing public sector financial liabilities), by selling financial assets such as shares in British Gas or British Telecom, or by selling off its property rights in North Sea oil. All these actions cause the government to compete with the domestic private sector, and the rest of the world, for financial resources. If government borrowing crowds out private borrowing then *so does the government's privatisation programme of asset sales*. Indeed, to the extent that British Telecom shares (for example) are closer substitutes for the shares of existing private firms than are government bonds, the effect of asset sales on the private sector's required rate of return on investment may well *exceed*, pound for pound, that of government borrowing. Never should the sale of existing assets be listed as an offset against current spending.

None of this has any implications for the desirability of privatisation or nationalisation. Leaving aside ideological or strategic considerations (which may override all other concerns) privatisation (nationalisation) of an industry or firm is desirable if the efficiency with which the industry's or firm's resources are utilised is greater in the private (public) sector. Efficiency is here understood in the wider sense of efficiency in meeting social objectives at minimum cost rather than the narrow objective of technical efficiency in the use of inputs. Thus a privatised monopoly may be technically more efficient but may lower social welfare through the abuse of its monopoly position. From the point of view of the balance sheet, all that matters about privatisation is whether the revenue raised by asset sales exceeds or falls short of the present value of future cash returns that would accrue if the industry or firm were to remain in the public sector. If it exceeds it, the solvency constraint is relaxed and spending programmes can be boosted, taxes can be cut and/or seigniorage can be reduced. If it falls short, the solvency constraint is tightened and measures in the opposite direction have to be taken.

Returning to equation (7.4), we note that the government's spending and revenue raising plans are inconsistent if the left-hand side exceeds the right-hand side. Unless spending plans are cut back, tax revenues are boosted or it is planned to have increased recourse to seigniorage revenue, elimination of the gap can only be effected by a (partial or complete) default on the public debt. While this is not out of the question in a number of deeply indebted developing countries, the United Kingdom does not seem to be a likely candidate for such a position. Figure 7.1 showed that the United Kingdom's national debt currently stands at a little under 50 per cent of GDP. This is low by UK historical standards (consider, for example, the ratio of 272 per cent of GDP achieved after the Second World War in 1947 and the ratio of 288 per cent of GDP after the Napoleonic War in 1821). It is also right in the middle of the pack in comparison with the other major industrial countries (see Figure 7.2).

Attempting to fill in the comprehensive balance sheet with actual figures is an ambitious enterprise. For the United Kingdom, John Hills[5] has made a brave attempt to put some orders of magnitude on a number of items in the comprehensive balance sheet. On the asset side, in addition to the usual financial assets, he included physical assets and the present value of future oil revenues. Rather than estimating the entire expected future stream of tax revenues, he included just the present value of 'deferred' taxes (tax liabilities already incurred by the private sector but not yet paid). On the liability side he included, in addition to the usual financial liabilities, the present value of state pensions and of unfunded public service pensions. For 1982 he estimated, in this partial balance sheet, a net liability of between £65 bn and £105 bn at March 1982 prices. This means that the remaining items in the comprehensive balance sheet (the present value of the taxes not included by Hills, plus the present value of seigniorage, plus the present value of public sector capital formation, minus the present value of the exhaustive public sector consumption programme, minus the present value of transfers, grants and subsidies not included by Hills) would have to add up to between £65 bn and £105 bn, for the government to have a consistent set of fiscal and financial plans.

Sustainability

It is important to note that there is nothing magical about public sector net worth or about any other subtotal in the comprehensive balance sheet. In particular, there is no reason, in general, for governments to pursue a policy of keeping net worth (or any other balance sheet subtotal) constant. A government may wish to pursue fiscal and financial policies resulting in a temporary or even a systematic long-term increase or decline in net worth. Without knowing the details of the spending, revenue raising, and other financial plans, one cannot judge their desirability. All that is necessary for the *feasibility* and *sustainability* of a fiscal-financial programme is that the left-hand side of (7.4) equals the right-hand side. Both sides may be rising or falling together.

If there is a discrepancy between the two sides of (7.4) a useful way of representing this *ex ante* inconsistency is to calculate its 'annuity value', or its real perpetuity equivalent. If G denotes the left-hand side of (7.4), that is, the present value of all government spending plans (in real terms) and W denotes the right-hand side of (7.4), that is, net worth (also in real terms), then the discrepancy is $G - W$ in present value terms. Its annuity value, which may by abuse of language be called the 'permanent deficit', is given by the term D below.

$$D = R(G - W). \tag{7.5}$$

Here R is the long-term real interest rate. If plans are consistent, then $G = W$ *ex ante*. If G does differ from W *ex ante*, one or more items in the balance sheet must give, to yield $G = W$ *ex post*. Although *ex ante* permanent deficits will not actually materialise, let alone be permanent, they represent the *permanent adjustment* that must be made, relative to the *ex ante* inconsistent plans, to the flows of spending, tax receipts or seigniorage in order to achieve solvency.

While, as we stated earlier, there is nothing especially virtuous about maintaining net worth intact, it is certainly of interest to trace the evolution of net worth over time, since this will determine the future fiscal elbow-room of the authorities. It can be shown quite easily that net worth increases (decreases) if the flow of total public spending over some period, g, is less than (exceeds) the value of its net worth at the beginning of that period multiplied by the current short-term real interest rate, r, that is:

$$\Delta W = rW - g, \tag{7.6}$$

where ΔW is the change in net worth. $\Delta W = 0$ is a useful benchmark, since it is obviously indefinitely sustainable. However, *any* set of fiscal and financial programmes that satisfy $G = W$ are consistent, feasible and sustainable, regardless of what happens to ΔW along the way.

A useful related benchmark is to calculate the maximum flow of real public spending that can be maintained indefinitely, let us call this g^p (for permanent government spending). It can be shown that $g^p = RW$ where R, as before, is the long-term real interest rate. If a government spends more (less) than this amount then future levels of permanent government spending will accordingly be lower (higher).

It is clear that the *permanent income deficit*, $g - RW$ (which equals $g - g^p$) looks like a deficit measure and so do $R(G - W)$ from (7.5) and $g - rW$ from (7.6). They are however very different from the usual budget deficit measures that simply record the actual flow of funds in any particular period. The revenues measured in RW or rW are 'average' current *and future* revenue flows, not just current revenues, and in the case of the permanent deficit in (7.5) spending flows too are measured as the average of current and expected future spending rather than just as current spending.

To give some idea of what a series for one of these measures looks like, Table 7.7 contains some estimates of the permanent income deficit, $g - RW$, calculated by David Begg (see footnote to table 7.7). This is constructed as follows. He first calculates a measure of the inflation-adjusted public sector financial deficit, and evaluates the

Table 7.7 The permanent income deficit compared with the public sector financial deficit and borrowing requirement (as a percentage of GDP)

	1970	*1975*	*1980*	*1981*	*1982*	*1983*	*1984*	*1985*
Permanent Income Deficit	−6.8	0.3	0.1	−0.2	−0.2	0.6	2.4	2.8
Public Sector Financial Deficit	−1.5	8.0	5.4	3.8	3.2	4.3	4.7	3.4
Public Sector Borrowing requirement	0.0	10.7	5.9	4.9	2.1	4.5	3.7	2.5

Sources: Begg, D.K.H. 'Fiscal Policy in Britain: Placing the MTFS in Context' in *Monetarism and Macro-Economics* (1987) Institute for Economic Affairs, and author's own calculations.

debt burden at real long-term rates of interest. He assumes that non-oil taxes remain constant, as a share of output, but takes account of declining revenues from North Sea oil by replacing them by their permanent income equivalent.[6] He also deducts half of public sector investment on the (conservative) assumption that half of public sector investment yields cash returns at the market rate. The series shows that only since 1984, when North Sea oil revenue was substantially but temporarily high, was there a significant permanent income deficit and hence fiscal policy was exacerbating the solvency problem for succeeding governments. Table 7.7 also demonstrates how little information concerning the solvency position of the government is contained in conventional measures such as the Public Sector Financial Deficit or the PSBR.

Finally, neither the conventional deficit measures nor the long-run measures introduced here are of *any* use as indicators of the short-run effects of fiscal and financial policy on aggregate demand. However the permanent deficit measure in (7.5) and the change in government net worth measured in (7.6) do at least have some usefulness as indicators of fiscal pain and changes in fiscal elbow-room respectively. Indeed the permanent deficit summarises the information contained in the current conventionally measured deficit and all future projected conventionally measured deficits. By itself, the conventionally measured deficit for any given year (that is, the Public Sector Financial Deficit and *a fortiori* the PSBR) is of interest to book-keepers but not to economists. Current cash-flow should matter to economic agents that are in danger of being cash-flow constrained, not to the government which has unparalleled access to credit as well as the power to print money. What *should be* of concern to the government is the effect of their actions on the cash-flow position of domestic private agents who may be or become cash-flow constrained and who in any case have access to credit on less favourable terms than the government.

7 WHEN TO RUN DEFICITS

The Prime Minister has been known to liken the public sector to a household. Prudent housekeeping, according to Mrs Thatcher, dictates that neither the public sector, nor the country, should live beyond its means. Yet where would multinationals such as IBM and British Petroleum be if they had relied on internally generated funds to finance investment? Even if we abstract from the stabilisation aspects of fiscal and financial policy, and assume that markets clear in the short run, sensible governments should be prepared to finance profitable investment projects by borrowing since the investments will ultimately pay for themselves. Similarly a government should not be concerned if the country is experiencing a trade deficit if that is due to an investment boom which is sucking in imports. The revenues generated by the investment will pay for the foreign debt that accumulates.

A world in which markets in both goods and labour continuously clear and in which there is unlimited access to capital and credit markets for consumers is, in fact, the one case where it could make sense for the government to stabilise the cyclically-corrected budget deficit. The welfare losses due to the distortions induced by taxes increase more than proportionately as tax rates increase (strictly speaking with the *square* of the tax rate). To minimise these losses it makes sense to maintain tax rates constant over time. If government spending and/or the tax base necessarily varies, for example because of wars or technological reasons, then the budget deficit will vary pro-cyclically.[7]

In practice wars are the major reason for increases in the debt–income ratio (see Figure 7.1). If this debt is 'repaid' by the 'surprise' inflating away of its value, the government may impair its ability to borrow in the future. This view suggests that in peace time the government should tend to run surpluses in order to reduce the debt–income ratio, in case of any future conflicts.

However, this is a very idealistic world which abstracts from the widespread imperfections in goods, labour and credit markets that we see about us. Exogenous falls in demand (perhaps due to adverse changes in the expectations of investors) and supply shocks (such as the two oil price hikes) are disturbances that the market mechanism deals with imperfectly. It takes time for workers who are laid off to retrain and relocate even if they can find work elsewhere. Incomplete insurance markets and limited access to credit prevent them maintaining their consumption while their income is transitorily low. This in turn exacerbates the decline in aggregate demand. By acting as a *lender of first resort* in such circumstances the government can use its unparalleled access to the international capital markets to substitute public borrowing for private borrowing, using the proceeds to sustain activity either through increases in expenditure or cuts in taxes. There is therefore an even stronger case for the government to run a deficit during a recession than under the 'tax-rate smoothing' story.

The obverse of this is that fiscal policy should be relatively contractionary in booms. Whether the budget should actually be in surplus depends on the average rate of inflation that the government thinks appropriate and the debt level it inherits. A relevant test is equation (7.2) relating inflation to the deficit and the debt–income ratio. In general there is no reason why the optimal average rate of inflation should be zero. In a world where all taxes are distortionary, the tax burden should be spread as widely as possible, and in principle that includes raising revenue through the 'inflation tax' as well. Nevertheless it seems unlikely that the optimal inflation rate is likely to be very far above zero and long-run price stability may be a reasonable target.

A target of *long-run* price stability does not, however, require continually maintaining a zero inflation rate. Unanticipated inflation does penalise holders of nominally denominated debt, but the unanticipated deflation of activity penalises those who have invested in real capital (entrepreneurs) and human capital (workers) rather than financial capital. Thus when there is an adverse supply shock – such as that imparted by the rise in oil prices – there is no reason why debt holders should not bear some of the burden in the form of some unanticipated inflation (or a contingent tax on interest income). Repeated bouts of unanticipated inflation would make people unwilling to buy government debt, but repeated bouts of unanticipated deflation will likewise discourage firms from investing in productive capital and workers from investing in specific skills.

The need to satisfy the government solvency constraint (equation (7.4)), ensures that periods of fiscal ease will need to be matched by periods of fiscal restraint as the level of activity varies. Stabilisation policy is, almost by definition, temporary in nature, and expansionary measures undertaken in a recession may turn out to be self-defeating if they engender expectations of a deficit–debt spiral and rising interest rates. Thus the credibility of the government when it undertakes a temporary fiscal expansion is essential. Some sorts of government spending, particularly on direct employment, may be very hard or unpopular to reverse, which suggests that attention be focussed on measures which are more easily put into reverse. Public investment projects, for instance, fit the bill since the gestation process means they come to an end naturally. Temporary subsidies to private investment have also been cited, since these naturally lead to a redistribution of expenditure over time. They both also have the virtue of enhancing the supply potential of the economy.

There is an abundance of evidence to suggest that the 'natural rate' of unemployment has risen somewhat in the last fifteen years.[8] However, whether it is 7 per cent or 9 per cent seems immaterial. There is still a significant margin of unused capacity in the economy and a *supply-friendly fiscal expansion* need not run into supply-side bottlenecks and engender a bout of renewed inflation. In this respect recent concern in the City that the economy is in danger of 'overheating' seems misplaced. While capacity utilisation is returning to more normal levels, it has not been accompanied by the tight labour market and raw material shortages that typified the 1973 boom. Industrialists themselves say there is no danger that they will not be able to meet demand. The real danger is that the longer the resources are left idle, the harder it is to bring them back into action and the more likely it is that an increase in demand will result in inflation. The economy may indeed now be into its seventh year of 'steady growth', but an average annual growth rate of 3 per cent is simply not sufficient to bring the unused resources back into activity. It is a *mathematical necessity* that there must be a period of *unsustainably rapid growth* if even moderately full employment is to be achieved. Given the still-depressed state of the economy it is in any case sensible to risk the possibility of even a little more inflation against the likelihood of the gain of a lot more output and employment.

It could be argued that the government should in any case be running a smaller deficit right now, because revenues are temporarily high on account of North Sea oil. These should be shared with future generations and one way of doing this is to use the revenues to reduce the future debt interest burden.[9] This would be true if other things were equal, but unfortunately this is not the case. The British economy has been suffering from a recession greater in magnitude even than that experienced between the wars. Maintaining government net worth constant by matching the tax revenues received as the oil is depleted against the debt would produce an unnecessarily contractionary stand at the present time.

In the last couple of years, by accelerating the privatisation programme, the government has indeed moved in this direction, and its programme of tax cuts and rising public expenditure suggests, for whatever motive, a conversion to a more expansionary fiscal policy. Yet the commitment is less than wholehearted and the measures inadequate in the context of the scale of the problem. A further shift in priorities is still required.

8 CONCLUSIONS

By way of conclusion let us summarise a few of the points that have emerged in the preceding pages.

(1) The *composition* of public spending and taxation is just as important as the overall size of the deficit, however measured. Transfer payments represent a *redistribution* of purchasing power within the population, whereas only current and capital expenditure on goods and services furnish a claim on the *real resources* of the economy.

(2) Spending and taxation decisions will usually have distributive implications and alter incentives as well as affecting the total level of demand. In general it will be impossible to separate the *distributional, allocative* and *stabilisation* effects of fiscal policy.

(3) *Financial* crowding out of a fiscal stimulus through interest rates or the exchange rate is a *policy choice* that is avoidable by pursuing a suitably accommodating monetary policy. *Real* crowding out because of supply bottlenecks on the other hand requires measures to expand *supply*.

(4) Private agents generally have access to capital markets on less favourable terms than governments. Thus the *time profile* of the government's taxation programme matters. The government should act as a *lender of first resort* during recessions by borrowing to cut taxes or increase spending.

(5) Temporary changes in government spending or taxes will generally have different effects on demand than permanent changes of the same magnitude. Permanent increases in spending may be more expansionary if they increase future profits and encourage investment, but they may also, if debt-financed, have adverse effects by raising long-term real interest rates. The *time profile* of spending and taxation is important, as well as the *credibility* of announcements of future fiscal plans.

(6) Accounting identities constrain fiscal and monetary policy in the long run. Any difference between the *present value* of spending and the *present value* of taxation must, at some time, be met by increased monetary expansion, if it cannot be met from initial assets. However, this *long-run* constraint need not prevent a government from pursuing sensible *short-run* counter-cyclical stabilisation policies.

(7) Increased public investment in projects yielding the market rate of return has *no* implications for the feasibility of future spending

and taxation programmes since the increased spending is exactly matched against a stream of future revenues from the investment. Investment in projects with low cash returns will require cuts in future spending or increases in future taxes. *Efficiency*, however, requires that a project be undertaken if the *social* benefit exceeds the (social) cost; implications for the exchequer finances are irrelevant.

(8) Privatisation is exactly like borrowing and should be regarded as a way of *financing* a given primary deficit, rather than as a negative capital expenditure. To the extent that the assets are sold for less than their market value and government debt and shares are imperfect substitutes, financing the primary deficit through privatisation will *intensify* crowding out pressures.

(9) There are *no* model-free measures of fiscal impact. However concepts such as the *permanent deficit* may be useful in the public expenditure planning process as a guide to fiscal elbow-room.

(10) Greater reliance on *indexed debt* will reduce the incentive for the government to reduce the real value of its liabilities through *unanticipated inflation*. However there is no reason why owners of human and productive capital should bear all the costs of adverse supply shocks. Equity demands that holders of government debt should also incur some of the costs, either through increased inflation or an increase in the tax rate on interest income.

(11) The national debt, as a proportion of national income, is at a historically *low* level and fear of a debt explosion need not constrain the government from borrowing to pursue an expansionary fiscal policy.

(12) Sound financial policy is not the sole preserve of Conservative governments. It is consistent with an infinity of debt–income ratios and political philosophies. *Sound* government is not synonymous with *small* government.

Notes

1. Charles Bean is Reader in Economics at the London School of Economics and Willem Buiter is Professor of Economics at the University of Yale. They are both Council Members of the Employment Institute. This text was first published in October 1987.
2. See Layard, P. R. G. and S. Nickell (1986) and Bean, C. R., P. R. G. Layard and S. Nickell (1986).
3. See Minford, P., D. Davies, M. Peel and A. Sprague, (1982); and S. Nickell's review in *Economic Journal*, 1984.

4. See Bean, C. R., 'The Macroeconomic Consequences of North Sea Oil', in R. Dornbusch and P. R. G. Layard (eds) (1987) for a detailed description and listing of the model.
5. See Hills, J. (1984).
6. See Odling-Smee, J. and C. J. Riley, (1985).
7. The 'tax-smoothing' view originates in R. Barro, (1979).
8. See Layard, P. R. G. and S. Nickell (1986).
9. See Odling-Smee, J. and C. J. Riley (1985).

Bibliography

Alogoskoufis, G. and C. A. Pissarides (1983) 'A Test of Price Sluggishness in the Simple Rational Expectations Model: UK 1950–1980', *Economic Journal* (September).

Attfield, C. L. F., D. Demery and N. W. Duck (1981a) 'Unanticipated Monetary Growth, Output and the Price Level: UK 1946–77', *European Economic Review* (June/July).

Attfield, C. L. F., D. Demery and N. W. Duck (1981b) 'A Quarterly Model of Unanticipated Monetary Growth, Output and the Price Level in the UK, 1963–78', *Journal of Monetary Economics* (November).

Attfield, C. L. F., D. Demery and N. W. Duck (1985) *Rational Expectations in Macroeconomics. An Introduction to Theory and Evidence* (Oxford: Basil Blackwell).

Azariadis, Costas (1981) 'Implicit Contracts and Related Topics: A Survey', in Z. Hornstein, J. Grice and A. Webb (eds), *The Economics of the Labour Market* (London: HMSO).

Azariadis, Costas and Joseph E. Stiglitz (1983) 'Implicit Contracts and Fixed Price Equilibria', *Quarterly Journal of Economics*, Supplement.

Baily, M. N. (1979) 'Implicit Contracts and Related Topics: A Survey: Comment', in Z. Hornstein, J. Grice and A. Webb, *The Economics of the Labour Market* (London: HMSO).

Baily, M. N. (1983) 'The Labour Market in the 1930s', in James Tobin (ed.), *Macroeconomics, Prices and Quantities* (Oxford: Basil Blackwell).

Barro, R. (1974) 'Are Government Bonds Net Wealth?', *Journal of Political Economy* (November/December).

Barro, R. (1977) 'Unanticipated Money Growth and Unemployment in the United States', *American Economic Review* (March).

Barro, R. (1978) 'Unanticipated Money, Output and the Price Level in the United States', *Journal of Political Economy* (June).

Barro, R. (1979) 'On the Determination of Public Debt', *Journal of Political Economy*.

Barro, R. (1984) *Macroeconomics* (New York: John Wiley).

Barro, R. and H. Grossman (1971) 'A General Disequilibrium Model of Income and Employment', *American Economic Review* (March).

Barro, R. and H. Grossman (1976) *Money, Employment and Inflation* (Cambridge University Press).

Barro, R. and M. Rush (1980) 'Unanticipated Money and Economic Activity' in S. Fischer (ed.), *Rational Expectations and Economic Activity* (University of Chicago Press).

Basevi, G., O. Blanchard, W. H. Buiter, R. Dornbusch and P. R. G. Layard (1984) *Europe: The Case for Unsustainable Growth* (Centre for European Policy Studies, No. 8/9).

Bean, C. R. (1983) *A Little Bit More Evidence on the Natural Rate Hypothesis From the UK* (Centre for Labour Economics Discussion Paper No. 149, February).

Bean, C. R., P. R. G. Layard and S. Nickell (1986) 'The Rise in Unemployment: A Multi-Country Study', *Economica*.

Beckerman, W. and T. Jenkinson (1985) 'Commodity Prices, Import Prices and the Inflation Slow-down: A Pooled Cross-Country Time Series Analysis', unpublished mimeo.

Begg, D. K. H. (1982a) *The Rational Expectations Revolution in Macroeconomics* (Oxford: Philip Allan).

Begg, D. K. H. (1982b) 'Rational Expectations, Wage Rigidity and Involuntary Unemployment', *Oxford Economic Papers* (March).

Begg, D. K. H. (1987) 'Fiscal Policy in Britain: Placing the Medium-Term Financial Strategy in Context', in *Readings 26: Monetarism and Macroeconomics* (London: Institute of Economic Affairs).

Blanchard, O. (1985) 'Monopolistic Competition, Small Menu Costs and Real Effects of Nominal Money', unpublished mimeo.

Blanchard, O., R. Dornbusch, J. Drèze, H. Giersch, P. R. G. Layard and M. Monti (1985) *Employment and Growth in Europe: A Two-Handed Approach* (Louvain: Centre for European Policy Studies, CEPS Papers No. 21).

Buiter, W. H. (1983) 'Real Effects of Anticipated Money: Some Problems of Estimation and Hypothesis Testing', *Journal of Monetary Economics* (March).

Charter For Jobs (1985) *We Can Cut Unemployment* (London: Charter for Jobs).

Davies, G. (1984) 'Comments on the Mais Lecture', *The Economics Analyst*, Simon and Coates, London (July).

Demery, D. (1984) 'Aggregate Demand, Rational Expectations and Real Output: Some New Evidence For the UK, 1963.2–1982.2', *Economic Journal* (December).

Department of Employment (1985) *Employment – The Challenge For The Nation*, Cmnd 9474 (London: HMSO).

Diamond, P. A. (1982) 'Aggregate Demand Management in Search Equilibrium', *Journal of Political Economy* (October).

Dimsdale, N. H. (1984) 'Employment and Real Wages in the Inter-War Period', *National Institute Economic Review* (November).

Dornbusch, R. and P. R. G. Layard (1987) *The Performance of the British Economy* (Oxford: Clavendon Press).

Eckstein, O. and D. Wyss (1972) *The Econometrics of Price Determination* (Washington: Board of Governors of the Federal Reserve System).

Fair, R. C. (1979) 'On Modelling the Effects of Government Policies', *American Economic Review*, Papers and Proceedings (May).

Figlewski, S. and P. Wachtel (1981) 'The Formation of Inflationary Expectations', *Review of Economics and Statistics* (February).

Geary, P. T. and J. Kennan (1982) 'The Employment–Real Wage Relationship: An International Study', *Journal of Political Economy* (August).

Gordon, R. J. (1982) 'Price Inertia and Policy Ineffectiveness in the United States, 1890–1980', *Journal of Political Economy* (December).

Gordon, R. J. (1983) 'A Century of Evidence on Wage and Price Stickiness in the United States, the United Kingdom and Japan', in James Tobin (ed.), *Macroeconomics, Prices and Quantities* (Oxford: Basil Blackwell).

Gordon, R. J. (1985) 'Wage-Price Dynamics and the Natural Rate of Unemployment in Europe, Japan and North America', paper delivered at the Centre For Economic Policy Research, 22 March.

Grubb, D. (1984) 'Wage Inflation and Unemployment: A Multi-Country Empirical Analysis' (Centre For Labour Economics, Working Paper No. 681).

Hahn, F. H. (1982), 'Why I Am Not A Monetarist', political economy lecture at Harvard University, reproduced in F. H. Hahn, *Equilibrium and Macroeconomics* (Oxford: Basil Blackwell).

Hahn, F. H. (1983) Review of 'The Rational Expectations Revolution in Macroeconomics', *Economic Journal* (December).

Hahn, F. H. (1984) *Equilibrium and Macroeconomics* (Oxford: Basil Blackwell).

Hart, O. (1982) 'A Model of Imperfect Competition with Keynesian Features', *Quarterly Journal of Economics* (February).

Hart, O. (1983) 'Optimal Labour Contracts Under Asymmetric Information: An Introduction', *Review of Economics Studies* (January).

H. M. Treasury (1985) *The Relationship Between Employment and Wages*, January.

Hills, J. (1984) 'Public Assets and Liabilities and the Presentation of Budgetary Policy' in *Public Finance and Perspectives* (London: Institute for Fiscal Studies).

Jackman, R. (1984) *Counter-Inflationary Policy in a Unionised Economy With Non-Synchronised Wage Setting* (Centre for Labour Economics Discussion Paper No. 207, October).

Keynes, J. M. (1978) *The Collected Writings of John Maynard Keynes*, Royal Economic Society.

Layard, P. R. G. and S. Nickell (1985) 'The Causes of British Unemployment', *National Institute Economic Review* (February).

Layard, P. R. G. and S. Nickell (1986) 'Unemployment in Britain', *Economica*.

Lucas, R. E. and L. A. Rapping (1970) 'Real Wages, Employment and Inflation', in E. S. Phelps (ed.), *Microeconomic Foundations of Employment and Inflation Theory* (New York: W. W. Norton).

Malinvaud, E. (1977) *The Theory of Unemployment Reconsidered* (Oxford: Basil Blackwell).

Middleton, R. (1981) 'The Constant Employment Budget Balance and British Budgetary Policy, 1929–39', *Economic History Review* (May).

Minford, P., D. Davies, D. Peel and A. Sprague (1982) *Unemployment: Cause and Cure* (Oxford: Basil Blackwell).

Mishkin, F. (1982a) 'Does Anticipated Monetary Policy Matter? An Economic Investigation', *Journal of Political Economy* (February).

Mishkin, F. (1982b) 'Does Anticipated Aggregate Demand Policy Matter?', *American Economic Review* (September).

Neary, J. P. and J. E. Stiglitz (1983) 'Towards a Reconstruction of Keynesian Economics: Expectations and Constrained Equilibria', *Quarterly Journal of Economics*, Supplement.

Odling-Smee, J. and C. J. Riley (1985) 'Approaches to the PSBR', *National Institute Economic Review*.

Okun, A. M. (1981) *Prices and Quantities* (Washington D.C.: The Brookings Institution).

Pesaran, M. H. (1982) 'A Critique of the Proposed Tests of the Natural Rate

– Rational Expectations Hypothesis', *Economic Journal* (September).

Robinson, W. (1985) 'How To Create New Jobs' (London Business School Forecast Release, vol. 9, no. 7, April).

Rosen, H. S. and R. E. Quandt (1978) 'Estimation of a Disequilibrium Aggregate Labour Market', *Review of Economics and Statistics* (August)

Shapiro, C. and J. E. Stiglitz (1984) 'Equilibrium Unemployment as a Worker Discipline Device', *American Economic Review* (June).

Snower, D. J. (1983) 'Imperfect Competition, Underemployment and Crowding Out', *Oxford Economic Papers* (November Supplement).

Startz, R. (1984) 'Prelude to Macroeconomics', *American Economic Review* (December).

Stromback, C. T. and P. K. Trivedi (1976) 'The Determinants of Ex-works Price Changes', in I. F. Pearce *et al.* (eds), *A Model of Output, Employment, Wages and Prices in the UK* (Cambridge University Press).

Symons, J. and P. R. G. Layard (1984) 'Neoclassical Demand For Labour Functions for Six Major Economies', *Economic Journal* (December).

Taylor, J. B. (1979) 'Staggered Wage Setting in Macroeconomic Models', *American Economic Review*, Papers and Proceedings (May).

Tobin, J. (1980) *Asset Accumulation and Economic Activity*, Yrjo Jahnsson Lectures (Oxford: Basil Blackwell).

Wallis, K. F. (ed.) (1984) *Models of the UK Economy* (Oxford University Press).

Weitzman, M. L. (1982) 'Increasing Returns and the Foundations of Unemployment Theory', *Economic Journal* (December).

Weitzman, M. L. (1984) *The Share Economy* (Harvard University Press).

Worswick, G. D. N. (1984) 'The Sources of Recovery in the UK in the 1930s', *National Institute Economic Review* (November).

Index